*Governing Science
and Technology
in a Democracy*

Governing Science and Technology in a Democracy

EDITED, WITH AN INTRODUCTION,
BY MALCOLM L. GOGGIN

WILLIAM A. BLANPIED

LEONARD A. COLE

DENNIS FLORIG

MALCOLM L. GOGGIN

HAROLD GREEN

RACHELLE D. HOLLANDER

BRUCE JENNINGS

SHELDON KRIMSKY

HELEN LESKOVAC

HELEN LONGINO

LEON E. TRACHTMAN

LEON WOFSY

THE UNIVERSITY OF TENNESSEE PRESS

The paper used in this book meets the minimum requirements of the
American National Standard for Permanence of Paper for Printed Library
Materials, Z39.48–1984. Binding materials have been chosen for
durability.

Library of Congress Cataloging-in-Publication Data
Governing science and technology in a democracy.
   Bibliography: p.
   Includes index.
   1. Science and state.   2. Science—Social aspects.
3. Technology and state.   4. Technology—Social aspects.
I. Goggin, Malcolm L., 1938-   .   II. Blanpied,
William A., 1933-   .
Q125.G68   1968   338.9′26   86-7074
ISBN 0-87049-506-2

To Mary-Margaret, my best friend

Contents

Tables

Foreword

It has become a cliché to observe that we live in an age of science. We see the signs of scientific inquiry and their ultimate applications in technology around us daily. But while this flow of knowledge proceeds with increasing momentum, there seems little evidence that the social sciences, in their mainstream activities at least, have taken serious note of the social, and especially the political, import of this new knowledge.

The social sciences have been slow to recognize that the age of science has strongly challenged the smug notion that the traditional disciplines are self-contained. Although it is of course true that the social sciences have adopted many of the methods and concepts of the natural sciences, these changes have not brought with them a corresponding sensitivity to the broad range of public policy issues that have emerged from the practice of science itself. Such issues are a natural concomitant of powerful new knowledge about behavior and technology coming from the natural sciences, especially biology. This knowledge is directly relevant to analyses of social behavior, but it is routinely ignored by most social scientists. Thus we find that the social sciences are frequently isolated from the most intellectually dynamic and socially challenging discoveries of twentieth century science, and this isolation has resulted in an inattentiveness to many of the public policy questions emanating from those discoveries and the research processes which led to them.

One promising exception to this rather sad state of affairs has been the founding in 1980 of the Association for Politics and the Life Sciences. This professional society, composed primarily of political scientists, has as its central mission to foster the incorporation of life science information into the study of political phenomena. Much of the work in this area has focused on exploring the biological dimensions of human political behavior; other work has emphasized the public policy issues emerging from new knowledge in the life sciences, e.g., in genetic and reproductive technologies.

But, again, the work fostered by the Association for Politics and the Life Sciences is the exception within the social sciences generally. Perhaps one reason for this situation is the all too prevalent scientific illiteracy that social scientists share with the general population. In consequence, the sensitivity of social scientists to science-based issues is minimal. Is it any wonder, then, that the social sciences often display an embarrassing inattentiveness to the central intellectual impulses of the age?

Malcolm Goggin has performed a genuine service for the humanistic, social, and natural science communities in editing this important volume drawing together knowledge about governance issues in science and technology. The issues addressed relate to questions of conflict of interest, locus of political control, censorship, the commercialization of the research process, and others. All of these issues have critical public policy dimensions with which social analysts and governmental policy makers must ultimately contend.

This volume, therefore, makes a genuine contribution to scientific literacy. The issues with which it deals are so important that one must hope the volume finds its way to the personal bookshelves of many professional social scientists and public policy makers. Beyond this, the volume should be required reading in the training of advanced students in the social sciences.

I commend Dr. Goggin and his coauthors for presenting us with a challenging set of readings. I am quite confident that their work will make a major contribution to the resolution of the many issues herein discussed.

Thomas C. Wiegele
Northern Illinois University

Preface

In the post–World War II era, debates over national science and technology policy have revolved principally around the manner in which basic and applied research and product development should be either encouraged or discouraged. From Vannebar Bush's 1945 report on the need for direct links between science and government, through post-Sputnik public and political pressure for more government support for science education in the public schools and Richard Nixon's early 1970s crusade for a national war on cancer, to the Reagan administration's latest pleas for cutbacks in funding for applied research in industry and increases in federal funds for defense-related basic research in the so-called hard sciences, the struggle has been over funding and regulation. For example, in the 1980s, under the banners of "deregulation" and "improved productivity," the relationship between science and government has changed to the extent that there are now fewer regulations and less government support for some kinds of research, especially in areas where the research holds little promise of either commercial or military application.

To define the major issues relating to the organization and management of modern science and technology solely in terms of funding and regulation is to ignore important problems of governance that are created by a science and technology—and a larger culture or society in which scientists and engineers practice their crafts—that is in constant flux. The biological revolution that began with Watson's and Crick's 1953 discovery of the DNA molecule; the widespread use of hazardous technologies since World War II; and ethical, moral, and constitutional dilemmas created by the use of life-extending technologies, research with human fetuses and artificial organs, and the recent resurgence of censorship in the creation and dissemination of new knowledge—all these underscore the need for institutions of governance that are appropriate for a science and a technology that are both diversified and dynamic. Problems of governance created by these developments, and the institutional arrangements for solving them, go well beyond issues of which scientific and technological projects should be encouraged by government at what level of support, and which activities should be restricted.

Running through the eleven original essays of this book are two fundamental assumptions about science, technology, and their governance. First, any scientific discovery or technological development has potential for benefit or harm. And second, because of the importance of science and technology to modern society, they are too important to be left solely to scientists and technologists, or to universities, corporate executives, or any one group, for that matter. In any "disputed" project aimed at discovering, extending, or using new knowledge, one will invariably find competing interests, often with legitimate but conflicting demands. More often than not, among the various interests that are importantly affected by a scientific discovery or its applications, there are those who are more optimistic and thus tend to have confidence in science's and technology's abilities to solve most problems that might arise. Because these optimists focus on the positive promise of research and development, they are more likely to support funding and discourage regulation. In contrast, there are others who are more pessimistic. Rather than seeing the brighter "benefits" side, they tend to dwell on the real or potential costs and risks that are posed; they are frequently more cautious and therefore press for more restrictions. Representatives of such "camps" can be found, for example, on the two sides of the controversy over recombinant DNA research in the 1970s, and on the National Institutes of Health advisory committee that oversees government-sponsored gene-splicing research.

The interesting *political* question of what is the most appropriate governing scheme for developing funding priorities, for regulating controversial technologies, or for settling disputes is rarely addressed in books on national research and development policies. It is its focus on issues related to the problems of governance that distinguishes this book from others about science and technology policy.

I first raised the questions of who should govern science and technology and how scientific and technical disputes should be settled in 1984 *Politics and the Life Sciences* journal article provocatively entitled "The Life Sciences and the Public: Is Science Too Important to Be Left to the Scientists?" My argument was that recent developments, especially in the biological sciences, have stimulated competing claims both for more autonomy *and* for more accountability that are not easily resolved, and that this situation has led to a number of proposed institutional reforms that are designed to improve policy making with respect to "disputed", i.e., controversial or risky, scientific research and technological development. I concluded that a political solution is indicated.

From the several comments that were published along with my article and my response, two things became clear. First, the article had raised a number of important questions, but a book would be required to say all the things that the commentators suggested should be added about how scientific inquiry is and should be governed. And second, because the issues are so complex and intellectually diverse, it would be difficult for a lone scholar, working from a narrow disciplinary perspective, to write a book of this nature. For these reasons I invited each of the distinguished commentators on my article — from the physical, biological, and social sciences, and from the law and the humanities — to contribute an original essay for a book that I would edit. With the exception of four of the original commentators who for various personal reasons declined to participate further, all agreed to contribute a chapter to this book.

After brief summer meetings in Berkeley, California, and Washington, D.C., the contributors met in Houston, Texas, in May 1985 for a two-day symposium on the governance of science and technology. The symposium, sponsored by the University of Houston's Institute for Higher Education Law and Governance, allowed papers to be presented, criticized by other invited scholars, and eventually revised.

If a multi-author volume can have a single point of view, this book's thesis is that recent developments in science, technology, and society, along with interrelationships among the three, have created a constellation of problems that require action on the part of government, universities, industry, and the public. While it is true that all these have responded to changing conditions, the current institutions for governing science and technology seem woefully inadequate and thus could and should be improved. The principal aims of this book, then, are to outline the nature of the changes that have taken place in recent years in science, technology, society, and their interrelationships, to draw the contours of the problems of governance that these changes have created, to illustrate how these emerging problems have been handled, to show the extent to which several institutional reforms have worked, and to propose specific remedies for a crisis in the governance of science and technology. Broadly speaking, our prescriptions for the crisis of governance are not, as some have suggested, to limit the social control of scientific research and technological development, but instead to expand the power base of the scientific enterprise so that it includes all of those who are importantly affected by the decisions and actions of scientists and engineers. We argue for the substantive, and not merely procedural, democratic governance of science and technology.

In prescribing a science and a technology that are designed to serve democracy, we specify various degrees and forms of public, professional, corporate, and political participation in policy making for science and technology, given the constraints imposed by the philosophical conception of the nature of the quest for truth, the norms that prescribe the behavior of scientists and technologists, and the political realities of the democratic imperative.

We expect the readers of this book, like the contributors to it, to come from a variety of disciplinary backgrounds. The individual chapters have been written with at least four types of readers in mind. First, we expect the book to be read by policy makers and policy managers at all levels of government. Second, we anticipate that our colleagues who are specialists in science and technology policy or in the policy sciences will find the multidisciplinary treatment of new material and novel perspectives more subtle than the usual single-author treatment of the topic, and more integrated than the conventional multi-author collection of convention papers or previously published articles. Third, students should find both the theoretical chapters and the case studies useful introductions to the latest thinking of seasoned scholars in this field. Fourth, members of the interested public should find much of practical significance in these pages. To make our arguments more comprehensible to this diverse audience, the individual authors have taken great care to avoid the use of jargon. To make the book more coherent and integrated, I have also provided introductory and concluding chapters and brief mini-introductions to each of the book's three parts.

Houston, Texas
January 1986

Malcolm L. Goggin
University of Houston

Acknowledgments

A multidisciplinary research project involving so many people has many debts to pay. The most important of these, of course,
are owed to the contributors to this volume, whose patience, understanding, and responsiveness to my suggested revisions and deadlines
are much appreciated. Many other people helped with this project, some
with encouragement and critical comments on all or parts of the manuscript, some with financial support, some with facilities and other resources, and still others with assistance in data collection and manuscript preparation.

For sustained encouragement and support, I thank Peter Corning,
Alexander George, Michael Olivas, and Harrell Rodgers, Jr. For editorial assistance with the original journal article which was the catalyst
for the entire project, I thank Peter Corning, Kathleen Shenkman, Tom
Wiegele, and three anonymous referees for *Politics and the Life Sciences.* I am also grateful for invitations to spend several summers as
visiting assistant professor and visiting scholar in the Department of
Political Science at Stanford University, and for this opportunity I wish
to thank Heinz Eulau and Arlee Ellis. The one person who supported
this project from the beginning and did everything she could to move
it toward completion and publication is Cynthia Maude-Gembler, acquisitions editor of the University of Tennessee Press. To her and to
the press's two outside readers, whose detailed suggestions for revisions
and encouraging comments helped shape the final manuscript, I am
especially grateful.

I was also helped considerably by financial support from several
sources, first with a Limited-Grant-in-Aid from the Office of Sponsored
Programs, University of Houston, and then with release time from teaching one course, made possible by salary support from the Institute for
Higher Education Law and Governance at the University of Houston.
Michael Olivas, the institute's director, was particularly supportive, not
only believing in the project but also making additional institute funds
available so I could convene the two-day symposium on the issue of

governing science and technology at the University of Houston in May 1985. Other institute staff members also aided the project. Carolyn Winter handled much of the correspondence with authors and symposium participants and helped prepare the book manuscript; Marilyn Nerem helped in planning the symposium; and Amouri Smith and Simon Gotchek videotaped the entire conference and provided valuable assistance with my own research. A research facilitation grant from the University of Houston's Center for Public Policy during summer 1985 and the hospitality extended to me by Steven Krasner and Arlee Ellis during my delightful summer stay at Stanford University made it possible for me to complete the final book revisions on schedule.

Several people read all or part of the manuscript, and I wish to thank this multidisciplinary group for its contribution. Todd La Porte and Sheila Slaughter read parts of the manuscript, as did a number of scholars who acted as chairs and discussants at three symposium panels in May 1985: Richard Barke, Lynton Caldwell, Richard Delgado, Roger Eichhorn, Eric Holtzman, Tom Mayor, Julie Norris, Emmett Redford, and Charles Walter. The list of those who helped me during the last year of research and writing would not be complete without mentioning Stanford graduate research assistants William Lowry and Rick Ulguin; and Peter Goggin, who not only aided me considerably in the early weeks with library research but also helped with final typescript preparation and proofreading.

In appreciation of her contribution, this book is dedicated to Mary-Margaret Goggin, who, even in the midst of completing her doctoral dissertation, listened patiently to my ideas about how to make science and technology serve democracy and helped me view these ideas from a more humanistic perspective.

Contributors

William Blanpied holds a doctorate in physics from Princeton University. He has held academic appointments at Harvard, Yale, and Case Western Reserve universities and previously served as the director of the National Science Foundation's Ethics and Values in Science and Technology program. He is currently international policy research specialist at the National Science Foundation.

Leonard Cole earned a DDS degree from the University of Pennsylvania and a Ph.D. in political science from Columbia University. A practicing dentist, he is an adjunct professor of political science at William Paterson College and at the New School for Social Research.

Dennis Florig is a political scientist who earned his doctorate at Stanford University. He has taught at the University of California, Santa Barbara, Providence College, and the University of Texas at Dallas. He is now an assistant professor of government at the University of Puget Sound.

Malcolm L. Goggin is a graduate of Haverford College and received his doctorate in political science from Stanford University. He has taught in the political science department and in the department of family, community, and preventive medicine in the School of Medicine at Stanford. He is currently an associate professor of political science and research associate at the Center for Public Policy at the University of Houston–University Park.

Harold Green is a graduate of the University of Chicago and the University of Chicago Law School. He is professor of law and associate dean for post-J.D. studies at the George Washington University National Law Center. He is a founding fellow of the Hastings Center in Hastings-on-Hudson, New York.

Rachelle D. Hollander received her Ph.D. in philosophy from the University of Maryland. She has directed the Science for Citizens program at the National Science Foundation and is currently the head of NSF's Program on Ethics and Values in Science and Technology.

Bruce Jennings is a graduate of Yale University and Princeton University. He received his Ph.D. in political science from Princeton and is currently associate for policy studies at the Hastings Center/Institute of Society, Ethics, and the Life Sciences. Before joining the Hastings Center staff he taught political theory and philosophy at Stockton State College in Pomona, New Jersey.

Sheldon Krimsky received his doctorate in philosophy and philosophy of science from Boston University. He also did post-doctoral work in economics. Presently an associate professor of urban and environmental policy at Tufts University, he has also taught philosophy at the University of South Florida.

Helen Leskovac received her J.D. degree from the University of California, Davis, where she was senior notes and comments editor of the *Law Review.* She is currently a research fellow at the Institute for Higher Education Law and Governance at the University of Houston–University Park.

Helen Longino earned her Ph.D. in philosophy from the Johns Hopkins University. With the aid of a National Science Foundation grant, she spent the 1985-86 academic year at the University of California, Berkeley, and is currently an associate professor of philosophy at Mills College in Oakland, California.

Leon Trachtman received his doctoral degree from the Johns Hopkins University. He is professor of communications and associate dean of the School of Humanities, Social Science, and Education at Purdue University. He also serves as general editor of *Science and Society,* a Purdue University Series in Science, Technology, and Human Values.

Leon Wofsy is a biologist who received his Ph.D. from Yale University. He is currently professor emeritus of microbiology and immunology at the University of California, Berkeley, where he was departmental chair from 1967 to 1972 and again from 1975 to 1977.

*Governing Science
and Technology
in a Democracy*

Introduction. Governing Science and Technology Democratically: A Conceptual Framework

MALCOLM L. GOGGIN

The United States is no longer the undisputed commercial and military world leader she once was,[1] and at least one influential group of corporate and academic chief executives believes that this slippage is due to faulty national policies for science and technology. According to the Business–Higher Education Forum, because of several factors — an inefficient "explosion" of regulations to protect health, safety, and the environment; *ad hoc* government policy making that encourages the pursuit of narrow, private interests rather than broader national goals; shortsighted businesses and labor unions: universities that, in emphasizing the pedagogical rather than the practical uses of knowledge, have not kept up with the times; and an adversarial public that distrusts business, labor, and government — the nation is facing a crisis of governance in science and technology. In April 1983, these business and educational leaders declared that if America is to avert a crisis of governance — if America is to achieve a just society, a high standard of living, and a strong national defense — major reforms in the institutions of governance are indicated.[2]

The crisis has been fueled by the failure to resolve the issues of *which* modern scientific and technological activities should be promoted or restricted; *who* should organize, direct, and manage those activities; and *which* institutions for governing science and technology are best able to serve broad, national interests. Whereas many Americans would agree that science and technology *by* the people may now be impossible, and whereas science and technology *without* the people is unacceptable, a fundamental question remains: how can a Western industrial democracy like the United States best balance the need for a healthy scientific re-

3

public with the imperative to maintain a robust democratic republic — how can government shape a science and technology that is *for* the people? Deciding on the best institutional arrangements for managing the scientific enterprise in the service of society is one of the major tasks of politics.

One of the principal tasks of this book is to sort out and evaluate alternative schemes for governing a scientific enterprise that is neither unified nor static. One needs only to review the history of the atomic energy movement to demonstrate that science as a social institution is not constant, but rather forms part of a dynamic configuration of public and private institutions.

It is with the knowledge that science and technology are ever-changing, that science governance is pluralistic, and that scientific inquiry is not a single process, that this book raises its central question: what institutional arrangements for governing science and technology — *who* should govern; *at what stage* of the process; *where, how,* and *to what ends* — best serve democracy and the needs of the American people? Before we can prescribe institutional reforms, however, a number of related questions must be addressed, both here and in the essays that follow:

1. What do "science," "technology," and "governance" mean, and how are science, technology, and society currently interrelated?
2. How have science, technology, and society changed in recent years?
3. What problems of governance have been created by these changes in the interrelationships between science and society?
4. How have federal, state, and local governments responded to these challenges?
5. To what extent have these responses been adequate?
6. What can be done to improve the present arrangements for governing science and technology?

These changes, challenges, and responses and their inadequacies are presented in this introductory chapter as a framework for analyzing the crisis of governance in science and technology and for evaluating alternative solutions to governance problems. The framework foreshadows the eleven original essays that make up this volume.

CONCEPTUAL CLARIFICATION

Before proceeding with an elaboration of the analytical framework, we need to clarify what is meant by democratic governance, science, and technology — the three concepts that make up the title of this book.

Governance as Problem-Solving. The verb "to govern" is derived from the Latin, *gubernare* and the Greek, *kybernan.* It means to steer or pilot—in this case, to steer the policy on a particular course, one designed to solve community problems.[3] And while the actions of governments are diverse, they are, according to Heinz Eulau and Kenneth Prewitt, the political means of settling—mediating—disputes between man and man and between man and his environment.

> The focus on governing conceived as problem-solving (but also problem-creating) and therefore mediating the relationship between units and their multiple environments make governance not a routine to be administered but a set of issues to be solved.[4]

Science and Technology as Social Activities. If governing behavior consists of problem-solving decisions and actions by those in positions of authority, what distinguishes the two social activities—science and technology—that are to be governed? For analytical purposes, they can be differentiated in terms of the *activities,* the *people* who "do" science or technology, and the *motives* these people have for doing what they do. This preliminary distinction serves merely as an introduction to Leon Trachtman's more extensive conceptual analysis in Chapter 6 of this volume.

Rather than independent and deterministic forces, science and technology are social activities, each with its own workers, usual work place, reference group, and norms. As historians of science and technology have noted, although it is convenient to make analytical distinctions between knowing and know-how, these distinctions are often overdrawn. Science and technology are inextricably linked, especially in physics, computer science, and molecular biology, the last being one of the areas of research and development on which this volume focuses.[5] In biotechnology, for example, the lines between science and technology are blurred. Recombinant DNA research has been conducted primarily in university laboratories, but increasingly is being carried out in the laboratories of private industry. Moreover, as Leon Wofsy points out in Chapter 5, the profit motive in the "new" biology has undermined traditional scientific norms.[6] This is part of what Robert Merton calls the "ambivalence" of scientists.[7]

Science celebrates the triumph of knowledge over ignorance. In its narrowest sense, science is a descriptive study of the laws of nature, with discovery of the truth concerning physical and biological reality—that is, concerning man, the universe around him, and man's relationship

5

to the universe—as its ultimate aim. Harvey Brooks, in an influential essay on the functions of scientific advisors in science-government relations, distinguishes between "science in policy" and "policy for science." In the former, science is an *instrument* of policy, "concerned with matters that are basically political or administrative but are significantly dependent upon technical factors."[8] The emphasis is on science and technology as they are used in the complex decision processes that translate society's preferences for a particular kind of science- and technology-driven environment, health care or educational system, defense strategy, or economic arrangement into public policies and programs. We see an example of "science in policy" in Chapter 9 of this volume—Sheldon Krimsky's discussion of the use of experts and informed laypersons in Cambridge, Massachusetts, to decide whether or not chemical weapons testing should be continued in a private laboratory within the city limits.

"Policy for science," on the other hand, is concerned "with the development of policies for the management and support of the national scientific enterprise and with the selection and evaluation of substantive scientific programs."[9] Here, science is the *object* of policy. In this sense, the emphasis is on the nature of specific preferred policies, relative to expenditure levels, levels of acceptable risk, or patterns for allocating scientific and technical benefits and burdens in a modern "mass" society that is not only radically different from the political communities that spawned "classical" and "representative" forms of democracy, but is even distinctive from the industrial society of the first half of this century.[10] Harold Green's discussion of recombinant DNA research and its regulation in Chapter 7 of this book is an example of a "policy for science." But clearly there are also elements of the use of scientific knowledge in deliberating about which regulatory structure is optimal.

If science is the quest for new knowledge, technology is the search for applications of knowledge for useful purposes. Narrowly defined, technology is the science of the industrial arts, the collection of production possibilities, techniques, methods, and processes by which resources are actually transformed by man to meet human wants. One of the most dominant forces in modern life, technology is, according to Jerome Weisner, "the engine that propels modern society."[11]

Scientists are the source of new discoveries. Claiming to be objective and precise, scientists supposedly pursue knowledge without regard to ends. Technologists, on the other hand, apply the discoveries of scientists in the service of economic and political ends. They see knowledge as solving socially defined problems. Actual behaviors, however, frequently belie these textbook distinctions between science and technology and between scientists and engineers.

A CONCEPTUAL FRAMEWORK

To cover many of the problems of governance that arise as a result of the complex and changing relationships between science and society, and to offer a framework within which proposed institutional reforms can be evaluated, Table 1.1 incorporates (1) *changes* in science, technology, and society; (2) *challenges* that these changes pose; (3) *responses* to the challenges and their inadequacies; and (4) *proposed solutions* to the crisis of governance. The framework that is schematized in Table 1.1 poses four questions addressed by the essays in this book. The first question relates to the changing nature of the relationship between science and technology, and society. Describing the dynamic setting within which most governance problems emerge is the main focus of this introductory chapter.

HOW HAVE SCIENCE AND SOCIETY CHANGED?

In the "postindustrial" era, the United States has enjoyed many benefits of scientific and technological progress, yet changes in basic and applied science and in process and product development have also introduced many risks, costs, and social dislocations. Ethical and value questions have also been raised concerning the social consequences, or negative external effects of scientific and technological activities — the bad results of private decisions that do not affect the decision maker. Many contemporary problems of governance can be traced to these sometimes unanticipated, untoward side-effects of an advanced science- and technology-based industrial state that is characterized by "the exponential growth and branching of science, the rise of a new intellectual technology, the creation of systematic research through R&D (research and development) budgets . . . and the codification of theoretical knowledge."[12] Three of the most significant changes in the nature of scientific progress in the post–World War II period are: (1) the scale and complexity of science, (2) the revolution in biology, and (3) the crossing of new frontiers in basic and applied research.

TABLE 1.1. Governing Science and Technology Democratically: A Conceptual Framework

Changes	Challenges	Responses	Solutions
1. Scale and complexity of science and technology	1a. Fraud and abuse of human subjects	1a. Committees	*Who* should govern? • A few • Many
	1b. Hazardous technologies	1b. New laws, agencies, and regulations	
	1c. Politicization of policy-making process	1c. Reassessment of peer review	
2. Revolution in biology	2a. Commercialization of biology and medicine	2. Litigation	*When* should governors govern? • Inception • Research protocol • Interpretation • Publication
	2b. Conflict of interest	2b. Committees	
3. New frontiers in basic and applied research	3a. Scientist-entrepreneur 3b. "Disputed" science and technology	3. Committees	
4. Crisis of confidence in science and technology	4. & 5. Antiscience/Anti-technology sentiment	4. & 5. Citizen participation	*Where* should authority be lodged? • Centralized • Decentralized *To what ends* should science and technology be directed? • Military and Commercial ends • Social ends
5. Scientific and technological illiteracy			
6. Nationalization of science and technology policy	6. Erosion of state and local control	6. New Federalism in science and technology	

Big Science and Science as Big Business. The first change to be noted is simply the increased scale, complexity, and sophistication of science and technology. Because of the pervasiveness of science and technology, the distribution of their benefits and burdens has come to be an important consideration in making choices about paths in research or development. Because of their scope, large-scale technological initiatives such as supercolliders, supercomputers, space stations, and the Strategic Defense Initiative entail massive future commitments as well as uncertain future risks, costs, and benefits. Therefore, public choices about questions relating to "big" science have, in many instances, become political as well as technical. Yet the size and complexity of science and technology have made them increasingly difficult for lay members of the public to comprehend; and the peer review process by which much science and technology policy is made has added to the problem by further insulating science from the public.

Research and development have become big business as well, with William Carey estimating that during the decade of the 1980s industry and government will combine to spend over $1 trillion or more.[13] The federal government will account for less than half of that total, but with annual combined industry and government spending of over $110 billion for research and development, R&D represents a valuable source of support for a substantial number of researchers and institutions. The point is well illustrated by the flood of applications from university scientists for $70 million dollars for initial Star Wars research.[14]

Furthermore, a trend towards more federal spending for defense- and space-related research is clearly discernable, and this development is not without political import. The most recent federal budget indicates that more than six of every ten federal dollars for research and development was spent for defense and military purposes in fiscal year (FY) 1984. In spite of a March 1985 report from the nation's under secretary of defense for research and engineering that the United States leads the Soviet Union in virtually every basic technology critical to defense,[15] the budget for FY 1986 shows that approximately three-quarters of the federal R&D budget are earmarked for military or space, the latter having become increasingly militarized since the beginning of the decade.[16]

The Department of Defense's presence on university campuses is on the rise as well. Since passage of the so-called Mansfield Amendment to the Military Procurement Authorization Bill of 1970, the Pentagon has been unable to fund university research that was not directly related to its mission. This, in effect, kept the Department of Defense (DOD)

9

off the nation's campuses in the immediate post–Viet Nam era, but by the mid-1980s the DOD had become a major investor in university research facilities. One such facility, which received 90% of its funding from the DOD, is the Center for Integrated Systems (CIS) at Stanford University. The research center is a joint government-industry-university project designed to maintain America's world leadership in supercomputers, electrical engineering, and materials science. In extemporaneous remarks at Stanford in the early stages of the project's development, Richard DeLauer, under secretary of defense for research and development, emphasized the important link between technology and defense by describing the DOD as the "daddy rabbit" of CIS, and characterizing technology as "at the forefront of our (national) security."[17]

With renewed emphasis on strengthening the nation's military and commercial competitive advantage, it is no wonder that, compared to the 1960s and early 1970s, science policy making in the 1980s is much less likely to take into account the "social relevance" of research and development. Rather, in recent years the choice of budget priorities has been determined in large part on the basis of potential military and commercial application.[18] Like the business and university executives in the Business–Higher Education Forum, George Keyworth, the former White House chief science advisor, believes that the United States' dominant position as "(leading) all industrial technologies" and "anchoring the security of the free world"[19] is waning; and in his 1985 State of the Union Address Keyworth's boss in the White House reiterated the administration's position that industrial revitalization and national security are the government's first responsibilities.

President Reagan has criticized the Carter administration for encouraging an adversarial relationship with business and has directed his own administration to improve relations between government and industry. Federal regulatory agencies have reduced the regulatory burden on the private sector, and greater use of cost-benefit analysis in regulatory decision making has undoubtedly forced policy makers and policy managers to make hard choices, for example, between jobs and the environment, or between health and safety and increased prices to the consumer.

That the incidence of choices of this nature is on the rise is due as much to the changing nature of science and technology as to changes in the regulatory climate in society, however. Since World War II there has been an enormous proliferation of processes and products that pose hazards to human health and safety and to the environment. Those with the greatest potential for a major catastrophe are nuclear, biological,

and chemical weapons, but other common products that have disbene-
fits as well as benefits are chemical fertilizers, pesticides, and food preservatives. One major problem for government (and industry) is the uncertainty that surrounds regulation of potentially hazardous technologies.[20]
For example, what is the probability of a catastrophe? What are the probable consequences? What levels of risk are acceptable? And how will
the risks and benefits be shared between government and industry? Attempts to rationalize this process by substituting economic incentives
for regulations and by increased use of cost-benefit analysis may have
relieved some industries of the regulatory burden, but at what cost to
the health and safety of the general public and to the environment?

The New Biology.   The second major change in science and technology
that has challenged government and raised the controversial political
question of the most appropriate role for government in directing and
regulating research is the biological revolution. Although its origins can
be traced to Watson's and Crick's 1953 discovery of the double helix —
the basic building block of life — the biological revolution did not reach
the public agenda until more than twenty years later. Because of nag-
ging questions about potential risks related to the most hazardous experiments with recombinant DNA (rDNA), in July 1974 some of the
most prominent molecular biologists in the country called for a self-
imposed moratorium on gene-splicing research, at least until the National Institutes of Health (NIH) could devise safeguards that would
insure that gene-splicing experiments would pose minimal risks to the
public health and safety.

Debate within the scientific community reached its peak in winter
1975, when over one hundred scientists and a few invited lawyers and
journalists met at Asilomar, a conference center in Pacific Grove, California, to discuss the next step. A few of the scientists who attended
the meeting were asked by NIH to serve on a Recombinant DNA Advisory Committee (RAC) to write guidelines for research using the rDNA
technique. Federal guidelines that applied only to government-sponsored
research were published in July 1976. Setting up RAC and writing NIH
guidelines did not quiet the controversy, however. Continuing throughout the 1970s, the flap surrounding genetic engineering turned largely
into a "freedom of scientific inquiry" debate,[21] and despite none of the
predicted catastrophes, the debate rages on in the 1980s.

While in the mid-1980s the central issues continue to be safety (the
low probability of creating new pathogens) and ethics (the ability to

11

change the human gene pool), the field as a whole has shifted its emphasis from the conduct of basic scientific research in laboratories to the use of the technique to screen employees, the release of genetically altered microorganisms into the environment, and the application of genetic engineering to manufacture products that will cure genetic diseases, eat pollutants, or protect perishable foods from frost damage.[22] Ironically, the powerful biotechnology industry which has grown up with molecular biology and which for more than a decade had urged government to stay out of its affairs in the laboratory now wants Congress to change patent, trade, and tax laws so that the industry can flourish. And, as Leon Wofsy points out in Chapter 5, what was once a fertile field for the generation of new knowledge, spawning Nobel prizes, is now the harvesting ground for products for industry and the military. The shift from university to industry as the "home" of much rDNA research and the emphasis on market mechanisms to determine the course of product development have made it exceedingly difficult for the public and their representatives in government to monitor or direct the uses of this new knowledge.

New Frontiers.   The third major change in the nature of the scientific enterprise is that scientists and engineers have crossed several important frontiers of knowledge during the past four decades. Nowhere is this more obvious than in the area of life-extending medical technology. Although several of these pathbreaking discoveries are capable of either increasing the number of middle-aged people who live to old age or increasing the maximum age to which people can live, new pharmaceutical products, diagnostic devices, life-extending machines, organ transplants, artificial organs, and surgical procedures, for example, have also created a number of challenges to government. Other "disputed" research and development, such as cloning, findings relating race and intelligence, or XYY chromosome experiments have either created safety problems or raised ethical and value questions.[23]

The sociocultural contexts within which national science and technology policies are made and implemented are also constantly changing. The economy has its periods of boom and bust; social classes migrate from city to suburb or from East to West; the population ages; the political pendulum swings from conservative to liberal and back to conservative again. Since the end of World War II, changes in social institutions, political climate, and the economy have had profound effects on what those who rule and those who are ruled say and do with respect to science and technology policy. Some of the changes that seem to have had the most profound effects on science and technology policy are: (1) a crisis of confidence in science and technology, (2) scientific and technological illiteracy, and (3) "nationalization" of public problems and the formulation of solutions to them. It is to an examination of these changes in society, all of which have erected barriers to active citizen participation in science and technology policy making, that we now turn.

A Crisis of Confidence in Science and Technology. The changes in the relations between science and society that are discussed in this Introduction — changes in science and technology and in the men and women who "do" them, and changes in the economic structure, the role of government, and the rate of diffusion of modern technologies — have created a substructure which social critics like Jergen Habermas have called "the legitimation crisis."[24] The crisis of legitimacy expresses itself, for example, in the rise of professionalism in the nineteenth century, in professionalism's increasing conflict with the public sector in the twentieth century, and, since the end of World War II, in the development of an exchange relationship between science and the rest of society. The crisis is also manifested in society's changing status from patron to partner and finally to servant of science as we enter the last decades of the twentieth century. The perception of a crisis of legitimacy is one of the principal reasons that governments are willing to experiment with institutional arrangements for governing science and technology that permit limited participation by non-experts in policy making.

Evidence of a crisis of legitimacy comes mainly from public opinion polls. Surveys show that, beginning in the mid-1960s and lasting until at least the early 1970s, public trust in institutions of authority — government, business, labor, and organized religion, for example — declined. About the time that trust should have been on the mend, a decade of poor economic performance (in the form of inflation, unemployment, and high interest rates) dampened public confidence, with a low point reached in November 1982.[25] According to Seymour Martin Lipset, since then Americans have been feeling better, and their faith in public institutions is improving.[26] But another political analyst reminds his readers that a majority of the public still lacks confidence in social institutions.[27] But what about America's confidence in science and technology? Is there a crisis of confidence?

As I have argued elsewhere, attitude surveys show that although most Americans still believe science is valuable to society, the public has also

13

lost confidence in science and even more in technology.[28] From data collected in 1972, Todd La Porte and Daniel Metlay concluded that while science was not a source of concern, there was "an undercurrent of skepticism about dependency on technology" that led many Americans to support regulation of technical development.[29] Allan Mazur has examined public attitudes towards science between 1966 and 1980 and concluded that confidence has waxed and waned, but there is an unmistakably positive, if qualified, view of science and technology.[30] Comparing surveys in 1957–58, 1972, 1974, and 1976, another study comes to quite a different conclusion: "Whereas in the late 1950s only about 10 percent of the population was anything but positive about science's social contribution, by 1976, the proportion of these negative and ambivalent responses had more than doubled to 22 percent."[31] This discrepancy in findings only underscores problems related to the quality of the data, which seem to indicate an ambivalence towards science and technology.

Scientific and Technological Illiteracy. Not unrelated to changing attitudes towards these social activities is a rise in scientific and technological illiteracy. It is one of the most serious problems facing the nation today. Science and technology have become so specialized and complex that many ordinary citizens cannot comprehend, and representative institutions cannot always control, science and technology without a knowledge of how they work. Without that knowledge it is exceedingly difficult to govern science and technology democratically.

Aristotle warned that a knowledge gap among members of the polity undermines the political integrity of the state; when knowledge discrepancies among citizens reach a point at which citizens no longer have the same "virtue," the state ceases to be constitutional. The depth and extent of scientific and technological illiteracy are alarming, especially when one considers that a majority of public policy issues that now get on the governmental agenda has scientific or technical content. And the crisis has reached alarming proportions. For example, a 1979 National Science Foundation survey of more than fifteen hundred adults showed that only seven percent of the respondents were scientifically literate, not a surprising statistic when one considers that in 1985 more than 27 million Americans were classified as functionally illiterate.[32]

Making Public Problems National Problems. In recent years governance problems have been exacerbated by a number of changes in the political climate as well. Two of these changes — increases in the size and

14

complexity of the units of government and the rise of the administrative state—are characteristic of American government in the twentieth century. Together they add up to a trend of greater government direction and responsibility for solving problems at the federal, rather than state or local, level of government.[33] The trend was reversed shortly after the 1980 presidential election.

According to Robert Dahl and Edward Tufte, these changes in the character of political units over the years have created a trade-off between *citizen effectiveness*—citizens acting responsibly to control the decisions of the polity—and *system capacity*—the ability of the polity to be responsive to the collective preferences of its citizens.[34] Increased size, complexity, and heterogeneity of the polity's members place serious limitations on the ability of citizens to manage their own affairs. On the other hand, small size, while enhancing citizen capacity for self-government, makes it exceedingly difficult for the polity to maintain its independence. Size and complexity, then, are two additional impediments to democratic governance.

Solving national problems has increasingly become the responsibility not just of government, but of the *federal* government. One of the major reasons that much policy for science and technology is made at the federal level is that 75 percent of the R&D spending goes to space and defense, both national issues. To put the relative importance of these issues in perspective, one need only compare the U.S. spending pattern to Japan's 2 percent and West Germany's 12 percent investment in security defense R&D.[35] The penchants for passing state and local problems on to the federal government for solution, and for delegating to federal technoscience agencies the responsibility for making decisions about which science and technology policies to support and to what degree, are typical of what is going on in other policy areas as well. Nationalization in the area of science and technology, which has been especially true in the era of "big" science, has obvious implications for the possibilities of democratic governance.

WHAT CHALLENGES HAVE THESE CHANGES CREATED?

In Table 1.1, the second column focuses on the nature of the problems of governance that have been created by these postwar developments in science and society. The most significant governance problems that emerge from these changes range from the negative externalities of haz-

15

ardous technologies to commercialization of biology to what to do about a substantial antiscience and antitechnology public sentiment. The following brief discussion of the governance problems that are listed in Table 1.1 anticipates the five chapters that make up Part I of this book.

Fraud, Abuse, and Hazardous Technologies.   The first three governance problems—fraud and abuse, hazardous technologies, and a renegotiated contract between science and its public—are created by the size, scope, and complexity of science and technology. The problems are exacerbated by a system of research sponsorship that leaves universities and individual scholars dependent upon outside financial support for their research and development undertakings. The most immediate problems are in the conduct of research, where there has been an alarming increase in the number of cases of investigator fraud—deliberate theft of information, plagiarism, distortion, misrepresentation, or fabrication of results—and abuse of human subjects.[36]

Writing about the hubris of science, biologist Lewis Thomas believes that the most serious problems of governance are created not by abuses perpetrated by scientists, but by first and second order risks.[37] Thus, technology and its applications, rather than moral indifference within the scientific community itself, lead to abuses in the research process. Therefore, technology cries out for restriction. In Thomas' view, when people and the environment are put at risk—for the most part from hazardous *technologies*—government intrusion is most easily justified. What the authors of the chapters in this book advocate is not wholesale regulation of technology but, instead, the need for a knowledge base about individual technological processes, their effects, and the public and private institutions that govern them. Leon Trachtman (Chapter 6) discusses a variety of processes and the risks each poses, and then proceeds to describe current arrangements for governing science and technology. His overview sets the stage for more detailed analyses of a number of problems of governance examined in Part I.

A Renegotiated Contract between Science and Its Public.   In Chapter 2, Helen Longino's epistemological argument that nonscientific contextual values shape the development of knowledge serves as an important reminder that in their pursuit of knowledge and its by-products, scientists and engineers are neither free from external control nor entitled to exclusive control of the scientific enterprise. What Longino and others in this volume (for example, Trachtman in Chapter 6) allude to is that some of the changes in the nature of science and technology that I have outlined above have undermined the longstanding compact between science and its public.[38]

The nature and extent of the change in the relationship between science and government since its "golden years" is documented in Chapter 3 in William Blanpied's and Rachelle Hollander's historical case study of the formation of the National Science Foundation (NSF). Their story of the early debate over the agency's organizational structure is also instructive. Again, the issue is control of the direction of a national science policy. As originally envisioned, the NSF was to be a centralized authority, following the model outlined by Michael Polanyi,[39] to make science self-governing by putting scientists in charge. But President Truman vetoed the bill that incorporated that idea, arguing for (and eventually getting) a funding agency whose director was under the control of the president and Congress instead. During the five-year debate over the structure of NSF, Congress created a number of other more specialized agencies, thus beginning the current pluralistic, decentralized system with multiple funding centers, each with its own constituency.

The Commercialization of Biology and Medicine. The revolution in biology and the increased importance and use of medical technologies have created a number of challenges to government, and most important of which are the effects that the rise of the scientist-entrepreneur and the increased scale of industry-university agreements have had upon the university. As several of the authors in this volume will argue, the lure of fame and fortune has significantly altered the relationships among industry sponsors, university researchers and administrators, and government officials. The commercial side of university-based science threatens to undermine the traditional quality control mechanism of peer review through the publication of findings in professional journals, has allowed industrial donors to patent university scientists' discoveries, and has redefined traditional notions of free inquiry and academic freedom.

Two things emerge as particularly problematic: first, the spectre of corporate control of science and technology; and second, conflict of interests for university scientists.

David Dickson argues that since the release of Vannebar Bush's 1945 report, *Science, the Endless Frontier,* the center of power that controls science has shifted from scientists and engineers to industrialists, and that in recent years the principal driving force behind science has been the profit motive.[40] Dickson's main point is that, to allow industry to

17

make a more substantial profit, government is reducing the weight of social controls on technological innovation. "The result," he writes in *The New Politics of Science,* "is that fundamental decisions concerning the direction of the nation's scientific enterprise are being steadily removed from the domain of active public decision-making."[41]

That science is no longer a public good, but a private commodity, is underscored by Dennis Florig's analysis in Chapter 4, of the role of the scientist-entrepreneur in the development of biotechnical and biomedical innovations. Florig examines the challenges to government posed by the development of the totally implantable artificial heart: first, what to do about its high cost; and second, how to distribute the device when the need for it is greater than the supply. Florig uses evidence from his case study to show that lay members of the public were excluded from any meaningful participation in deliberations about the course of that device's development. He makes a strong case for more public involvement, arguing for institutional reforms that would transfer the power to make decisions about product development from producers to consumers and their representatives. This is in sharp contrast to arguments made by Simon Rottenberg and others that these types of decisions should be left to the market.[42]

Indeed, the revolution in biology has created a second problem, especially for universities. It is conflict of interest. And this conflict takes several forms, many of which are described by Florig in Chapter 4, Leon Wofsy in Chapter 5, and Helen Leskovac in Chapter 8. Unlike most European nations, where there is apparently a happy marriage between business and the university, in the United States, industry funding of university research has created a great deal of friction. This is because the proprietary interest of private corporations, the secrecy that surrounds many industry-university agreements, and the restrictions that some patrons impose on investigators are in direct conflict with both the norms of science and the purposes of the academy.[43] One of the distortions that is currently plaguing departments of biological sciences where gene-splicing research is conducted is that individualism and competition are crowding out the traditional communal values of collegiality and cooperation. It would be incorrect to say that what is happening in molecular genetics is also happening in all of biology or all of science. Nevertheless, since virtually all of the people who are engaged in basic and applied research are funded by someone, one can assume that most have at least pondered conflict of interest issues.

Fraud, abuse, threats to human health and the environment that are

18

posed by hazardous technologies, the politicization of science and technology, and a research and development agenda dictated by the pursuit of profit are just a few of the many challenges that have been created at least in part by changes in the nature of science and technology in postwar America. At least two other governance problems stem from changes in our culture, for example, in the way people perceive science and technology and those who do them, in the depth and extent of people's knowledge of matters scientific and technological, and in prevailing attitudes towards the role of government in contemporary society. Institutions that govern science and technology can no longer take for granted blind faith in the beneficence of science or technology, for they have to contend with a public that has a more realistic view of what science and technology can and cannot accomplish. Nor can state or local governing institutions take for granted that the federal government is going to look out for their best interests. State legislatures and governors have come to realize that states and localities must develop their own capability to manage and direct modern science and technology within their jurisdictional boundaries.

Antiscience and Antitechnology Sentiments.   Public ambivalence about science and, even more, about some technologies, and the alarming rate of scientific and technological illiteracy in the United States stand directly in the way of the democratic governance of science and technology. If a large proportion of the public is apathetic at best and hostile at worst and also uneducated in the ways of science and technology, many questions are raised about the possibility of public governance of science and technology.[44]

For instance, does the average American know enough to play a role in public policy making, especially about things as esoteric as science and technology? Are lay members of the public going to have access only to the democratic institutions of Congress, or will they have opportunities to influence policy wherever it is made? Will non-experts take an active part in shaping not only the ends of science and technology policy but also the means? If laypersons do become involved, will they merely serve in the capacity of a minority, legitimizing decisions that are made by a majority of experts? How one answers questions about the widsom and civic virtue of average Americans has a lot to do with how one defines the important issue of the power relationships between those who govern and those who are governed. Some of these questions will be answered in the concluding chapter.

Although there is some disagreement about just how negative the American public is about science and technology,[45] Arthur Kornberg has complained that in spite of the fact that science is a public responsibility, the public has not supported science enough and

> the support of science has been visibly ebbing. Funds for important research have been cut at a time when inflation and advanced technology require increases; the support for training of our best young scientists has been abruptly eliminated. . . . The support for science, so absolutely vital to our future, has been and must remain the responsibility of society. It is too important and too complex a problem to be left to scientists.[46]

Critics of science and technology come from the entire political spectrum. Liberals see science as a tool of corporate interests; establishment scientists criticize the scientific enterprise for its irrelevance, its emphasis on knowledge for the sake of knowledge; and conservatives are loathe to support research, especially research in the social sciences, that, in the words of George Keyworth, does "not offer enough intellectual excellence or industrial potential."[47] Obviously, there is a governance problem here; a public that is antiscience and antitechnology is unlikely to support increases in funding for scientific research and development, and with fewer funds to go around, the number of projects to be funded declines and the entire scientific edifice begins to crumble.[48]

State and Local Capability to Manage Science and Technology. In the 1970s the controversy over recombinant DNA raised the spectre of federal preemption, and chemical weapons testing in the 1980s has revitalized the issue. Sheldon Krimsky's essay (Chapter 9) demonstrates how, in our federal system of government, state and local needs often come into conflict with a national government mission. In this case, the Cambridge, Massachusetts, City Council wanted to use its police power to stop supertoxins testing that threatened public health and safety. The Department of Defense, however, wanted the local company, Arthur D. Little, to fulfill its contractual obligations to test the toxic material as part of a national defense mission. National interest took precedence over local concerns.

A second governance problem challenging states and localities is how to manage bourgeoning science- and technology-based health care and educational systems, or energy or agricultural sectors of local economies, for example. In recent years, states, cities, and towns around the country have had to face hardships — unemployment, toxic waste, national disasters, or the dangers of nuclear power, for example — that often require scientific and technological solutions. Harvey Sapolsky's inventory of the states' capacities to govern science and technology indicates considerable variability in state capacity for self-governance.[49] And monumental changes have taken place in recent years, especially in high-technology industries such as computers, which many states view as a panacea that will solve state and local economic woes. The governance problems for states are that many of them have difficulty bargaining with the federal government and many are struggling to manage either the negative externalities that industries produce or the opportunities for economic growth that industry offers.

HOW HAS GOVERNMENT RESPONDED?

The accumulated weight of these governance problems has forced the federal government to reexamine its existing governing institutions and experiment with new ones. As Table 1.1 shows, the federal government has responded in a number of ways. First, Congress has passed new legislation and created new government agencies to control the most offensive effects of hazardous technologies. Second, the courts have settled disputes as disparate as creationism, benzene, and hazardous waste. Third, peer review, the internal mechanism for the democratic control of science, has been reexamined and new structures for assuring accountability have been put in place. Fourth, "bipartisan" commissions and federal advisory committees that include a broader base of representation have been created. And fifth, as part of the Reagan administration's New Federalism, states and localities have improved their capacity to make and implement intelligent science and technology policy. Each of the chapters in Part II is a case study of a specific government response to some of the problems of governance: the NIH's experiences regulating government-sponsored gene-splicing research; the State of California's efforts to deal with conflicts of interest of scientists and technologists in state universities' employ; and in Massachusetts the City of Cambridge's response to a private company's plans to fulfill a DOD contract to test chemical weapons.

Legislation, Regulations, and Litigation. The legislation and executive branches of government have responded to the challenges created by changes in science and society by passing new laws and regulations to inhibit or enhance scientific research and technological development. Examples include the Superfund, the NIH guidelines to regulate research with recombinant DNA, and requirements for environmental impact statements. When frustrated by its inability to deal effectively with emerging problems in the areas of science and technology, the Congress has even created new agencies, one of the most notorious being the Department of Energy, created at the height of the energy crisis. Staff support agencies such as the Office of Technology Assessment in the legislative branch and the Office of Science and Technology Policy in the White House were also created as a result of a changing society—one that is increasingly dependent on science and technology.

Finally, several new scientific and technological developments have raised controversial issues for public debate. Fetal research gave rise to a National Commission for the Protection of Human Subjects in Biomedical and Behavioral Research; the transplant of a baboon's heart in Baby Fae put this item on the agendas of many Institutional Review Boards (IRBs); and gene therapy has spawned a new, broadly based committee to examine the ethical dilemmas created by this breakthrough. All of these sensational developments, and the institutional responses to them, have increased public awareness of the social consequences of science and technology and forced the institutions that govern science and technology to ask themselves how they can encourage scientists and engineers to be more socially responsible.

Peer Review and Conflict of Interest.   I have already noted that the rise of "big" science, the commercialization of biology, and increased military and industry funding of university research have created conflicts of interest, particularly for scientists. In Chapter 8, Helen Leskovac shows how California's university system handled its problem internally. Following a conflict of interest case on the University of California, Davis, campus in 1981, the state's conflict of interest regulations were amended, obligating university faculty to disclose financial interests, if any, in the non-governmental sponsors of their research. Potential conflicts of interest are now reviewed by a campus committee.

Some would argue that such conflict is an internal matter and that IRBs, the peer review system, and censure by professional associations are adequate to minimize the conflict of interest problem. When these internal democratic controls are functioning properly, there is accountability within science, and thus no need for external checks. But several scholars have raised questions about the effectiveness of these institutions. The objectivity of IRBs, for instance, has been called into question. And several studies of the peer review system have indicated that these controls can be both undemocratic and subjective.[50]

Citizen Participation. One response, especially to the crisis of legitimacy, is to democratize governing institutions by including either members of the public or advocates for the public interest in the policy making process. Several statutes mandate public participation in policy deliberations; and citizens can be found on committees that give advice to government agencies in virtually every policy area, including nuclear energy, hazardous waste, pharmaceutical products, or engineering projects.[51] Several experimental governing arrangements for settling scientific and technical disputes also make provisions for the participation of lay members of the public. As Sherry Arnstein and others have noted, participation does not equal power. Among other things, power depends upon the strength of public opinion, the point in the decision-making process when participation occurs, the ratio of expert to non-expert members of the deliberating body, the decision rules that the body adopts, and the technical competence of the participants.[52] The case studies of federal, state, and local governments trying to settle a scientific dispute and Leonard Cole's analysis of at least one experimental governing scheme that includes public members will give the reader an inkling of the variety of ways in which non-expert members of the public get involved in scientific controversies and the extent to which they are effective at influencing policy.

State and Local Control. The chapters in Part II discuss the role for state and local governing institutions as well. Although many issues with scientific and technological content are, in fact, national policy questions, for some time now, states have been building a capacity to make informed decisions about directing and regulating science and technology within their borders. The Reagan administration's New Federalism policies and the recent emphasis on greater self-sufficiency for state and local governments have also motivated state legislatures and governors' offices to seek autonomy through local technical competence.

In spite of the relentless nationalization of public policy that began shortly after the Civil War, that was stimulated by depressions and wars, and that continued apace until recently, states have traditionally been active in employment and science manpower issues. More recently, states have also taken the initiative in many policies for science and technol-

23

ogy. As Helen Leskovac notes in Chapter 8, science advisory committees to governors and state legislatures are now the rule.

Federal, state, and local governments have tried to solve governance problems in a number of ways. For the most part, the responses have taken the form of nonstructural or reformist, rather than structural, reform.[53] Typically, when problems arise "bipartisan" or "pluralistic" committees or commissions are formed; and their recommendations are taken into consideration when policy is eventually made. While there are many examples that could be cited, three institutional responses to the challenges that have been created by changes in science, technology, and society are studied in depth in this second part of the book.

TO WHAT EXTENT HAVE THESE EXPERIMENTS WORKED?

Our overall assessment of these responses is that they have been woefully inadequate, particularly when democratic standards are applied. They simply have failed to solve the crisis of legitimacy. This is because most of what passes for democratic or social control of science is merely ceremonial—window dressing aimed principally at ratifying decisions *post hoc* and gaining public support. In describing a number of experiments in public participation in technological decisions, Dorothy Nelkin and Michael Pollak write:

> (Most forums) are directed more toward co-opting public support than changing decisions; more toward seeking informed consent than expanding democratic choice. Determination to implement preconceived decisions leads officials to ignore, to debunk, or simply to be unaware of opposition. And this results in the transfer of conflict from the hearings to the courts, and often to the streets.[54]

While some of the experiments that Nelkin and Pollak cite satisfy the *procedural* aspects of democracy, they do not satisfy *substantive* ones. This is the thesis of Bruce Jennings' Chapter 10. In essence, the responses to governing problems that have been discussed above have been inadequate because of who governs, where, when, and how. Part III of the book examines these questions in depth.

HOW CAN THESE INADEQUACIES BE REMEDIED?

The remaining issue that is addressed in the conceptual framework that is schematized in Table 1.1 is the question of what can be done to make science and technology *and* democracy work better. How can science and technology be governed democratically? This is the organizing question for Part III, which consists of an assessment of the ways in which existing institutions fail democracy and specific recommendations regarding *preconditions* for democratic governance and *strategies* for reform.

But before specifying new institutional mechanisms and prescriptions for reforms in existing institutions, Jennings presents an elegant philosophical argument for the democratic governance of science and technology. He recognizes the weaknesses of existing institutions that are discussed in Cole's analysis (Chapter 11) of the "nuts and bolts" of a number of proposals and experiments for dealing with science and technology controversies. Although Cole's discussion deals only with a small subset of the problems of governance, his analysis of alternative proposed processes for resolving scientific and trans-scientific questions[55] leads one quickly to the conclusion that there are no easy answers to the problems of governance.

Even after my analysis of the nature of changes, challenges, and responses to governance problems in this chapter, and after Jennings' assessment of the inadequacies of current governing institutions, a number of questions are still left unanswered. The most important of these are summarized in Table 1.1. In Chapter 12, I address the questions of who should govern, when, where, how, and to what ends. The concluding chapter not only is a logical extension to the analyses in the other essays; it also serves as an agenda for future research into the question of what are optimal institutional arrangements for governing science and technology so that they will serve democracy.

CONCLUSION

Given the philosophical conceptions of science, technology, and democratic governance, direct democracy has been dismissed as unworkable; and a strict division of labor between the few who have a monopoly of power by virture of their skills at politics or science and the many who have little of this power has been rejected as an alternative because it offends our democratic impulses. What this book seeks to find is a political compromise — a middle way — that will attempt to balance the interests of preserving the integrity of the Republic of Science while advancing collective interests.[56]

In the chapters that follow, twelve contributors trained in the natural and social sciences, the law, and philosophy will examine a variety of empirical and normative questions that relate to the governance of science and technology in a democracy. From their collective wisdom one hopes to be able to learn enough about what works, what does not work, and what might work in order to prescribe a set of institutional reforms that, if implemented successfully, will increase the chances that science and technology will be governed more democratically in the future.

NOTES

1. See National Science Board, *Science Indicators, 1982* (Washington, D.C.: National Science Foundation, 1983), for details of the nature and magnitude of the decline. For possible reasons for the decline, see American Council on Education, *America's Competitive Challenge: The Need for a National Response* (Washington, D.C.: Business-Higher Education Forum, Apr. 1983); Simon Ramo, *America's Technological Slip* (New York: Wiley, 1980); and "Science and Public Policy: A Seminar with William D. Carey," *Science, Technology, and Human Values* 10 (Winter 1985): 7–16.

2. Letter from the Business — Higher Education Forum accompanying its report to the president of the United States, in American Council on Education, *America's Competitive Challenge.*

3. *Cassell's New Latin Dictionary,* 269. For further discussion, see Heinz Eulau and Kenneth Prewitt, *The Labyrinths of Democracy: Adaptations, Linkages, Representation, and Policies in the United States* (Indianapolis: Bobbs-Merrill, 1973), 13–14.

4. Eulau and Prewitt, *Labyrinths of Democracy,* 17. One of the most important issues in democratic theory is how power relationships between rulers and ruled are defined. Dennis Thompson, in *The Democratic Citizen* (Cambridge: Cambridge Univ. Press, 1970), distinguishes between democratic theorists who emphasize the mediating role of interest groups, political parties, and elections (elite democrats) from theorists who stress the need for direct public participation (citizen democrats). There is considerable controversy over the meaning of "public participation," however. For a brief discussion of the concept in the early days of the controversy surrounding genetic engineering, see U.S., Congress, House, Committee on Science and Technology, Subcommittee on Science, Research, and Technology, *Genetic Engineering, Human Genetics, and Cell Biology: Evolution of Technological Issues,* 94th Cong., 2d sess. (Washington, D.C.: Government Printing Office, Dec. 1976). For a broader view of political participation, see Sidney Verba and Norman Nie, *Participation in America* (New York: Harper & Row, 1971).

5. Edward Layton, "Mirror-Image Twins," *Technology and Culture* 12 (Oct. 1971): 562–80.

6. Robert Merton, *Social Theory and Social Structure* (New York: Free Press, 1968), 606–15. Those norms have been revised in recent years, reflecting countervailing values in science.

7. Robert Merton, "The Ambivalence of Scientists," *Bulletin of the Johns Hopkins Hospital* 112 (Feb. 1963): 77–97.

8. Harvey Brooks, "The Scientific Advisor," in *Scientists and National Policy-Making,* ed. Robert Gilpin and Christopher Wright (New York: Columbia Univ. Press, 1964).

9. Ibid., 76.

10. Mass society is a society in which masses are available for participation and elites are accessible. This view of society can be found in William Kornhauser, *The Politics of Mass Society* (Glencoe, Ill.: Free Press, 1959). According to Kornhauser, a mass society tries to reconcile aristocratic and democratic traditions by creating intermediary groups such as political parties and interest groups — mediators between rulers and ruled. For a critique of the concept of mass society, see Maurice Pinard, *The Rise of a Third Party* (Englewood Cliffs, N.J.: Prentice-Hall, 1971).

11. Jerome B. Weisner, *Where Science and Politics Meet* (New York: McGraw-Hill, 1965), 30.

12. Daniel Bell, *The Coming of Post-Industrial Society* (New York: Basic, 1973), 44.

13. William Carey, "Charting a Course for Science," *Science* 212 (26 June 1981): 1455.

14. This is merely a fraction of the $26 billion that is allocated for initial research and product testing. See R. Jeffrey Smith, "Star Wars Grants Attract Universities," *Science* 228 (10 May 1985). Some of the first awards were classified, but no work on university campuses will be classified unless the university agrees to it. It will be interesting to see if the movement on some campuses to ban SDI research will spread.

15. For a completely different view, see U.S. Department of Defense, *Soviet Military Power,* 4d ed. (Apr. 1985).

16. This compares to about one-half when the Reagan administration took office, and represents an increase from $51 billion in FY1985 to $57.6 billion — more than 10% — just in FY 1986. Office of Management and Budget, *Budget of the United States Government, Fiscal Year 1986* (Washington, D.C.: U.S. Government Printing Office, Feb. 1985): K-5. Colin Norman, "The Science Budget: A Dose of Austerity," *Science* 227 (15 February 1985): 726-8. For an analysis of the militarization of high technology, including space technology, see John Tirman, ed., *The Militarization of High Technology* (Cambridge, Mass.: Ballinger, 1985.)

17. "DeLauer Says CIS Provides Model for U.S." Stanford University *Campus Reports,* 25 May, 1983: p. 1, 22. For a comprehensive analysis of university-industry agreements in the area of biotechnology, see Martin Kenney, *Biotechnology: The Birth of an Industry* (New Haven: Yale Univ. Press, forthcoming).

18. George A. Keyworth III, "Science and Technology Policy: The Next Four Years," *Technology Review* 88 (Feb./Mar. 1985), esp. the tables on p. 48. For a critique of administration policy, see David Dickson, *The New Politics of Science* (New York: Pantheon, 1984).

19. Keyworth, "Science and Technology Policy: The Next Four Years," 45–46. For an assessment of the conservative administration's science policy, see Will Lepkowski, "The Making of a Conservative Science Policy," *Technology Review* 8 (Jan. 1984): 39–46.

20. In order to be a source of power in society, expertise must be able to reduce uncertainty. See J. French, Jr., and B. Raven, "The Bases for Social Power," in *Studies in Social Power,* ed. D. Cartwright (Ann Arbor: Institute for Social Research, Univ. of Michigan, 1959). Citizens who lacked expertise in molecular biology showed that they were also capable of wielding power, as was illustrated by the role they played on the Cambridge Experimentation Review Board in the rDNA dispute. As part of the body politic, lay members of the public are no less qualified than scientists or technologists to decide the moral, social, and political consequences of research and development.

21. Gerald Holton and Robert S. Morison, eds., *Limits of Scientific Inquiry* (New York: Norton, 1979).

27

22. U.S., Congress, House, Committee on Science and Technology, *Committee Report*, Feb. 1984.

23. "Disputed" science and technology are defined as activities where risks of unknown probability to human health and safety or to the environment are posed, or regarding which there is a scientific or ethical controversy. Harvey Brooks distinguishes between: (1) the resolution of disputes by separating political and technical components; and (2) the resolution of disputes by assuming that all controversies are value-laden. Harvey Brooks, "The Resolution of Technically Intensive Public Policy Disputes," *Science, Technology, and Human Values* 9 (Winter 1984): 39–50. For further discussion of the relationship between facts and values in science policy making, see Alvin Weinberg, "Science and Trans-Science," *Minerva,* 10 (Apr. 1972): 209–22; Dorothy Nelkin, *Technological Decisions and Democracy: European Experiments in Public Participation* (Beverly Hills: Sage, 1977); Allan Mazur, *The Dynamics of Technical Controversy* (Washington, D.C.: Communications Press, 1981); Dorothy Nelkin, ed. *Controversy: Politics of Technical Decisions,* 2d ed. (Beverly Hills: Sage, 1984); and James C. Petersen and Gerald M. Markle, "Politics and Science in the Laetrile Controversy," *Social Studies of Science* 9 (Feb. 1979): 139–66.

24. For a sampling of views on the legitimation crisis, see Kornhauser, *Politics of Mass Society;* Jurgen Habermas, *The Legitimation Crisis* (Boston: Beacon, 1975); James P. Freeman, *Crisis and Legitimacy* (Cambridge: Cambridge Univ. Press, 1978); Richard Rose, *Challenge to Governance* (Beverly Hills: Sage, 1980); Leon Lindberg et al., eds., *Stress and Contradictions in Modern Society* (Lexington, Mass.: Lexington Books, 1971); Arthur Vidich and Ronald Glassman, eds., *Conflict and Control: Challenge to the Legitimacy of Modern Governments* (Beverly Hills: Sage, 1979); and Alan Wolfe, *The Limits of Legitimacy: Political Contradictions of Contemporary Capitalism* (New York: Free Press, 1977).

25. Seymour Martin Lipset, "Feeling Better: Measuring the Nation's Confidence," *Public Opinion* 8 (Apr./May 1985): 9. Also see Seymour Martin Lipset and William Schneider, *The Confidence Gap: Business, Labor, and Government in the Public Mind* (New York: Free Press, 1983).

26. Lipset, "Feeling Better,":6–9, 56–58.

27. Arthur Miller, "Is Confidence Rebounding?", *Public Opinion* 6 (June/July 1983), 20.

28. See Malcolm L. Goggin, "The Life Sciences and the Public: Is Science Too Important to Be Left to the Scientists?" *Politics and the Life Sciences* 3 (Aug. 1984): 28–40. The most comprehensive examination of public opinion about science and technology can be found in Jon D. Miller, Robert W. Suchner, and Alan M. Voelker, *Citizenship in an Age of Science: Changing Attitudes Among Young Adults* (New York: Pergamon, 1980).

29. Todd R. La Porte and Daniel Metlay, "Technology Observed: Attitudes of a Wary Public," *Science* 188 (11 Apr. 1975):123. Genetic engineering and nuclear power have been singled out as particularly problematical. In Miller, Suchner, and Voelker, *Citizenship in an Age of Science,* the authors report that the public was willing to restrict research that created new life forms. And in a cross-national study of attitudes towards nuclear power, Ronald Inglehart has shown that fears of nuclear technology stem from misconceptions, which public education might correct. Ronald Inglehart, "The Fear of Living Dangerously: Public Attitudes Toward Nuclear Power," *Public Opinion* 7 (Feb./March 1984):41–44.

30. Allan Mazur, "Commentary: Opinion Poll Measurement of American Confidence

in Science," *Science, Technology, and Human Values* 6 (Summer 1981): 18. For an even more upbeat interpretation of the data, see L. John Martin, "Science and the Successful Society," *Public Opinion* 4 (June/July 1981): 17, 56.

31. Georgine M. Pion and Mark W. Lipsey, "Public Attitudes Toward Science and Technology: What Have the Surveys Told Us?" *Public Opinion Quarterly* 45 (Fall 1981): 305.

32. See B. Shen, "Scientific Literacy and the Public Understanding of Science," in *Communication of Scientific Information,* ed. S. Day (Basel: Karger, 1975); Miller, Suchner, and Voelker, *Citizenship in an Age of Science;* and Jon D. Miller, "Scientific Literacy: A Conceptual and Empirical Review," *Daedalus* 112 (Spring 1983): Table 5.

33. Theodore J. Lowi and Alan Stone, eds., *Nationalizing Government: Public Policies in America* (Beverly Hills: Sage, 1978); and John Hanus, ed., *The Nationalization of State Government* (Lexington, Mass.: D.C. Heath, 1981). There are, of course, trends that run counter to increased centralization and nationalization, for example, the block grant programs that were established with the passage of the Omnibus Budget Reconciliation Act of 1981. For an analysis of these "New Federalism" block grants in theory and in practice, see Malcolm L. Goggin, David Cownie, David Romero, Larry Gonzalez, and Susan Williams, "Block Grants and the New Federalism: Theory and Practice," paper presented at the 1985 Annual Meeting of the Southwestern Social Sciences Association, Houston, Texas, March 1985.

34. Robert A. Dahl and Edward R. Tufte, *Size and Democracy* (Stanford, Calif.: Stanford Univ. Press, 1973). There are various ways for citizens to express their collective preferences on technological matters. Some of these mechanisms are discussed in U.S. Army Corps of Engineers, *Public Involvement Techniques* (Washington, D.C.: Government Printing Office, 1983). See James Carroll, "Participatory Technology," *Science* 171 (19 Feb. 1971): 647–53; and Sherry Arnstein, "A Ladder of Public Participation," *Journal of the American Institute of Planning* 35 (July 1969): 216–24.

35. National Science Board, *Science Indicators, 1982.*

36. Several examples are cited in Goggin, *"Is Science too Important?",* and in Leonard A. Cole, *Politics and the Restraint of Science* (Totowa, N.J.: Rowman and Allanheld, 1983). Scientists who cheat are threatening further to undermine public confidence in science, so scientists are trying to police themselves. For example, the NIH has held a symposium on the issue; and the AAAS organized a related panel at its 1985 annual meeting. See R. Jeffrey Smith, "Scientific Fraud Probed at AAAS Meeting," *Science* 228 (14 June 1985): 1292–93; and George How Colt, "Too Good to Be True," *Harvard Magazine* 85 (July/Aug. 1983): 22–28, 54.

37. Lewis Thomas, "Hubris in Science?" *Science* 200 (30 June 1978): 1459–62.

38. Alice K. Smith, *A Peril and a Hope* (Chicago: Univ. of Chicago Press, 1965); Dorothy Nelkin, "Threats and Promises: Negotiating the Control of Research," *Daedalus* 107 (Spring 1978): 191–211; and Barbara Culliton, "Science's Restive Public," *Daedalus* 107 (Spring 1978): 152–155.

39. Michael Polanyi, "The Republic of Science," *Minerva* 1 (Aug. 1962): 54–73.

40. Dickson, *The New Politics of Science.* In July 1984 a for-profit hospital, Humana Inc., pledged "many millions of dollars" to Dr. William C. DeVries. Within a month, Humana's stock price had increased by approximately 25 percent.

41. Ibid., 5.

42. Simon Rottenberg, "The Economy of Science: The Proper Role of Government in the Growth of Science," *Minerva* 19 (Spring 1981): 43–71. Polanyi, "The Republic of

Science," argues along similar lines, with scientists determining the most promising projects to fund.

43. See Malcolm L. Goggin, "Threats to Freedom from a Tyranny of the Minority," *Politics and the Life Sciences* 3 (Aug. 1984): 68–75.

44. Donald S. Fredrickson, "The Public Governance of Science," *Man and Medicine* 3 (1978): 77–88.

45. Contrast Lawrence Lessing, "The Senseless War on Science," *Fortune* 83 (Mar. 1971): 87–91, 153; and, more recently, John P. Dickinson, *Science and Scientific Researchers in Modern Society* (Paris: UNESCO, 1984); with Dorothy Nelkin, "Eye to the Rosy Lens," *Nature* 313 (28 Feb. 1985): 825.

46. Arthur Kornberg, "The Support of Science," *Science* 180 (1 June 1973): 909.

47. Keyworth compared exciting projects in neurobiology, particle physics, and space science with areas of research that in his opinion offered no excitement, for example, social science research. Keyworth, "Science and Technology Policy," 50.

48. In FY 1985, the Reagan administration, upon the advice of the Office of Management and Budget, had attempted to reduce the total number of grants awarded by 500. After a pitched battle with scientists, the 500 grants were finally reinstated.

49. Harvey Sapolsky, "Science Advice for State and Local Government," *Science* 160 (19 Apr. 1968): 280–84.

50. Diana B. Dutton and John L. Hochheimer, "Institutional Biosafety Committees and Public Participation: Assessing the Experiment," *Nature* 297 (6 May 1982): 11–15; and William Hines, "Peer Review: Fostering an Old Boy Network or Policing Scientific Research?", *San Francisco Chronicle,* 5 July, 1981; a series of articles by John Walsh, which appeared in *Science* in 1975; and recent criticisms by Stephen Cole and his colleagues. See Malcolm L. Goggin, "Science Policy Governance: Experts and Laymen," paper delivered at the Annual Meeting of the American Political Science Association, New York, Sept. 1981, pp. 4–6.

51. See, for example, James C. Petersen, ed., *Citizen Participation in Science Policy* (Amherst: Univ. of Massachusetts Press, 1984); John Lester and Ann O'Malley Bowman, eds., *The Politics of Hazardous Waste Management* (Durham, N.C.: Duke Univ. Press, 1983); Steven Ebbin and Raphael Kasper, *Citizen Groups and the Nuclear Power Controversy: Use of Scientific and Technological Information* (Cambridge: MIT Press, 1974); Lynton K. Caldwell et al., *Citizens and The Environment: Case Studies in Popular Action* (Bloomington: Indiana Univ. Press, 1976); Daniel Mazmanian and Jeanne Nienaber, *Can Organizations Change?* (Washington, D.C.: Brookings, 1979); and Dorothy Nelkin and Susan Fallows, "The Evolution of the Nuclear Debate: The Role of Public Participation," *Annual Review of Energy* 3 (1978): 275–312.

52. Malcolm L. Goggin and Ralph Silber, "Public Participation: Society's Right to Decide," paper prepared for the Stanford University School of Medicine EVIST Project, 1980.

53. André Gorz, *Strategy for Labor* (Boston: Beacon Press, 1967).

54. People with little or no technical expertise are challenging the priests of science by demanding to be let into science's ecclesiastical court. There are many articles and a few books on the role of the public in science policy making, the most comprehensive and subtle of which is James C. Petersen, *Citizen Participation in Science Policy.* Petersen's edited volume pays more attention than this book to the mechanisms for citizen participation.

55. Weinberg, "Science and Trans-Science."
56. Goggin, "Is Science Too Important?," 39. Also see Duncan MacRae, Jr., "Science and the Formation of Policy in a Democracy," *Minerva* 11 (Apr. 1973) 230; Duncan MacRae, Jr., *Policy Indicators: Links between Social Science and Public Debate* (Chapel Hill: Univ. of North Carolina Press, 1985), Chs. 2 and 10; and Henry Lambright, *Governing Science and Technology* (New York: Oxford Univ. Press: 1976), 202–3.

PART I

THE CRISIS OF GOVERNANCE IN SCIENCE AND TECHNOLOGY

The five chapters in Part I examine a variety of challenges to the institutions that organize and direct modern science in a democracy, and provide the philosophical, historical, political, and economic contexts within which these challenges arise.

One of the most perplexing aspects of this crisis of governance is the tension created by demands that those who "do" science and technology be granted more autonomy *and* that they also be held to account for their activities to a larger public. The tension is created by the very nature of American government: under some conditions and in some policy domains the influence of the people's representatives is significant whereas under other circumstances political leaders are more responsive to the wishes of their constituents. For example, it has long been recognized that the president of the United States and legislators in Washington act more independently of their constituents in making foreign policy decisions than in making social welfare policy choices.

Like foreign policy and national security, science and technology are policy domains in which technical advisors to Congress and the president and non-elected officials in government agencies — in this case scientists and engineers from universities and industry — make most of the important policy decisions. According to Lincoln Kirsten, these scientific and technological experts live by elite, not democratic criteria. Besides the constitutional argument for self-rule, the principal sociological justification of science's autonomy is that scientific inquiry is already subject to internal democratic controls through a strong set of norms and a viable peer review system.

Part I of this book takes up several issues related to two central con-

33

cerns of this book — the crisis of governance in science and technology and reforms in the institutions of governance that could strengthen *both* the scientific republic *and* democracy. In the first chapter, I raise the normative question of who *should* govern in a science- and technology-based advanced industrial state that is seeking to be just and democratic. I describe what I believe are the parameters of the democratic imperative in a modern society whose size and complexity have necessitated a representative form of democracy; and from the democratic imperative I infer a number of necessary and sufficient conditions of citizenship. These citizenship requirements pertain to both expert and non-expert members of the public. By juxtaposing to this philosophical view of republican democracy a modern conception of science and technology, I make the argument that the wide variety of claims that are made on science and technology may be competing and contradictory. In fact, they are often mutually exclusive.

After enumerating the demands and supports of competing claimants and their justifications, I conclude that the scientists' and technologists' constitutionally protected right to academic freedom and the pursuit of inquiry are not absolute. Rights must be mediated so that a balance can be struck between (1) the requirements for participation and for autonomous inquiry in a working democracy, and (2) the need for scientists and technologists to account for their activities to a larger public, especially when public monies are involved or when the health and safety of members of the public and of the environment are at risk. To emerge from this paradoxical situation a political solution is offered, a solution that specifies the degree and type of participation in policy making of a wide variety of interests who have a stake in the choice of research topic, the research protocol, the dissemination of findings, and the application of new knowledge for the achievement of practical ends.

Several recent developments in science and technology and in their relationship to society threaten to undermine the autonomy of basic and applied research, and they are discussed in the chapters in this part of the book. In the 1980s, restrictions of scientific inquiry are both external and internal, and they are made in the name of the need for greater social responsibility and national security, or for maintaining a competitive edge in international markets. Moreover, these encroachments on autonomy are no longer confined to the choice of research subject or method, but affect the dissemination of research results as well.

Beyond the common theme of autonomy and accountability that underlies all of the chapters of this book, the five chapters in this section focus on problems of governance—what they are, how they have come about, and what can be done to solve them. One governance issue dealt with in two of the chapters is the relationship between science and government. Helen Longino's essay not only sets the philosophical context within which the many processes that constitute scientific inquiry take place, but also documents the executive branch's recent efforts to limit the free flow of information. William Blanpied and Rachelle Hollander, who provide the historical context of policy for science and technology, review the changing position of scientists and engineers in the political bargaining process. By bringing their history of the development of the National Science Foundation up to date, they point out that the process for setting priorities for science and technology has, since 1981, resulted in policies that favor defense- and mission-oriented research at the expense of other types of R&D. And these new research priorities may redefine a new contract between science and government.

Other governance problems stem from the commercialization of biology. One problem is the increase in the number of scientist-entrepreneurs, and what Dennis Florig, in his analysis of the political and economic contexts of research and development, describes as the contradictions between the scientist, with an intellectual commitment to pursue knowledge, and the entrepreneur, with a material commitment to making a profit.

A second problem is the increase in the number of university-industry agreements, a special case of the scientist-entrepreneur syndrome. In giving a working university scientist's perspective on a number of governing problems that have emerged as a result of growing commercialization of research and development, especially in molecular biology, Leon Wofsy draws attention to the interdependence of industry and the military, on the one hand, and the university on the other. While there are many parallels in other branches of science, one should not conclude that what is happening in genetic biology is typical of the whole of science.

Wofsy notes that ties between academia and industry have already resulted in changes. Secret agreements that provide patent protection to new life forms, or transfer ownership of inventions and other intellectual property to the corporation in exchange for personal financial rewards, have made making money a new criterion of success for biologists. These agreements have also forced many biologists to look upon their colleagues as competitors and lured younger scientists into areas of research that can be exploited commercially. Like the other chapters in this section, Wofsy's pinpoints a fundamental contradiction between the norms of the university and the norms of the military and industry sponsors of university research. And this, Wofsy argues, is bound to lead to conflicts of interest — another problem with which the institutions that govern science and technology have to contend. Both the rise of the scientist-entrepreneur and increase in the number of university-industry agreements pose a potential threat to the autonomy of scientific inquiry; and both are part of a constellation of recent challenges to governing institutions.

There are also a number of other problems of governance that are raised by all the authors who have contributed chapters to Part I. First, all would agree that in this information age, science and technology are pervasive. Moreover, science and technology are complex social activities that represent several processes. Despite this diversity, however, these activities are far from autonomous. Instead, there are many nonscientific "contextual" values — for example, prepublication review requirements as a "string" attached to external government funding, or industry requirements that publication of results be delayed until a discovery can be exploited commercially — that shape the development and use of knowledge. By threatening the autonomy of inquiry, all such constraints have contributed to the crisis of governance in science and technology.

The authors in Part I underscore the point that science is being overrun, and some lay the blame for that development on the *ad hoc* nature of the science policymaking process itself. Blanpied and Hollander agree that policy for science and technology is fragmented, disjointed, and uncoordinated. Other contributors to this book point out that the integrity of science is being challenged for other reasons: the institutions of governance are following neither the norms of science nor the sound management practice of separating the promotion of a technology from its regulation.

While these chapters have many themes in common, there is at least one point about which some of the authors who have contributed to Part I cannot agree. It is the nature of the solution to the problem of governance. Florig and Wofsy opt for more decentralized governance of science; and Blanpied and Hollander would like to see more central coordination. These differences in proposed solutions to the problems of governance will be addressed in Part III.

1. Science and Technology: Who Should Govern?

MALCOLM L. GOGGIN

That there is a "crisis of governance" in science- and technology-driven western industrialized democracies is widely accepted! Whether there is agreement about the nature of the crisis and its causes, or about the steps that should be taken to resolve the crisis, is another matter. There are at least two conflicting views as to what the crisis is, how and why it developed, and what can be done about it. The first view, which I shall call *the alienation hypothesis,* argues that the role of ordinary citizens in governance has been too limited. The second view, *the overload hypothesis,* sees active participation of mass publics as a threat to democracy, and therefore, argues that participation of the public in governance should be curtailed.

Both the alienation and the overload hypotheses treat the crisis of governance as a crisis of democracy, generally manifesting itself in virtually every policy domain. But nowhere is the crisis more acute than in the making and carrying out of public policies with high scientific and technical content. The crisis of governance in science and technology policy is a microcosm of the larger problem of democratic governance. The purposes of this chapter are to explore two alternative explanations for the crisis of governance, to examine the competing claims of those who wish to share in the governing of science and technology, and to analyze the linkages between the many who wish to influence the direction, funding, and regulation of basic and applied research and technological development and the few whose responsibility it is to make and implement those kinds of decisions. How rulers and ruled relate to one another is the essence of democratic governance.

THE CRISIS OF GOVERNANCE

Why do we have a "crisis of governance"?

The first explanation is that a "cult of expertise"[2] has intimidated large segments of the voting-age population, forcing them to sit out the game of politics. The lack of political participation has alienated these spectators and left them without a sense of political efficacy. Alienation, in turn, has led to declines in public confidence in the institutions of authority in general and in government in particular. Educating these "apathetics" in the ways of politics will restore their trust in government, to be manifested in correspondingly higher levels of support and approval.[3] The essence of this line of argument is that a lack of political participation, or apathy, on the part of a large percentage of the public threaten to kill democracy. This is the alienation hypothesis.

Alienation Breeds Distrust. This "alienation breeds distrust" argument has relevance for the democratic governance of science and technology as well. Loss of control over one's own destiny is engendered by a society in which (1) the units of government have become larger, more complex, more centralized, more bureaucratic, and thus more impersonal; (2) where many problems that previously had been handled locally are now resolved by non-elected technocrats at the national level; and (3) where many public policy decisions contain a high level of scientific and technological content that ordinary citizens are ill-prepared to comprehend. Frustrated and alienated by this loss of control, a critical minority of the mass public has lost some of its confidence in science and especially in some forms of technology as panaceas for society's ills. In the wake of constant media coverage of the negative consequences when science and technology go awry, demands for more regulation and accountability have increased, as have demands that limits be placed on some types of research and some technologies. A more antiscience and antitechnology public, now generally more skeptical, is more reluctant to support investment in some types of research and development and more willing to impose restrictions on scientists and technologists.

Since in this version of the crisis the root cause of apathy and alienation is scientific and technical illiteracy (this form of literacy includes being "learned" and able to read and write about science and technology),[4] one solution is to educate citizens so that the public's understanding of science and technology is both deepened and expanded. But achieving the goal of scientific and technical literacy is not simple, and it requires more than book-learning. According to Kenneth Prewitt, people have to acquire a common-sense "street savvy" about the subject.[5] A slightly different solution is offered by Dorothy Nelkin, namely "democratization" of sectoral and national policy making, or "efforts to make political systems more responsive to the general public by incorporating diverse citizen interests in the formulation and implementation of national policies for science and technology."[6]

The problems of scientific illiteracy and mass apathy are not unique to the United States. In Britain, for example, scientific and technical illiteracy has become a major barrier to understanding and communication. Referring specifically to the situation in Britain, Bruce Williams writes,

> If we are to become a well-educated and effective society, we need a much wider understanding of science and technology and of the interactions between science, technology and society. Just why we more than other countries go on allowing our schools to practise a sort of educational apartheid, by the early selection and separation of literary sheep and numerate goats, and what should be done about it, are issues that deserve more discussion and action.[7]

Participation Breeds Disrespect for Authority. The second explanation for the crisis of governance is that not too little but too much democracy threatens to kill democracy. A "cult of equality"[8] has aroused a restive public which in turn has threatened the privileged status of those in positions of authority. They can no longer claim superiority by virtue of their "age, rank, status, character, or talents."[9] And they see cherished traditional values under fire from an unruly mass public whose members engage in unconventional (i.e., outside the electoral process) modes of political participation. This "democratic surge," as Samuel Huntington of the Trilateral Commission characterizes it, results in a substantial decrease in governmental authority.[10] Participatory strategies such as "maximum feasible participation" or "consumer control" have created a new class of gladiators, who threaten to disrupt the system's equilibrium and therefore hold the potential for creating disorder within the system.

What are the consequences of this democratic distemper? Budget deficits, strikes by public employees, economic nationalism, and the government's inability to require its citizens to sacrifice in the face of military and economic threats from abroad are but a few outcomes of too much democracy. But above all else, this type of system overload results in

39

disrespect for authority. What is the proposed solution to this change in the relative influence of elites and non-elites? If it were possible, elites would like to restore normalcy — in the form of mass apathy — as a way to preserve traditional values, reinstate elites in their traditional positions in superiority, and restore American power and influence in the world. This is the overload hypothesis.

The overload hypothesis has an analogue in the governance of science and technology. And it can be illustrated by events connected with the ten-year debate over the question of how, if at all, gene-splicing research should be regulated. The adversaries in this political struggle were establishment scientists and executives, venture capitalist connected with an emerging biotechnology industry, and the university (elites), on the one hand; and dissident scientists and members of the attentive public (counter-elites), on the other. Employing a strategy based on E. E. Schattschneider's advice on party politics, the insurgents attempted to "expand the scope of the conflict."[11] Relying on experts of their own, dissident scientists politicized the issue by linking questions of hazards and ethics related to the recombinant technique to concerns of immediate importance to social movements of the 1970s, for example, consumers and environmentalists. By politicizing the issue, those in the minority hoped to enlist the support of politically powerful organized interests and mobilize large segments of the American public to support restrictions on gene-splicing research. In this manner, the minority hoped to become the majority.

Fearing a tyranny of the majority in the form of a "democratic surge," molecular biologists and establishment scientists in other disciplines lobbied Congress to prevent legislation that would have given lay members of the public a meaningful role in policy making.[12] Instead, they pressed for a compromise solution that would have maintained the status quo, that is, kept the Recombinant DNA Advisory Committee (RAC) within the National Institutes of Health (NIH), with limited power over university researchers and no power over industry, as the only regulatory institution for gene-splicing research.[13] This solution would both channel the debate into this single forum, where members of the lay public were by law in a minority status, and confine the discussion to safety issues. Moreover, the NIH guidelines, which specifically exempted industry research from government regulation, and the designation of RAC as the principal forum in which disputes would have to be settled preempted the efforts of municipal governments to restrict research that was being conducted within local political jurisdictions.

LIMITS TO FREEDOM OF INQUIRY

One of the battlegrounds of the crisis of governance is over the following questions: Is the freedom to inquire absolute? If it is not, under what circumstances should free inquiry be limited? Is freedom of inquiry protected under the Constitution?[14]

Scientists and technologists have had no difficulty accepting peer review and informed consent as restraints on inquiry. But most have resisted other incursions into autonomous inquiry, which, although the matter has not yet been decided in the courts, many believe is an extension of free expression.[15] In answering the question of what, if any, kinds of research should be limited because of the danger that new knowledge presents to the established or desired order, David Baltimore has opposed limiting science, writing that science should not be the servant of any ideology.

> I believe that there are two simple, and almost universally acceptable answers. First, the criteria determining what areas to restrain invariably express certain sociopolitical attitudes and reflect a dominant ideology . . . Second, attempts to restrain directions of scientific inquiry are more likely to be generally disruptive of science rather than to provide the desired specific restraint.[16]

There are, however, certain types of experiments — for example, when human or animal subjects are used, or when the community is put at risk — when regulation of inquiry is morally and constitutionally indicated.[17]

In the 1960s, the issue of limits to freedom was raised by antiwar activists who questioned whether *some* university researchers were, in fact, apolitical (especially with respect to the Vietnam War), threatened to shut down the university, and forced defense-related contract research off most campuses. But the withdrawal of troops from Southeast Asia and the rapid developments in molecular biology changed the parameters of the limits-of-inquiry debate.

In the 1970s, the major restrictions on free inquiry were initiated by dissident scientists and members of the attentive public — those persons who were willing to take the time and make the effort to inform themselves about issues in a specialized area.[18] The first targets of regulation were potentially hazardous research like recombinant DNA, where local authorities invoked the state's police power to protect human health and safety.[19] The second target of restraint was research that Richard Delgado and David Millen have termed "inopportune" — research that

41

the state would like to limit because it "considers the area of inquiry itself inappropriate or suspect."[20] Examples are research on the XYY syndrome, the genetics of human intelligence, and sociobiology. Rather than technology, science was the object of most of the regulatory effort. The end result was that in the 1970s many more restrictions were imposed and several new institutions of accountability—from the federal RAC to university biohazards committees, institutional review boards, and human subjects committees—were put in place.[21]

The field of public discourse over the question of limitations on the pursuit of knowledge changed again when, in 1980, Ronald Reagan was elected president, and the power to govern was transferred to a more conservative administration. One general tendency distinguished governance in the 1980s from governance in the 1970s. Conservatives have become more politically active. Business groups have organized to lobby Congress and the president and to publicize the benefits of free enterprise, and conservative Political Action Committees have become a potent (and often negative) force in electoral politics. Furthermore, organized fundamentalist religious groups have attacked theories of evolution and "secular humanism" in the nation's public schools. Beginning in Reagan's first year as president and continuing at least until 1986, the limitations that had been placed on scientific research and technological development in the 1970s were extended from the choice of research topic and the research protocol to the dissemination of scientific information as well. And established authority, in the form of federal agencies such as the Departments of State, Commerce, and Defense, replaced students, dissident scientists, public interest groups, and active members of the public—the gladiators—as the principal limiters of inquiry. It is to these new examples of limitations on free inquiry that we now turn.

Limits to Academic Freedom.   There are four basic areas in which the state has imposed restrictions on the freedom of scholars to express and exchange their ideas:[22] (1) prepublication review and contract constraint, (2) increased security classification, (3) export controls, and (4) restrictions on foreign scholars. The examples cited demonstrate the nature of and extent to which federal authority is now being exercised in order to restrict and disrupt the free flow of ideas.[23]

Prior Restraint.   Through National Security Decision Directive 84, dated March 11, 1983, the Reagan administration required more than

120,000 government employees to sign lifetime prepublication agreements as a condition for gaining access to certain classified information. In addition, under this directive government agencies are authorized to order polygraph tests when appropriate and to regulate government employee contacts with the media.[24] As part of this trend towards greater state censorship, several federal agencies are requiring recipients of grants to sign prepublication review clauses in contracts as a condition of funding their research. As the Harvard Report on Federal Restrictions notes, "the imposition of censorship has grown substantially beyond the boundaries of the traditional wartime national security exception to the ban on prior restraints that has long been a fundamental element of First Amendment doctrine."[25]

Classification.   President Reagan's 1982 Executive Order 12356 was issued to revise the security classification system of previous administrations.[26] Beginning in 1982, the classifier need only have a reasonable expectation that by not classifying the material, national security might be damaged. The new order also eliminated automatic declassification. Moreover, material could be classified at any time. This latter provision may have a chilling effect on certain types of sensitive research, for an investigator may not wish to make a long-term intellectual investment in an area of research that may suddenly become classified.

Export Control.   During the Carter administration, Export Administration Regulations were promulgated as part of the Export Administration Act of 1979. The regulations were intended to prevent "technological data" from getting into the hands of the Soviets and other nations hostile to the United States. This act supplemented the International Traffic in Arms Regulations of 1968. Traditionally, publications of university researchers have been exempted from the regulations. But with the 1979 rules, "correspondence, attendance at or participation in meetings" and "instructions in academic laboratories" were also placed off limits. As part of this new policy, shortly after Ronald Reagan took office the department of state sent a form letter to many universities inquiring into the activities of some of their foreign scholars. In other cases, especially in the area of laser optics, government agencies have pulled scholars' papers from professional meetings.[27]

Restrictions on Foreign Scholars.   Under the McCarran Act, foreign nationals may be denied entry to the United States on the basis of what they say or believe. The Harvard Report on Federal Restrictions cites three cases of foreign nationals who, because of their beliefs, were denied asylum or reentry to the United States. In all three cases, the government used classified information to plead its case. Many other foreign scholars have had their freedoms restricted.[28]

WHO SHOULD GOVERN?

It should be clear from this brief description of recent developments in the debate over restricting the freedom to inquire that in a democracy the governance of science and technology should not be in the hands of any one group, and clearer still that state control should be vigorously opposed. Nor is there a simple choice between oligarchy (leaving science and technology to scientists and engineers) and democracy (leaving science and technology to the people). Ours is a society of plural interests, each with competing claims and each claim with a certain degree of validity and legitimacy.

This is not to deny that some interests — for example, those represented in what President Dwight Eisenhower, upon leaving office, called the "military-industrial complex"[29] — are more powerful than others. The case of early government funding and development of one medical device, the totally implantable artificial heart, illustrates the proposition that choices of particular paths of development for technologies are determined by experts in the field and by commercial interests. And there is ample evidence that, depending on the nature of the support it received during the election campaign, every administration in Washington is going to be more sympathetic to the claims of some groups and less responsive to the petitions of others.

Governments govern, yet multiple interests are involved in the "tangled web" of science and technology governance. Through support, demands, and consent, a bevy of interests, some organized and some not, some more powerful or more articulate than others, press their cases for one national science and technology policy configuration or another. And governors respond to varying degrees with a series of decisions and actions, in the form of public policies.

This leads to the question of who should govern science and technology. Who has a legitimate case for control over the direction and funding of research and development, and what arguments are used to justify and legitimize a claim? As a framework for answering this question, we introduce the notion of a science and technology policy system,[30] consisting of congressional committees and subcommittees, industry, and the university as *patrons*; the scientists and technologists as *providers*; and expert and non-expert citizen *consumers* as the people who benefit from, and are exposed to the risks and harms of, basic and applied research and technological development and deployment. Each party has a claim to be represented at the bargaining table where policies for science and technology are formulated and adopted. And the bargaining takes place in the context of a decision environment that includes elements of the national political economy, such as the federal technoscience agencies, interest groups, power wielders, labor unions, public opinion, the media, and many more.

The Patrons.   There are many patrons of the sciences and technology, and funds for research come from many sources. The principal donors, however, are Congress and its agents, the executive branch agencies and bureaus, industry, and the university. As investors, each has a strong claim to be a major, controlling voice in any decisions about the course and conduct of research and development.

The most obvious donor is Congress. The Constitution grants Congress the power of the purse, which means that its members are empowered to raise revenues and budget and appropriate funds. Congress performs not only a law making but also a representational function. As representatives of constituencies within their districts, congresspersons have a responsibility for determining the preferences of those they represent. Perhaps it is this notion of constituency, an aggregate of persons who appoint others to act for them as attorneys-in-fact, that comes closest to the idea of a public, for "the" public is an inclusive concept made up of many publics, for example, bench scientists, engineers, business and labor leaders, university presidents, rank and file workers, and the poor and the unemployed, to name a few. Congresspersons have a direct claim to govern — to make policy and, through their oversight responsibilities, many of which have been delegated to non-elected government officials, to see that their plans are successfully put into effect. The president, as the only representative of all the people, can also make legitimate demands to be represented in any major decisions about the course and conduct of science and technology. There are many cases when he has exercised that right, such as President Nixon's involvement in the Cancer Crusade and President Ford's ill-fated association with the Swine Flu Immunization Program of 1976.

Another patron is corporate capital. In comparison to senators, representatives, and agency officials administering policies and programs, who in theory are motivated by the public interest but in practice may be motivated by a desire to be reelected or to land a plumb job in private industry after leaving public service, capitalists emphasize private interests and invest resources for the purposes of getting a reasonable rate of return on their investments. Hence, corporate interests use knowledge and know-how for a profit, hoping to privatize the gain and socialize any bad externalities, for example, risks of hazard or harm to the public health. One way to accomplish this objective is to use the university and the genius of its faculty as a means of improving corporate profit.[31]

Through their sponsorship, patrons influence providers of new discoveries and applications; their choices of research questions, methods, and protocols; and when and through what channels they will communicate their results. Scientists and technologists, like most people, are self-interested individuals whose choices invariably reflect the interests and concerns of their patrons, whether these be the military, "study sections" in federal agencies, capitalists sponsoring research, or leaders in their own professional circles. These patrons are elites in the sense that they set the standards for what constitutes scientific progress. As David Noble describes the relationship between technologists and their patrons, "The power relations of society . . . define to a considerable extent what is technically possible."[32] An anecdote will underscore the point. In a 1982 talk with MIT students on the subject of the social responsibility of the university, Ralph Nader told students of his experience when, as a law student at Harvard University, he was doing research for his book, *Unsafe at Any Speed.*[33] Nader wanted to consult with some MIT faculty members on automotive safety but could not find a single person on the MIT campus who was doing research in this area.

The university, which Nader believes is becoming the "vanguard of mercantilism,"[34] has also become a patron in the science and technology policy system. In a March 1985 talk to students and faculty in the University of Houston Honors Program, Nobel Laureate Paul Berg expressed concern that the university is changing its traditional role vis-à-vis its faculty. At least in those areas of biology that are becoming increasingly commercialized, Berg felt that the university was becoming too aggressive, both as a venture capitalist and as a patent attorney. These new roles for the university are, according to Berg, taking their toll on the research faculty. They detract from research (by a preoccupation with what is patentable and what is not), and they stifle curiosity and true creative genius. Berg is apparently worried that the university is too anxious to exploit the genius of its faculty as a product upon which a profit can be turned. Of course, industry is the largest consumer of such a marketable product. These developments raise the perplexing questions of whether or not the entire research process is being driven by the quest for commercial gain, and whether the primary purpose of the university is to serve industry or to pursue knowledge and nourish the young that it is committed to educate.

Providers.[35] Because they are the providers of scientific discoveries and new products and processes, scientists and technologists also have a claim to govern. They justify their claim on philosophical, constitutional, and contractual grounds, invoking the norms of scientific activity, provisions of the Constitution, and the terms of an implicit contract in which the governed have given to experts their consent to make policy decisions for science and technology on their behalf.

The arguments for autonomy that are advanced by these experts rest on the assumption that the vast majority of those who do various types of science act responsibly, living by what Robert Merton calls "institutional imperatives," or the "ethos of science."[36] If a scientist is irresponsible, the peer review system, a "sensible arrangement for enlisting volunteer referees to call balls and strikes on proposals pitched by the funding agencies,"[37] is there to censure her or him. The use of peacetime scientific discoveries for wartime destructive purposes and the value questions raised by research in genetics and population control have given rise to a reformulation of earlier norms of science. These developments raised questions about the moral and social consequences of basic scientific research, and pointed out the reality that scientists are not always, as the earlier work of Merton suggests, objective and disinterested in how their discoveries are used.[38]

A second line of argument that is used by producers of scientific discoveries and their applications is that scientific inquiry is an "implicit" First Amendment right.[39] According to Ira Carmen, "serious constitutional questions arise when public officials adopt regulations which limit our capacity to comprehend the nature of the physical universe and its biological phenomena."[40] This is because all those who "do" science and technology are involved in "expressive" activities — words, ideas, attitudes, values, and emotions — all of which are protected by the U.S. Constitution. If this argument is applied to the rDNA case, NIH has no right to limit the freedom of expression of scientists in the molecular biology laboratory.

In confining his argument to the scientists' expressive activities and to the relationship between science and society, Carmen's arguments seem unduly narrow; faculty members' academic freedoms — to inquire, to write, and to speak as well as to act — are also constitutionally protected, and the personal freedom of faculty members from the discretionary powers of university administrators need to be given recognition.[41] The central question is whether scientific freedom and academic freedom are absolute, or whether there ought to be boundaries to inquiry. Is there, as Walter Metzger has suggested, "the kind of research so inimical to health or so morally degrading as to justify an outright ban?"[42] In answering his own question, Metzger suggests that what is needed most in writing guidelines to regulate science is wisdom — derived from the ethos and moral history of science, from libertarian philosophy, and from the "give and take" bargaining which is so central to the democratic process.[43]

Thus far, the essence of the providers' justification for expert self-rule is that they *are* accountable, if only to others who, by virtue of their expertise, qualify as judges. Scientists and engineers can also claim a rightful place at the negotiating table over the funding and direction of research and development on the basis of a negotiated contract with the public.[44] This amounts to a social contract: lay citizens willingly give up their democratic rights to control science and technology, delegating to expert citizens the tasks of passing judgment on the direction of basic and applied research and the appropriateness of research methods, deciding on the research's scientific merit, and allocating funds on the basis of this evaluation. In exchange for this delegation of power, scientists and technologists promise to deliver future benefits of science and technology that will improve society's well-being.

The Consumer. Those who benefit from, pay for with their tax dollars, or are exposed to the risks of science and technology also make a claim to govern. They press their case using economic, constitutional, and political arguments. Rather than science in the hands of the experts, most organized consumers opt for a cooperative arrangement for governing science and technology, one which gives priority to communal interest.

The most straightforward argument for citizen participation in science policy making is a practical economic one. Taxation with representation is an integral part of our republican form of democracy. Since a large portion of scientific research is funded by the federal government and is conducted in publicly-funded universities throughout the fifty states, taxpayers — and not only scientist taxpayers — are entitled to be represented in any governing scheme.

A second argument for citizen involvement is equally compelling. Science and technology are social activities, with broad social and moral consequences as well as potentially good and bad health effects.[45] Because they are social enterprises, they should be governed democratically. Therefore, citizen participation in the science policy-making process is part of a constitutionally protected right to informed consent.[46]

A third argument is a populist one. Populism stresses direct, equal participation by all.[47] A democratic tradition that has its origins in the French Revolution, populism "was founded on the principle that there can be no genuine meeting of minds where one party negotiates on an assumption of superiority that the other party regards as gratuitous."[48] The essence of the populist argument is that in order to be democratic, a society must open all of its authority structures to the public. Among these would be the science and technology policy-making apparatus. The democratization of policy making — where independent equals share power equally[49] — allows for the possibility that individuals can control their own destinies.

This third argument in favor of making members of the public an equal partner in policymaking is an argument for "participatory technology":[50] broad, direct participation in making decisions which have widespread social impact is *necessary* for self-development and self-government. In this sense, participation performs a practical educative function. For democracy to survive, and for the potential of self-government to be realized, it is necessary for a large proportion of the population to develop a "democratic character." Democratic character can only be nurtured and developed by active involvement in decision-making — not only by choosing among two competing elites in elections, but also by deciding day-to-day matters which affect individuals' lives. Therefore, individuals learn to be democratic by acting democratically — for example, by being directly involved in deciding policy relative to science and technology.[51]

LINKAGES

Problems arise when some claims — for example, those of providers that they be allowed to govern themselves and competing claims of lay members of the public that they be permitted to govern by having meaningful access to science and technology policy-making institutions — are mutually exclusive. This is where politics, which is predicted on mutual consent and which requires reciprocal agreements between the specialists who do science and technology and lay members of the public, comes in to resolve the dispute. Politics is the instrument for resolving claims that are both legitimate *and* mutually exclusive. The result of politics might be a compromise solution that preserves the autonomy of inquiry that scientists and technologists value so highly, while at the same time giving members of the public a meaningful voice in making and implementing policy for science and technology.

To examine the *political* aspects of competing claims requires an examination of the linkages between the rulers and the ruled, whether in connection with a local dispute about chemical weapons testing in Cambridge, Massachusetts; a dispute over conflicts of interest of university faculty members at the University of California, Davis; or a controversy between the university and its faculty members over the appropriate role for scientist entrepreneurs or industry in the academy. These linkages not only lie at the heart of democratic governance but also form the basis of most proposals for institutional reform. In the concluding paragraphs of this chapter we turn to the issue of linkages between rulers and ruled.

CONCLUSION

Public participation can be defined in terms of who is participating and to what effect.[52] Assuming that in a democratic system of governance political equality and majority rule are the operative rules, the public is defined as any individual or group that takes the time and effort to promote or inhibit the particular social activity (science and technology) in question. Whether the behavior actually affects decisions about funding, development, or direction of discoveries and their applications is inconsequential. What matters is that the behavior is purposeful.

Employing Don. K. Price's familiar "truth to power" continuum, we acknowledge that in those matters that come closest to the "truth" end of the spectrum (what Alvin Weinberg calls "scientific" issues), specialists have a more legitimate claim than nonspecialists; and in matters that come closest to the "power" end of the spectrum (what Alvin Weinberg labels "trans-scientific" issues), nonspecialists have a more legitimate claim.[53] The problem is that it is not often easy to distinguish scientific issues from trans-scientific ones. In fact, most issues have both fact and value components. Modes of political participation in formulating and implementing policies for science and technology are the linkages between those who make the decisions and those who are attempting to influence them.

Some of these linkages are stronger than others. Consistent with the findings of others who have studied representational linkages in democratic governance, there is a hierarchy of modes of participation.[54] Some modes are more effective than others. And effectiveness is not usually a function of the quantity of participation but rather the quality. Quality is judged by the impact of the participatory behavior. What are some of the characteristics of public participation that are likely to make a difference in quality, and therefore in effect?

First and foremost, active participation is usually more effective than passive participation. Participation *early* in policy deliberations—for example, when problems are defined as either technical or political or before funding has been committed to a particular technology path—is usually more effective than participation later in the policy process. When a pluralistic body such as an advisory committee is organized, *majority status* makes participation more effective than minority status. Indeed, giving advice is not as likely to influence the content of policy as is actually *making the decision.*

Moreover, participation that is *organized* is generally more effective than participation that is individualistic; and if organized groups are *large and powerful,* that is, rich in resources, they have a better chance of influencing policy than groups without these attributes. Two key resources are money and knowledge, so interests that have *financial resources* are more likely to be effective than those who do not. And citizens who are *informed,* and have authority on their side, are going to be more effective negotiators than members of the public who have difficulty comprehending either the technical aspects of a decision or the ways in which science and technology impinge on their lives. If informed citizens can show how the effects of a new discovery or a new technology are linked to other effects that are important to other organized

51

interests, the chances for a *coalition* are improved, and those who are part of a coalition of interests are more likely to affect policy than those who act on their own. Finally, individuals and groups who can show that they will be *affected* directly by a particular course of action or inaction have more legitimate claims than those interests that will probably not be affected at all.

Specific case studies of the many linkages between those who make and implement policy for science and technology or use science and technology in policy making, and those who try to influence such people are examined in the chapters that follow. In the course of this examination, a mental image of the relations between rulers and ruled should emerge. From this mental image one should also be able to construct a theory of governance of science and technology that depicts what democratic governance is and what it can and should be.

NOTES

1. In an article in the Spring 1983 issue of *Daedalus,* Kenneth Prewitt refers to the crisis of governance, and summarizes the alienation hypothesis. See Kenneth Prewitt, "Scientific Illiteracy and Democratic Theory," *Daedalus* 112 (Spring 1983): 49-64. For another view of the crisis of governance, and details of the overload hypothesis, see Michael Crozier, Samuel P. Huntington, and Joji Watanuki, *The Crisis of Democracy: Report on the Governability of Democracies to the Trilateral Commission* (New York: New York Univ. Press, 1975).

2. Samuel Beer, "In Search of a New Public Philosophy," in *The New American Political System,* ed. Anthony King (Washington, D.C.: American Enterprise Institute, 1978).

3. Dorothy Nelkin and Michael Pollak, "Public Participation in Technological Decisions: Reality or Grand Illusion?" *Technology Review* 80 (1978): 55.

4. Jon D. Miller, "Scientific Literacy: A Conceptual and Empirical Framework," *Daedalus* 112 (Spring 1983): 29–48.

5. Prewitt, "Scientific Illiteracy and Democratic Theory."

6. Dorothy Nelkin, *Technological Decisions and Democracy: European Experiments in Democracy* (Beverly Hills: Sage, 1977), 12–13.

7. Bruce Williams, "Living Better with Technology," *Minerva* 21 (Winter 1983): 386.

8. Beer, "In Search of a New Public Philosophy."

9. Samuel Huntington, in Crozier, et al., *The Crisis of Democracy,* 64.

10. Samuel P. Huntington, "The Democratic Distemper," in *The American Commonwealth–1976,* ed. Nathan Glazer and Irving Kristol (New York: Basic Books, 1976), 10.

11. E.E. Schattschneider, *The Semi-Sovereign People* (New York: Holt, 1960).

12. Huntington, in Crozier, et al., *The Crisis of Democracy,* 64.

13. For an excellent summary of the more general national debate, see Clifford Grobstein, *A Double Image of the Double Helix: The Recombinant DNA Debate*; Clifford Grobstein, "The Recombinant DNA Debate," *Environment* 20 (May 1978): 7–41. For insights into the congressional debates, see Barbara Culliton, "Recombinant DNA Bill De-

railed: Congress Still Trying to Pass a Law," *Science* 199 (Jan. 20, 1978): 274–77; Nicholas Wade, "Congress Set to Grapple Again with Gene Splicing," *Science* 199 (Mar. 24, 1978): 1319–22; and David Dickson, "Friends of DNA Fight Back," *Nature* 272 (April 20, 1978): 664–65.

14. See Walter Metzger, "Academic Freedom and Scientific Freedom," *Daedalus* 107 (Spring 1978): 93–114; and David Baltimore, "Limiting Science: A Biologist's Perspective," *Daedalus* 107 (Spring 1978): 37–45.

15. For a variety of opinion on the issue of the constitutionality of limiting laboratory research with recombined genes, see Ira H. Carmen, "The Constitution in the Laboratory: Recombinant DNA as 'Free Expression'," *Journal of Politics* 43 (1981): 737–62; Marc Lappé and Patricia Archibald Martin, "The Place of the Public in the Conduct of Science," *Southern California Review* 52 (1978): 1535–54; Harold Green, "The Boundaries of Scientific Freedom," in *Regulation of Scientific Inquiry: Societal Concerns with Research,* ed. Keith M. Wulff (Washington, D.C.: AAAS, 1979); Thomas I. Emerson, "The Constitution and Regulation of Research," in *Regulation of Scientific Inquiry: Societal Concerns with Research,* ed. Keith M. Wulff (Washington, D.C.: AAAS, 1979): John A. Robertson, "The Scientists' Right to Research: A Constitutional Analysis," *Southern California Law Review* 51 (Sept. 1978): 1203; and Richard Delgado and David R. Millen, "God, Galileo, and Government: Toward Constitutional Protection for Scientific Inquiry," *Washington Law Review* 53 (1978): 349–404.

16. Baltimore, "Limiting Science," 41.

17. Green, "The Boundaries of Scientific Freedom," 18; and Hans Jonas, "Freedom of Scientific Inquiry: The Accountability of Science," *The Hastings Center Report* (Aug. 1976): 15–17.

18. Gabriel A. Almond, *The American People and Foreign Policy* (New York: Praeger, 1960). James Rosenau further differentiated the concept of an attentive public by dividing this group in a "mobilized" and a "nonmobilized" public. James Rosenau, *Citizenship Between Elections* (New York: Free Press, 1974). For a discussion of the role of attentive publics in science policy, see Jon D. Miller, Robert W. Suchner, and Alan M. Voelker, *Citizenship in an Age of Science: Changing Attitudes Among Young Adults* (New York: Pergamon, 1980).

19. Several municipalities passed ordinances regulating gene splicing research in local communities. Others used existing laws to regulate certain types of experiments. Cambridge, Mass., was the first (Feb. 7, 1977), and Amherst, Mass., the borough of Princeton, N.J., and Berkeley, Calif., quickly followed.

20. Delgado and Millen, "God, Galileo, and Government," 352. Richard Delgado, et al., "Can Science Be Inopportune? Constitutional Validity of Governmental Restrictions on Race-IQ Research," *UCLA Law Review* 31 (1983): 128–225; and Clifford Grobstein, "Recombinant DNA Research: Beyond the NIH Guidelines," 1134.

21. See Philip L. Bereano, "Institutional Biosafety Committees and the Inadequacies of Risk Regulation," *Science, Technology, & Human Values* 9 (Fall 1984): 16–34; Bradford H. Gray, Robert A. Cooke, and Arnold S. Tannenbaum, "Research Involving Human Subjects," *Science* 201 (Sept. 22, 1978): 1094–1101; and Diana Dutton and John L. Hochheimer, "Institutional Biosafety Committees and Public Participation: Assessing an Experiment," *Nature* 297 (6 May, 1982): 11–15; on the role of advisory committees in the governance of science and technology see Malcolm L. Goggin, "Science Policy Governance: Experts and Laymen," paper presented at the 1981 annual meeting of the American Political Science Association, New York, 1981; and Malcolm L. Goggin, "Commission

Government: Collective Decision Making in the Executive Branch," Houston: University of Houston Center for Public Policy, May 1984.

22. The following section draws heavily from "Federal Restrictions on the Free Flow of Information and Ideas," prepared by John Shattuck, and reprinted in *The Chronicle of Higher Education.* "Harvard Report: Freedom of Scholars to Exchange Ideas is 'Essential'," *The Chronicle of Higher Education* (Jan. 9, 1985): 13–17 (hereafter referred to as the Harvard Report on Federal Restrictions). Also see George Brown, "Administration Policies on Government Control of Information," *Congressional Record* 97th Cong., 2d sess., 128, no. 16 (Feb. 25, 1982), H511. Stephen H. Unger, "The Growing Threat of Government Secrecy," *Technology Review* (Feb./Mar. 1982): 31–39; 84–85.

23. Harvard Report on Federal Restrictions, 17.

24. See Allan Adler, "Unclassified Secrets," *Bulletin of the Atomic Scientists* (Mar. 1985): 26–28. The tensions between the military and the research community were relieved somewhat when Under Secretary of Defense Richard DeLauer issued a memorandum on October 1, 1984, which effectively called off the Department of Defense's efforts to restrict the dissemination of results of "fundamental" scientific research that is sensitive militarily. The problem is that the meaning of "fundamental" is not entirely clear. See "Pentagon Lowers Heat on Science Secrecy—Maybe," *Physics Today* 37 (1984): 57–59.

25. Harvard Report on Federal Restrictions, 14.

26. See U.S. Congress, House of Representatives, Committee on Government Operations, *Report on the President's Executive Order on Security Classification* 97th Cong. 2d sess., 16 Aug. 1982 (Washington, D.C.: U.S. Government Printing Office, 1982); and National Academy of Sciences, *Scientific Communication and National Security* (Washington, D.C.: National Academy Press, 1982).

27. Also see "FBI Upsets AVS Arresting East German at Meeting," *Physics Today* (1984): 53–54; Gina Kolata, "Export Control Threat Upsets Meeting," *Science* 217 (24 Sept. 1982): 1233–34.

28. Material on file from Rosemary Chalk, AAAS.

29. David Dickson has mounted a convincing case that the universities have joined the military and industrial forces to coopt those who, in the 1960s and 1970s, were calling for the public governance of science and technology. See David Dickson, *The New Politics of Science* (New York: Pantheon, 1984).

30. For the application of a policy system for welfare policies, see Leonard Goodwin, *Can Social Science Help Resolve National Problems? Welfare, A Case in Point* (New York: Free Press, 1975). Goodwin adds administrators to his system, but in the case of science and technology governance, the lines between donors and administrators are blurred. Several observers of the practices of policy making have noted that in the case of science and technology, control over both policy formation and expenditure has increasingly devolved to nonlegislative agencies that are free of electoral control. The principal justifications for claims by administrators that they should control science and technology policy are expertise and administrative efficiency. I have treated public officials who work in the technoscience agencies as patrons.

31. David F. Noble, *American by Design: Science, Technology and the Rise of Corporate Capitalism* (New York: Knopf, 1977), and David F. Noble, *Forces of Production: A Social History of Industrial Automation* (New York: Knopf, 1984).

32. Noble, *Forces of Production,* 44.

33. "Democracy in America," *Technology Review* 85 (July 1982): 81.

34. Ibid. For an insightful analysis of the entrepreneurial university and university

scientist, see Henry Etzkowitz, "Entrepreneurial Scientists and Entrepreneurial Universities in American Academic Science."

35. See Goggin, "Life Sciences and the Public" for fuller discussion.

36. The following paragraph is based on the writings of Robert Merton. See Robert K. Merton, *Social Theory and Social Structure* (New York: Free Press, 1968). Later, more variegated versions capture both the rational and irrational aspects of the practice of scientific inquiry. See Robert K. Merton, "The Ambivalence of Scientists," *American Scientist* 57 (1969): 1–23; and Robert K. Merton and Elinor Barber, "Sociological Ambivalence," in *Sociological Theory, Values, and Socio-cultural Change*, ed. Edward A. Tiryakian (New York: Free Press, 1963).

37. William D. Carey, "Peer Review Revisited," *Science* 189 (1975): 331. Also see Don K. Price, "Endless Frontier or Bureaucratic Morass," *Daedalus* 107, no. 2 (1978): 82.

38. For a critique of science as a "value-free" enterprise, see Ira Mitroff, *The Subjective Side of Science* (New York: Elsevier, 1974).

39. Dewitt Stetton, Jr., "Freedom of Inquiry," *Science* 189 (1975): 953; and letters to the editor of *Science* in the following issue: Letters, *Science* 190 (1975): 326–30. Also see Hans Jonas, "Freedom of Inquiry and the Public Interest," *Hastings Center Report* (Aug. 1976): 15–17; and Harold Green, "The Boundaries of Scientific Freedom," *Harvard University Newsletter on Science, Technology and Human Values* 20 (1977): 17–21.

40. Ira H. Carmen, "The Constitution in the Laboratory: Recombinant DNA Research as 'Free Expression'," *Journal of Politics* 43 (1981): 738. For a recount of the DNA contratemps, see John Lear, *Recombinant DNA* (New York: Crown, 1978).

41. On several occasions, the court has acknowledged a constitutionally-protected academic freedom. See Harold W. Chase and Craig R. Ducat, *Corwin's The Constitution and What It Means Today*, 14th ed. (1978), p. 338. This issue is best illustrated by the Overton decision in Arkansas, and the recent opinion of Justice Black with reference to the creation science controversy.

42. Walter Metzger, "Academic Freedom and Scientific Freedom," *Daedalus* 107 (Spring 1978): 109.

43. Ibid., 110.

44. See Alice K. Smith, *A Peril and a Hope* (Chicago: Univ. of Chicago Press, 1965) for an historical perspective. Further discussion of the contract can be found in Donald Brown, "Quality and Relevance," *The Hastings Center Report* 5 (1975): 7–8; and David Baltimore, "Limiting Science: A Biologist's Perspective," *Daedalus* 107, No. 2 (1978): 37.

45. Lappé and Martin, "The Place of the Public," 1542.

46. Ibid., 1554.

47. George H. Sabine, "The Two Democratic Traditions," in Michael P. Smith, ed. *American Politics and Public Policy* (New York: Random House, 1973), 29–40.

48. Ibid., 40.

49. By equality, I mean equality of opportunity, where everyone has equal access to decision-making. For a variety of reasons only a few choose to exercise this opportunity.

50. James D. Carroll, "Participatory Technology," *Science* 171 (19 Feb. 1971): 647–53.

51. Carole Pateman, *Participation and Democratic Theory* (Cambridge: Cambridge Univ. Press, 1970); Peter Bachrach, *The Theory of Democratic Elitism: A Critique* (Boston: Little, Brown, 1967); and Robert Dahl, *A Preface to Democratic Theory* (Chicago: Univ. of Chicago, 1963), ch. 2.

52. For the classic definition of political participation, see Sidney Verba and Norman H. Nie, *Participation in America: Political Democracy and Social Equality* (New

York: Harper & Row, 1972). For a reformulation, see Robert R. Alford and Roger Fried-land, "Political Participation and Public Policy," in *Annual Review of Sociology* (Palo Alto, Calif.: Annual Review Books, 1975).

53. Don K. Price, *The Scientific Estate* (New York: Oxford Univ. Press, 1965), 137; and Alvin Weinberg, "Science and Trans-Science," *Minerva* 10 (1972); 209–22. Even Wein-berg, who has on several occasions characterized the public governance of science as a threat to liberty, sees a role for members of the public in making "trans-scientific" de-cisions. The question is, how many purely scientific questions are there? For a discussion of the use of federal advisory committees to address scientific and trans-scientific issues, see Malcolm L. Goggin, "Commission Government."

54. Verba and Nie, *Participation in American;* and Sherry Arnstein, "A Ladder of Citizen Participation," *Journal of the American Institute of Planning* 35 (July 1969): 216–24.

2. Science Overrun: Threats to Freedom from External Control

HELEN LONGINO

The claim to autonomy by the practitioners of science is, as I understand it, the claim to a right to exclusive control over what one does as a scientist and a denial of accountability to a public outside the scientific community. In the contemporary United States setting, the claim to autonomy is made both by individual scientists for themselves and by members of the scientific community for that community. The individual researcher's autonomy should only be limited by properly constituted bodies within and acting for the community, for example, review committees for funding agencies who can decide whether a research project will proceed, or professional standards or ethics committees who may place limits on acceptable experimental procedures.

I intend, in this chapter, to review this claim from the perspective of the philosophy of science. I shall discuss three contemporary approaches to understanding the nature of scientific inquiry, exploring in particular their implications for the claim to autonomy. Brief analyses of selected cases in recent and contemporary scientific research will illustrate the philosophical ideas and clarify their relevance to the question of autonomy. I will suggest that arguments for autonomy are based on an oversimplified conception of inquiry. I will also argue that, nevertheless, the types of control of inquiry, through restriction of scientific communication, imposed by the current presidential administration are also based on a misconception of science.

THE PHILOSOPHICAL AND MATERIAL BASIS
OF SCIENTIFIC AUTONOMY

The claim to autonomy rests on a conjunction of philosophical and material grounds. The conceptual or philosophical legitimation that is offered presupposes a certain account of the nature of inquiry and the satisfaction of certain material conditions. I will argue that neither presupposition survives examination.

The philosophical basis of claims for scientific self-governance, rather than external control or accountability, is an ideal of freedom of inquiry in which scientific research is perceived as continuous with other forms of inquiry, for example, research in the humanities. Scientific research is perceived as contributing to the human understanding of self and environment. The guardian of quality is the process of peer review. Freedom of inquiry means freedom in choice of subject matter and of questions asked of that subject matter, freedom in choice of methods and to pursue those methods to their logical results or conclusions, freedom in choice of traditions within which to work. A corollary to these freedoms is freedom of access to ideas. The scientist who enjoys these liberties is usually imagined to be an academic scientist, employed in a university like most researchers in the humanities. Like these latter scholars, the scientist is subject to the judgment of her or his peers. Any limitations on the above freedoms can be legitimately imposed only by those peers, and only for reasons connected to the central mission of the university, the pursuit of understanding. Thus peer review of journal articles and grant proposals is intended to insure that informally and internally established standards of research design (including appropriateness of subject matter and of methods) are adhered to. The suggestion, however, that a scientist ought to have an eye to potential harmful applications of her or his research is brushed aside by noting, first, that all knowledge can be turned to good or bad ends, but that knowledge itself and the research that produces it is neutral with respect to the modes of its application in the real world and, second, that the consequences of any particular bit of scientific research are unpredictable.

Why is freedom of inquiry (within the limits indicated above) an ideal? In the case of the natural sciences freedom of inquiry is perceived to be a good because we assume that inquiry will lead to the truth of things. The methods of science, properly pursued, will lead us toward truth and (or, for Popperians, only) away from error. Constraints imposed by an uninformed lay public will only hinder that progress. The

58

spectre of Lysenkoism, that is, of wishful state doctrine wrongheadedly and brutally imposed on a scientific research community, is frequently called up to support the claim that public involvement is an impediment. Indeed, much discussion of scientific autonomy and responsibility suggests that the tension is between a scientific community protecting its integrity and a public seeking to limit scientific freedoms out of fear or ignorance or a combination of both![1]

Several features of contemporary science in the United States undermine this picture. On the one side, peer review is, by some accounts, failing in its task. Several recent studies have raised questions about the reliability of the screening such review provides. One of the most startling suggests that the reputation of the investigator and her or his home institution are more influential in determining publication than quality of submission.[2] Secondly, as contributors to this volume note, most scientists already operate under considerable constraints, imposed by the need to find funds to support research.[3] The government, including the military, and private industry are the primary sources of financial support for scientific research. As primary funders, they exercise *de facto* control over research. While scientists often plead eloquently for support of basic research that has no foreseeable applications,[4] the proportion of basic to applied work that actually receives funding fluctuates depending on the perceived needs of the donors. Moreover, the gap between basic and applied research is narrowing to the vanishing point in many fields, as Leon Wofsy points out in Chapter 5 of this volume.

In light of the very real control exercised by the facilitating funders of science, it becomes even more crucial to examine the philosophical underpinnings of the ideal of freedom of inquiry. I suggested above that the idea of freedom of inquiry is supported by the belief that scientific inquiry left to its own devices is a reliable way to discover the truth of things. This must be stated more precisely in order to carry the weight assigned to it. Scientific inquiry must be of such a nature as not to be influenced by social, cultural, or political beliefs, assumptions, and values. It must be of such a nature that only epistemic values, that is, the values associated with truth, play a formative role. If Lysenkoism is the spectre associated with public control of science, what can assure us that the authority of science is not simply being bought by the funders of science? This is not a question about the need to avoid or detect fraud in scientific studies. Rather the question is, What can assure us that the world-pictures given us by science do anything more than reflect the wishes and values of its funders?

IS SCIENCE VALUE-FREE?

The philosophy of science offers several competing accounts of the nature of scientific inquiry that are relevant to this question. I will discuss the empiricist account, the wholist account developed in reaction to it, and a third contextualist view. These approaches to thinking about inquiry differ on key philosophical issues. I will show how, from the perspective of each, it is nevertheless possible to delineate ways in which contextual values, that is, values belonging to the social, economic, and cultural environment of science, shape the development of knowledge.[5] I will then offer examples from the recent practice of science that fit the analytic spaces sculpted by the philosophical analyses.

Among scientists themselves the most influential account is the family of analyses grouped under the rubric of logical empiricism. Logical empiricists distinguish between a context of discovery and a context of justification. The context of discovery refers to the set of circumstances surrounding the initial formulation of a hypothesis or theory, that of justification to the circumstances surrounding its confirmation. In the context of justification, hypotheses are tested by observation and experiment. In the accounts of confirmation offered by these theorists, hypotheses are related syntactically to statements describing their evidence. The most famous definition of confirmation in this tradition is offered by Carl Hempel.[6] He proposed that an observation report (B) confirms an hypothesis (H) if B is entailed by what is called "the development of H for the class of objects mentioned in B."[7] The development of an hypothesis for a class is a sentence asserting for the members of that class what the hypothesis asserts for objects in general. Thus, "All bodies, falling from rest, fall with uniform acceleration" is confirmed by the observation report, "This hammer, when released at t, fell with uniform acceleration," because the development of "All bodies, falling from rest, fall with uniform acceleration," for the class consisting of the hammer released at t, entails the observation report by being identical with it.

The tight relationship purported to hold between evidence and hypotheses in the context of justification would mean that we can be assured that all nonscientific, contextual considerations have been eliminated from the scientific reasoning relevant to theory and hypothesis acceptance.

The selection of hypotheses for this sort of testing, however, is relegated to the context of discovery, which is not subject to logical constraints. Philosophers in this tradition are wont to tell stories of scientific insights occurring in dreams and fantasy (as in Kekulé's discovery of the structure of the benzene molecule) and to argue that the context of discovery could not be a locus of inference and reasoning. The empiricist analysis, then, would allow that contextual considerations could influence which hypotheses were under consideration, but not which hypotheses survived testing in the context of justification. External influence is limited, on this view, to shaping the areas in which knowledge expands.

The empiricist view came under major criticism when historians of science began to argue that in certain periods the same body of data was appealed to in support of conflicting hypotheses. The observational and experimental evidence was insufficient at the time of the controversies to distinguish between the Ptolemaic and Copernican theories, Priestley's phlogiston theory and Lavoisier's quantitative chemistry, the Lorenz contraction hypothesis and Einstein's special relativity theory. Some theorists have explained this phenomenon by use of the idea of theory-ladenness: observation itself is theory-laden, and the terms describing observation are defined in reference to theoretical terms.[8] Adherents of two conflicting theories observe or describe their observations under constraints imposed by the theories. This explains their apparent use of the same body of data, which in fact is not the same but is redescribed, restructured, even reperceived, in the context of different theories. This account would suggest that science is highly vulnerable to influence by contextual interests because choice of theory must logically precede the experimentation and observation that would test it. Most philosophers have found telling objections to any extreme or literal reading of the idea of the theory-ladenness of observation.[9]

The original historical phenomena giving rise to this view nevertheless remain as a challenge to traditional accounts and have made possible an acknowledgment of the underdetermination, in general, of theories by their evidence. This expression is used to refer to the fact that for any given body of data, it is possible to articulate a number of theories that are empirically indistinguishable with respect to that data. To see how this might be so, consider again Hempel's account of confirmation. One of the problems is that it is only applicable to situations in which a hypothesis and statement of evidence share the same descriptive terms. For the most part, however, scientific theories and hypotheses are expressed in language that cannot be used to describe the evidence adduced for them (without begging the question). Our theories

61

and hypotheses make reference to items too small, too large, or too remote to be observed in any ordinary sense of that term, and hence to be brought into descriptions of the evidence for those theories. This means that the relevance of data to hypotheses must be established by means of nonformal linkages. A fact F becomes evidence for some hypothesis H only in light of some background assumptions that assert a connection between the kind of fact F is and the kind of situation described by H'. A change of background assumption can mean that F is no longer taken to support H, but to support some other hypothesis H'. So, as the underdetermination thesis asserts, the same data can support conflicting hypotheses. But if background assumptions mediate the relation between hypotheses and their evidence, then if any facts are evidentially relevant to the background assumptions, this relevance can itself only be ascertained in light of further background assumptions.[10]

The above argument shows that the rules of scientific inquiry are not adequate totally to eliminate from a theory assumptions that are not mandated by the "facts," and the argument also supports a contextualist account of inquiry. This means that we cannot appeal to general features of scientific inquiry or of the structure of science as guarantors of freedom from contextual influence. If a given inquiry is value-free, this is local, accidental, not a result of its conformity to certain methodological rules.

This discussion, of course, does not yet show that past or present scientific research bears the marks of its cultural and economic context. To generate a possibility by means of a philosophical argument is not yet to show that it is instantiated. I believe, however, that contemporary science is, in fact, deeply marked by its context. I will offer several examples of inquiry that is significantly affected by values and commitments. For convenience, I will categorize the cases using the discovery/justification distinction just mentioned.

Cases Belonging to the Context of Discovery. I am including as issues belonging to the context of discovery decisions as to *what* to research — ranging from choices of area or field to choices of hypotheses for testing. In giving examples of both types of choice, I wish to show that nonscientific interests (what I have been calling contextual values and commitments belonging to the environment of science) play a major role in shaping knowledge in the examples I cite.

It has become customary to subject new drugs to various tests for health effects other than the primary intended function of the drug. Such "side effects" can be positive or negative. In review of the testing that preceded the commercial introduction of the systemic contraceptive, "Enovid," Carol Korenbrot argued that the choice of effects to test for showed a consistent preference for positive effects such as relief from dysmenorrhea and prevention of breast cancer and against negative effects such as thromboembolism.[11] Korenbrot also criticized the research procedure for passivity with respect to its subjects. Only those women who returned to the dispensing clinic in the experimental trials in Puerto Rico were the source of information about side effects. Many did not return and may have stayed away precisely because of negative effects. On the basis of these preliminary tests, "Enovid" could be marketed as a drug which not only enabled its user to control her fertility but had beneficial side effects as well. This clearly serves the interests of the corporation which manufactured the drug (and, incidentally, supported the research in question). The association with healthful side effects could, however, also be very useful in promoting the drug in cultures resistant to reducing births—cultures primarily of the very third world populations for which birth control technology is intended. Korenbrot argued that the bias in choice of effects to test for is very much a function of these contextual interests and very little a matter of the internal logic of research on synthetic estrogens. Contextual values shaped knowledge in such a way that, until the occurrence of adverse side-effects in white middle-class women of Great Britian and the United States became obvious, knowledge about the beneficial health effects of synthetic estrogens exceeded and overshadowed knowledge about their dangers.

This sorry history of "Enovid" testing has been repeated with variations in the testing of other drugs intended for fertility control. In a discussion of Depo-Provera testing, for instance, Phillida Bunkle points out that women's experiences that are not recognizable disease syndromes, but are nevertheless disabling, such as excessively heavy bleeding, depression, weight gain, and loss of libido are discounted by the male medical research establishment.[12] Here it is masculine experience, or rather lack of it, that shapes knowledge, excluding side-effects devastating to their victims from the class of those to be investigated. The history of systemic contraceptives may not represent all drug testing. The belated attention to harmful side-effects of antipsychotic drugs, however, considered in conjunction with this history, suggests that various extraneous contextual values can affect the choice of hypotheses to test when prospective users of a substance are not adequately represented in the scientific community doing the testing.

Another class of questions is raised by two "hotter" research areas: molecular biology, specifically rDNA research, and computer science. The first is increasingly supported by corporate industry, the second increasingly by the military. Here contextual interests and values shape knowledge both through their influence on what will be researched and through their impact on scientific communication. It is the latter effect on which I will comment primarily.

Both commercial and national security needs require the secrecy of certain kinds of information. That all members in certain university departments of biology are attached (as consultants or partners) to some biotechnology company or other and that, those being different companies, the academics can no longer converse about their research, is passing into the folklore of contemporary biology. David Dickson, in the recent *The New Politics of Science*, has detailed the ways in which the ever larger interest of industry in the basic research underlying biotechnology has resulted in a growing privatization of knowledge.[13] Research cannot be communicated through the ordinary channels of journals and conferences until it is known not to have commercial applications or its ownership is established through the application for and granting of a patent.

Dickson also discusses how the military and national security establishments are claiming larger and larger areas of basic research as potentially of military value and so subject to control even when not actually classified.[14] The International Traffic in Arms Regulation (ITAR) section of the 1976 Arms Export Control Act has been invoked a number of times recently in attempts to prevent publication of work in cryptography and work on very high speed integrated circuits (VHSIC — critical to the Cruise missile guidance system). ITAR also is invoked to restrict the circulation of this work through means other than publication, for example, by demands that "foreign nationals" be excluded from participation in projects or conferences concerning this research. If we live in a system of nation-states, some of which are hostile to others, there is clearly a national security interest in keeping some information secret. As the areas of research in which the military takes an interest expand, however, so does the scope of its secrecy claims.[15]

The withholding of research also shapes knowledge. Heretofore, scientific knowledge has been thought of as essentially public and as requiring unfettered communication. Research projects are chosen and hypotheses are formulated in light of the current state of knowledge and speculation. When significant portions of current ongoing research are not publicly available, obviously choice of project and formulation of hypothesis to test are affected.

There is, of course, another more familiar aspect to the intimacy between the military and security establishment and the scientific community. Government support of scientific research in any form historically has been justified by its potential value to the military and in maintaining U.S. competitiveness internationally. (The benefits to science of the Soviets' early success with Sputnik are just a recent example.) After a downturn in the late 1960s and 1970s, military support of science research on university campuses is growing, contributing 16.4 percent of the total research budget of U.S. colleges and universities in 1983.[16] During the first Reagan term, budget proposals for the Department of Defense included 45 percent increases in R&D spending from 1981 to 1983.[17] An example of the uses of such funds is the five-year Strategic Computing Initiative announced in October 1983. This $600 million plan, perceived as a first phase, involves artificial intelligence applications for each branch of the armed forces and has been called the "largest and most ambitious coordinated artificial intelligence project in U.S. history."[18] While this may from one point of view be seen as a corrective to the loss of other federal funds during the Reagan administration, Dickson notes that such support creates a certain inevitable dynamic:

> Military support for basic research must inevitably be committed on a long term basis if it is to achieve significant results. For universities, this has the advantage of providing a stable base for future planning. At the same time, however, it builds them into the structure of a weapons economy that they have an active interest in helping to maintain and expand.[19]

The consequence again is that interests and values external to science and coincidentally related to the pursuit of knowledge shape scientific knowledge by requiring it to grow in certain directions as opposed to others. Computer science and artificial intelligence research will develop in the directions envisioned by the Defense Department's Strategic Computing Initiative rather than towards more peaceful civilian applications because that is where researchers will find support. As long as there are people who wish to make their living doing science, knowledge will grow in the directions in which it is encouraged to do so by those with the resources to support it.

Cases Belonging to the Context of Justification. Molding the shape of knowledge through the pressures exerted in the context of discovery is only half the story. I will cite just two kinds of examples. One, like the systemic contraceptives case, involves seemingly routine carcinogenicity testing, while the other is a more theoretical endeavor—the attempt to show biological bases of behavioral sex differences. Both areas exhibit the logical gap between evidence and hypotheses that requires mediation by auxiliary assumptions and hence allows for the influence of contextual interests and values.

The first case is quite simple in structural outline.[20] One of the main questions about health effects of ionizing radiation concerns its carcinogenicity at low doses. Estimates of the risk of increased cancer incidence at low doses are desirable because most people likely to be exposed to radiation (barring a catastrophic accident or war) are likely to be exposed at low doses (workers at plants, waste dumps, or mines; people living near such facilities). The data that serve as primary evidence, however, are those of cancer incidence and fatality among survivors of the atomic bombings of Hiroshima and Nagasaki at the end of World War II. Most of these exposures are at much higher doses than the doses for which estimates are sought. This means that a dose response model must be employed which enables inferences from cancer incidence and fatality at high doses to cancer incidence and fatality at low doses. Several such models have been in official contention (i.e. considered by the National Research Council's Committee on Biological Effects of Ionizing Radiation [BEIR]), and another has been suggested by researcher John Gofman.[21] The linear model predicts the same incidence per rad at high and low doses; the quadratic model predicts much lower per rad incidence at lower doses than at high doses; the linear-quadratic model predicts somewhat fewer per rad at low than at high doses; and Gofman's supralinear model predicts a higher per rad incidence at low doses than at high doses.

The problem is that there is no decisive evidence in favor of any of these models. There are various considerations advanced in support of each of them, but none is overwhelming (given the arguments for the others), and these considerations are based in different fields of research, which makes comparative evaluation difficult. This means that a choice of models, if it is not to be arbitrary, must be based on non-evidential contextual considerations. Study of the most recent report from the BEIR Committee suggests a number of contextual considerations that may have: 1) swayed committee members to one or another model; and 2) prompted the committee's ultimate endorsement of the linear-quadratic model. The first category includes commitment to different fields, e.g., epidemiology versus radiology; preexistent ideas about the social value of nuclear technologies; and subjective perceptions of risk, among others. As for the second category, I suspect that, whatever the leanings of committee members making the choice, the most effective concern was an urge to settle on some estimate and to compromise in order to do so. The middle way, however, while it may be the path of virtue, is not necessarily the path of truth. Whether or not this is an accurate rendition of what happened in committee, it should be clear that this is just the kind of case in which contextual values *can* play a major role in shaping reasoning.

The second type of case involves research attempting to show biological bases of behavioral sex differences in humans.[22] This work includes a broad range of studies in fields from physical anthropology to endocrinology. Let me just mention two areas and some of the work that feminist scientists have done to expose their contextual determination.

In physical anthropology, it was until quite recently common to use the "Man-the-Hunter" framework to relate the fragmentary data relevant to hypotheses of human evolution. The key idea in this framework is that male hunting was the crucial behavioral adaptation that favored the selection for bipedalism, upright posture, changes in dentition, and ultimately larger brain size. So the assignation of a date of use to manuports and chipped stones is, in this approach, taken as evidence of male invention of tools by this date for use in hunting and the preparation of animal carcasses. This is the automatic interpretation given of these archeological remains. In the last ten years, another framework has been developed, that of "Woman-the-Gatherer." In this approach, female gathering behavior is the key adaptation favoring selection for those anatomical features characteristic of hominids. In this framework, women are the inventors of tools for gathering, digging, and self-defense; and the stones are taken as evidence for a point by which they had begun to develop stone tools in addition to the organic tools already in use. Whether or not this latter account is correct, it serves to show the non-necessity of the "Man-the-Hunter" framework. The assumptions of this approach gain their plausibility from the androcentricity of its adherents, not from any data. Ideas of masculine initiative, aggressivity, and independence are deeply tied to the Man-the-Hunter story. The Woman-the-Gatherer model suggests that men have no exclusive claim to these qualities, at least from an evolutionary perspective.

67

Students of research attempting to show a hormonal basis for perceived behavioral differences have criticized the data collection practices of researchers in this field and have also questioned the assumptions by which workers in the field move from studies in animals to statements about humans. Critics have focused in particular on the validity of the physiological determinist model, in which the behavioral and physiological data can be interpreted as evidence of the causal role of fetal gonadal hormone levels in the expression of adult gender role differences. The result of this questioning is to make the model visible and to emphasize the fragility of its evidential support. Although animal studies have been done in order to support the hypothesis that hormones play a causal role in the expression of gender differences, the disanalogies between humans and other animals in the relevant factors mean that these studies cannot be used to support similar causal chains in humans. The question raised, then, is whether the adoption of the physiological model is not as much a function of a need to understand male and female differences as biologically deep and permanent as it is a function of the data. That is, rather than being read from the data, the model is used to interpret it. And the choice of that model is a function of values of the cultural context in which the research is done.

Issues Bridging Both Contexts.   Finally, I would like to raise an issue that straddles both discovery and justification. Scientists and students of science are beginning to distinguish two fundamental modes of scientific investigatory practice.[23] The reductive mode seeks to understand natural processes in terms of mechanical motions of their least parts, for example, the development of organisms as the expression of information encoded in the DNA molecule. By contrast, the interactive or "wholist" mode seeks to understand natural processes in terms of their relation to their environments, for example, gene action triggered by changes in the cellular environment, the organism as maker of and made by its environment. These seem to be complementary ways of understanding, yet the reductive mode is far more extensively practiced than the interactive mode. I suspect one reason for this is the clearer relation of reductive science to production. Reductive science facilitates our intervention in and manipulation of natural processes much more than does interactive wholist science. The effect of its being more widely practiced is to promote the idea that its partial view of nature is the correct one. And yet it may be more widely practiced not because it employs the exclusively correct view of natural processes but because it is the kind of science that promises practical returns for its funders, whether these be corporate industry, the military, or the public.

DISCUSSION

I have covered some very different areas of scientific research in an attempt to show that over a wide range of issues contextual values can shape scientific knowledge, both by directing research to some areas and hypotheses over others and by influencing the choice of background or auxiliary assumptions mediating the relations between data and hypotheses. Let me now bring this analysis to bear on the central questions of this book, namely the issues of science governance. The analysis outlined has implications for three questions in particular: scientific autonomy, current administration science policies, and the various proposals regarding mechanisms of science governance.

Scientific Autonomy. Could scientific inquiry ever be free and autonomous? The answer surely depends in part on what is meant by those terms. The burden of my argument has been to show that contemporary science is not autonomous. Our romantic picture of the dedicated rugged individual bucking the mainstream in search of understanding is left over from another era. The twentieth century is the age of big science, of science projects too expensive to be supported by the resources of any one individual or even one university, and too complex to be executed by any single individual. This means that those who would do science must rely on externally generated funds. Regardless of the ease with which some individual researchers may find support for their projects, overall the content and direction of U.S. science is significantly influenced by external choices and interests. The point of my argument about value-free science is that those interests can be expressed in the overall conceptual framework that guides a given research program as well as in the kinds of research programs funded or undertaken.

Even if scientists were freed from the direct and indirect pressures exerted by product-oriented sponsors, they would not be free from the cultural baggage borne by any historically conditioned human being (and that includes all of us). A second consequence of the argument regarding value-free science is that there is no formal criterion by appeal to which we can say that science incorporating contextual values

69

is "bad," as opposed to "good" science. The structures of science, therefore, cannot be so closed as to exclude contextual influences. Rather, inquiry should be organized in such a way that such influence can be recognized and subjected to scrutiny. This methodological precept, it might be noted, requires unhampered communication. It also suggests that we should design our scientific institutions to insure representation of divergent points of view in scientific fields. Thus enlarging the formal scientific community would have two positive results. It would, in the first place, promote the kind of criticism that makes contextual influence visible. Since such influence is often covert, actively making it visible is necessary to give the scientific community the opportunity to debate the issues involved. Secondly, questions marginal to the interests of today's "establishment" or mainstream science, but central to feminist or third world concerns, would not be frozen out of the resource distribution network.

Current Administration Science Policies. External interests can also be expressed in the processes of inquiry, as when concern about individual rights restricts experimentation on human subjects, humanitarian concern restricts experimentation on other animal subjects, or concern regarding national security restrains scientific communication. While all of these forms of restraint pose deep and provocative questions regarding the nature and purpose of scientific inquiry and the imperatives of human curiosity, there is a fundamental asymmetry between the first two types of restriction and the third. The former impose limits on the scope of scientific inquiry and knowledge. Certain things in certain circumstances may not be the subject of direct investigation— for example, how much physical pain of a certain sort can a person bear, on average, before losing consciousness? The latter form of restriction, because it interferes with the self-corrective processes of inquiry, distorts knowledge. The argument of this chapter means that the self-corrective processes cannot guarantee that unbiased truth will be achieved. As noted above, however, this very fact means that inquiry, if it is formally organized, must be organized in such a way that the possibilities of mutual criticism are maximized. This requires free and open communication. Recent Reagan administration directives, which, apart from priorities expressed in funding decisions, seem to constitute the bulk of administration science policy, go in just the opposite direction.

A presidential directive issued in December 1982 instructed the Office of Science and Technology Policy (OSTP) to initiate a review of ways to control the publication of unclassified but "sensitive" information.[24] This review was apparently in response to the National Academy of Sciences report, *Scientific Communication and National Security,* which urged that basic research be conducted in as free an atmosphere as possible. In contrast, the directive to the OSTP required it to study the feasibility of prepublication review of all federally funded research. Another document, National Security Decision Directive 84 (NSDD 84), does require employees of the federal government to sign agreements containing prepublication review clauses as a condition of access to certain classified materials.[25] A report issued in January 1985 by Harvard University, "Federal Restrictions on the Free Flow of Academic Information and Ideas," reviews the controls, including NSDD 84, on scientific and scholarly communication imposed by the Reagan administration.[26] It notes, for instance, that a number of federal agencies, including the National Institutes of Health, the National Institute of Education, the Department of Housing and Urban Development, and the Food and Drug Administration, have included prepublication review clauses in contracts even for unclassified research. In addition, a regulation proposed in April 1983, "Identification and Protection of Unclassified Controlled Nuclear Information" (UCNI), would have required all institutions possessing or creating such information to impose strict criteria (such as U.S. citizenship) for access to it. The report commented that this regulation would make "known and unclassified information secret" and that it was so sweeping as to include basic course materials in physics and other sciences.[27] While this particular regulation has since been modified, the report makes clear that the range of federal administration efforts amounts to a pattern of control in conflict with university regulations and traditions regarding the accessibility of research. By reducing the possibilities for critical interchange, these efforts threaten, as well, to tear the heart out of science.

Mechanisms of Science Governance. I have argued that the logical structure of inquiry renders science vulnerable to external interests of the sort represented by corporate industry and the defense establishment. I have also suggested that such current science policies as there are threaten to overrun science rather than strengthen it. As science is reduced to an instrument of policy, it loses its role in the search for understanding. Are there any implications for the sorts of policies and institutions we should have?[28] I have already mentioned the importance of institutional mechanisms to maximize critical interchange. Beyond that, the variety in the examples I've mentioned should serve to remind us that scientific inquiry is not a single kind of process that can be described in general terms. Scientific research projects differ from one another in their aims and procedures as well as in their subject matter. They also differ in the ways in which they intersect with governance questions. Scientific disagreement over factual matters relevant to public policy decisions, such as the disagreement regarding low-level radiation, poses one kind of issue. The siting and performance of potentially hazardous experiments poses another. Decisions about what kinds of biomedical research ought to be done — e.g., research supporting high-tech intervention versus that supporting low-tech prevention — pose yet another. The institutional mechanisms appropriate to one will generally not be those appropriate to another.

Finally, it should be clear that the adversaries in the conflict over science governance are incorrectly described as scientists on one side and the public on the other. The tensions in this debate reflect tensions in the larger society — tensions between military and corporate special interests, tensions between them and members of the public seeking greater control over the conditions of their lives (and the disposition of their taxes). Science and its institutions are among the fields on which these different adversaries engage each other. Scientists, universities, and research institutions also have interests of their own to pursue in these struggles. The resulting complex dependencies and antagonisms must be accounted for in any attempts to resolve the conflicts that are emerging.

NOTES

1. See David Baltimore, "Limiting Science: A Biologist's Perspective," 37–45, and Goggin, "Is Science Too Important?"

2. Steven Harnad, ed., *Peer Commentary on Peer Review,* (Cambridge: Cambridge Univ. Press, 1983). See also James Lloyd, "Selling Scholarship Down the River: The Pernicious Aspects of Peer Review," *Chronicle of Higher Education,* 26 June 1985, p. 64.

3. See chs. 5 and 8 of this volume.

4. See, for instance, Lewis Thomas, *The Lives of a Cell* (New York: Bantam, 1975), for an exceptionally eloquent statement, and Leon M. Lederman, "The Value of Fundamental Science," *Scientific American* 251 (Nov. 1984): 40–47.

5. I contrast contextual values with constitutive values, which are internal to a science and include, among others, epistemic values. See Helen E. Longino, "Beyond 'Bad Science'," *Science, Technology, and Human Values* 8 (Winter 1983): 7–17, for a fuller discussion.

6. Carl G. Hempel, "Studies in the Logic of Confirmation," in Carl G. Hempel, *As-

pects of Scientific Explanation and other Essays in the Philosophy of Science (New York: Free Press, 1965), 3–51.

7. Ibid., 37.

8. See, for example, Thomas Kuhn, *The Structure of Scientific Revolutions* 2d ed., enl. (Chicago: Univ. of Chicago Press, 1975), and Norwood Hanson, *Patterns of Discovery* (Cambridge: Cambridge Univ. Press, 1958).

9. See Peter Achinstein, *Concepts of Science* (Baltimore: Johns Hopkins Univ. Press, 1968), 91–98.

10. See Helen E. Longino, "Evidence and Hypothesis," *Philosophy of Science* 46 (Mar. 1979): 35–56, and "Scientific Objectivity and the Logics of Science," *Inquiry* 26 (Mar. 1983): 85–106. For a more general discussion of the underdetermination problem, see Mary Hesse, *Revolutions and Reconstructions in the Philosophy of Science* (Bloomington: Univ. of Indiana Press, 1980).

11. Carol Korenbrot, "Experiences with Systemic Contraceptives," in *Toxic Substances: Decisions and Values, Conference II: Information Flow* (Washington, D.C.: Technical Information Project, 1979), 11–42.

12. Phillida Bunkle, "Calling the Shots? The International Politics of Depo-Provera," in *Test-Tube Women,* ed. Rita Arditti, Renata Duelli-Klein, and Shelley Minden (Boston: Routledge and Kegan Paul, 1984), 165–187.

13. David Dickson, *The New Politics of Science,* 56–106. See also Longino, "Beyond 'Bad Science'," and ch. 10 of this volume.

14. Dickson, *The New Politics of Science,* 107–62.

15. Dickson, ibid., quotes memoranda, speeches, and reports that cite basic research in lasers, electronics, materials sciences and genetic engineering among others as potentially subject to control.

16. Ibid., 109.

17. Colin Norman, "Reagan's Science Policy," *Science* 218 (12 Nov. 1982): 659.

18. Paul N. Edwards, "Are 'Intelligent Weapons' Feasible?", *Nation* 240 (2 Feb. 1985): 110–12.

19. Dickson, *The New Politics of Science,* 114–15.

20. See Helen E. Longino, "Hazardous Technologies: How Are the Hazards Measured?", *Research in Philosophy and Technology* 8 (forthcoming), for a fuller discussion.

21. Committee on the Biological Effects of Ionizing Radiation, *The Effects on Populations of Exposure to Low Levels of Ionizing Radiation: 1980* (Washington, D.C.: National Academy Press, 1980); and John Gofman, *Radiation and Human Health* (San Francisco: Sierra Books, 1981), 368–407.

22. See Helen E. Longino and Ruth Doell, "Body, Bias and Behavior," *Signs* 9 (Winter 1983): 206–27, for a fuller discussion.

23. See Evelyn Keller, "The Force of the Pacemaker Concept in Theories of Aggregation in Cellular Slime Mold," *Perspectives in Biology and Medicine* 26 (Summer 1983): 515–21. See also papers in Conrad H. Waddington, ed., *Towards a Theoretical Biology* (Chicago: Aldine, 1968–72).

24. Colin Norman, "Briefing: Reagan Orders Review of Controls on Research," *Science* 219 (4 Feb. 1983): 473.

25. "Federal Agencies' Effort to Muzzle Scholars Are Growing, Harvard Report Charges," *Chronicle of Higher Education,* 9 Jan. 1985, p. 1, 13.

26. Harvard Report on Federal Restrictions, 13–17. For a constitutional perspective, see James R. Ferguson, "National Security Controls on Technological Knowledge: A

Constitutional Perspective," *Science, Technology, and Human Values* 10 (Spring 1985): 87– 98.

27. Harvard Report on Federal Restrictions, 16.

28. I consider here only policy *about* science. The issues discussed also have implications for the use of science *in* policy making. For discussion of policy making under conditions of uncertainty, see, among others, "Technological Uncertainty in Policy Analysis," (1982), unpublished manuscript available from the Department of Engineering and Public Policy, Carnegie-Mellon Univ., Pittsburgh; Baruch Fischoff et al., *Acceptable Risk* (Cambridge: Cambridge Univ. Press, 1981); Todd La Porte, "Managing Nuclear Waste," *Society* 18 (1981): 57–65; and Richard Wilson, "Risks and Their Acceptability," *Science, Technology, and Human Values* 9 (Spring 1984): 11–22.

3. *The Political Non-Politics of U.S. Science Policy*

WILLIAM A. BLANPIED AND RACHELLE D. HOLLANDER*

In this chapter we sketch the origins and development of some of the tensions that currently exist in the United States between science and government, the principal patron of basic research in universities, as well as the principal arbiter of the country's extensive, if diffuse, research and development (R&D) enterprise. Those tensions, we believe, are intimately related to issues of autonomy and accountability. Because the policy framework for government support of scientific research emerged in the wake of World War II, our principal focus will be on the past forty years. We will demonstrate that the relationships between science and government were at that time, and continue to be, politically negotiated relationships. We will then argue that an appropriate balance between scientific autonomy and accountability may be better served by including a broader representation at the table where the negotiations between science and government take place.

Problems of balancing autonomy and accountability are not new. Indeed, they predate by more than three centuries the post–World War II compact that continues to provide the framework for negotiations between science and government. They are already evident in Francis Bacon's seventeenth century vision. Bacon, then lord chancellor of England, selected, as the frontispiece of the 1620 edition of his *Novum Organum,* a woodcut of a ship bound on a voyage of discovery and a prophecy from the Book of Daniel: "And many shall go forth, and knowledge shall increase."[1] So the metaphor of scientific progress as equivalent to a physical voyage into *terra incognito* was present in

*The views expressed by the authors are their own and do not necessarily reflect the policies of the National Science Foundation.

one of the first detailed articulations of science as an organized group activity.

Both the substance and the rhetoric of his vision indicate that, to Bacon, an increase in knowledge — or what today would be called the progress of science — was a necessary prerequisite to social progress. A systematic program to increase knowledge would require the disciplined efforts of self-selected groups — the "many" — who would be granted autonomy by the larger society. In other words, they would have the right to conduct their activities according to their own established rules, on the expectation that those activities would, in fact, ultimately lead to social benefits. It was the expectation of such social progress that provided the principal rationale for seeking to increase knowledge.[2]

A secularized version of the Baconism vision of scientific progress persists into our own era. Scientific progress is inevitably linked with social progress, and autonomy for scientific communities is viewed as a necessary prerequisite to scientific progress. The persistence of this article of faith is strikingly illustrated in the subject matter and style of *Science — the Endless Frontier*, a report which Vannevar Bush, President Franklin Roosevelt's wartime science adviser, submitted to President Harry Truman in July 1945 as a blueprint for a continuing peacetime relationship between science and government.[3] Bush's argument links scientific progress to social progress, arguing that "without scientific progress no amount of achievement in other directions can insure our health, prosperity, and security as a nation in the modern world."[4] Genuine scientific progress requires autonomous, self-governing communities, since "Scientific progress on a broad front results from the free play of free intellects, working on subjects of their own choice, in the manner dictated by the curiosity for exploration of the unknown. Freedom of inquiry must be preserved under any plan for Government support of science . . ."[5]

Most strikingly, perhaps, our Baconian cultural heritage is evident in Bush's invocation of the U.S. government's longstanding support for oceanic ventures to legitimize the concept of public support to open new frontiers of science. In rearticulating this metaphor and the traditional assumptions concerning the necessary autonomy and self-governance of science, Bush provided the rationale for policies established in the late 1940s to link nongovernmental scientific institutions in the United States more closely with the federal government.[6]

Both of Bush's assumptions — that scientific progress leads inevitably to social progress, and that scientific progress requires the autonomy of scientific communities — can be questioned, however. The first assumption overlooks the negative effects that can arise within and as a result of scientific activity. The second overlooks the possibility that the values scientists themselves hold may limit their ability to select appropriate priorities for research, even basic research, in the best interests of the larger society. It also ignores the need for broad-based and informed support for research and for procedures by which appropriate research agendas can be selected. It is these deficiencies that underlie many of the historical and current strains in the relationships among science, government, and society.

PRECEDENTS FOR NEGOTIATIONS BETWEEN SCIENCE AND GOVERNMENT

From the perspective of the current debate over accountability and autonomy, two explicit arguments set forth in *Science — The Endless Frontier* should be noted.

First, Bush argued that the innovative contract system created during World War II ought to be established on a permanent, peacetime basis.[7] This system placed the capabilities of nongovernmental scientific institutions at the disposal of government in order to help it fulfill specific mission-oriented objectives, such as military research and development. An essential feature of Bush's argument was that scientists should, to the greatest extent possible, conduct such mission-oriented activities in their home institutions — private industry and particularly universities — so that they could enjoy the maximum possible measure of autonomy even while conducting work for government.

Second, and at the time more controversially, Bush argued that science had become so important to society that the public interest demanded maintenance of a strong scientific infrastructure. When the conduct of undirected, curiosity-driven research — that is, the quest for knowledge for its own sake, or basic research — drives the entire scientific enterprise, the support of basic research, particularly in universities, becomes a legitimate concern of government. Therefore, it has become essential for the federal government to provide direct support for non-mission-oriented scientific research and education in universities. But since the concept of public support of university research was so novel in the United States, a new comprehensive agency would have to be created to carry out that mission.

77

Although the idea that the United States government should provide direct support for research in universities may have been novel in 1945, negotiated links between science and government were certainly not. In 1660 a group of self-anointed Baconian amateurs banded together in London to establish the Royal Society of London, with the objective of making "faithful Records of all the Works of Nature, or Art, which can come within their reach."[8] That event marked the first tentative beginning of science as an organized group activity in the English-speaking world. During its first hundred years, the Royal Society (and similar amateur scientific societies elsewhere) developed an internal governance system to further the accumulation of useful knowledge. In essence, this system was a "republican" or "town meeting" system in which authority was in principle shared equally among all members, but in practice was granted to those who made the most significant contributions to the society's work.[9]

Very early in its history the Royal Society exhibited a tension—like that evident today—between the desire for autonomy from, and the need for acceptance by, the larger society and the political authorities that governed it. Mindful of Galileo's recent ordeal, the society abjured any intention of probing matters "affecting Church and State," regarding that concession necessary to guarantee that the state would respect its internal autonomy. On the other hand, members of the Royal Society believed that their labors would inevitably benefit the larger society, and in 1660 they sought and obtained an official charter from King Charles II. As early as 1667 they were also lamenting that the king and his councilors did not regard their work with sufficient seriousness.[10] One might argue that the Royal Society thus compromised its autonomy from the outset. Yet such a compromise *had* to be made if the activities of the Baconians were to have significant effects on the larger society, and the fellows of the society confidently believed they would.

Science as an organized activity first emerged in the American colonies in 1743, when Benjamin Franklin drafted a charter for the American Philosophical Society, the first Baconian group in North America. His words expressed the self-assurance of what was soon to emerge as a new nation founded upon principles of scientific rationality. Franklin's new society proposed to further both science for its own sake and science as a means to socially beneficial ends, by cultivating "all philosophical experiments that let light into the nature of things, tend to increase the power of man over matter, and multiply the conveniences and pleasures of life."[11] Inevitably, then, science in America, as in England, would have to negotiate with government over issues of autonomy and accountability.

In fact, pivotal negotiations took place at the Constitutional Convention in 1787, when several prominent delegates proposed to grant to the federal government broad powers to support and encourage scientific activity, including authority to "establish seminaries for the promotion of literature and the arts and sciences," to "grant charters of incorporation," to "grant patents for useful inventions," and to "establish public institutions, rewards and immunities for the promotion of agriculture, commerce, trade and manufactures."[12] These and other provisions failed to be incorporated into the Constitution, not because a majority of delegates opposed their legitimacy, but rather because they were coupled, in the thinking of the delegates, with other proposals that would have granted authority to the federal government to build roads and canals, an authority which the smaller states were loath to concede. Had the advocates for science succeeded in their negotiations in 1787, there would have been no need for Vannevar Bush to argue, a century and a half later, that the federal government had implicit authority to provide direct support for scientific research and education in universities.

NEGOTIATION OF THE CURRENT
SCIENCE-GOVERNMENT RELATIONSHIP

In July 1945 Bush proposed the creation of a National Research Foundation to provide direct support for basic research and education in universities.[13] Negotiations about the nature of the federal government's role extended from then until May 1950, when President Truman signed a modified version of Bush's proposal into law and thus established the National Science Foundation. The character and outcome of these negotiations were influenced by the experiences of scientists and officials in both the executive and legislative branches of government in negotiating the issue of civilian versus military control over the development of atomic energy during 1946.[14]

From the perspective of the present analysis, the atomic energy debate was notable because it witnessed the emergence of a group of atomic scientists as an effective lobby. These atomic scientists were willing and able not only to take their case for civilian control to the public, but also to seek and forge alliances on specific issues within the political system itself. They forged such an alliance with liberal elements in the

Congress by convincing them that military control would impede the development of atomic energy for peaceful purposes. In contrast, they argued, civilian control would assure that Congress could maintain greater oversight authority, while vesting more autonomy for determining scientific priorities with research scientists. The atomic scientists also forged an alliance with the Bureau of the Budget (which had the president's mandate to weld the federal bureaucracy into an instrument to carry out his policies) by persuading the bureau that a presidentially-appointed Atomic Energy Commission of five civilian members would be more accountable to the president than the mammoth, difficult-to-manage Department of Defense.

Why were five years required to establish a National Science Foundation for the support of basic research and education, in contrast with the intense but relatively brief period of negotiation over the control of atomic energy development? First, of course, there was the postwar desire to harness "evil" for "good" and to demilitarize. Also, the atomic energy case could be regarded as an extension of the wartime emergency contract system on a continuing, peacetime basis. In contrast, the idea of direct federal support for non-mission-oriented basic research in universities was, in the United States, completely new. Thus the debate over the terms under which government could provide and universities could accept such support on behalf of their scientists challenged deeply-held beliefs in both science and government about issues of governance, accountability, autonomy, and the proper definition and defense of public interests. Several troublesome questions were not completely resolved at the time and remain unresolved today. For example, what constitutes the public interests that presumably are to be served by closer links between science and government? Who should define those interests, and how should they be advanced and guarded? What constitutes an unwarranted intrusion into scientific autonomy and under what conditions? And who should control the detailed selection of priorities for scientific research and procedures for the conduct of that research?

Negotiations over the establishment of a policy framework for federal support of scientific research in nongovernmental institutions involved two phases. Each phase centered on a different but related issue within the contest of acccountability and autonomy questions. During the first phase, from July 1945 through August 1947, the principal issue was, Who are the stakeholders who should have a voice in congressional and executive determinations of priorities for federally-supported research? Should those stakeholders be limited to scientists and others in the institutional settings where research is conducted? A positive answer could be supported by invoking the three-century-old autonomy model of the relationship between science and society. Or should other social groups be given a voice in determining research priorities? This set of issues was resolved in favor of the traditional, narrow, autonomy model of science within the larger society.

During the second phase of the debate, from August 1947 through May 1950, the principal issue was, How can the insistence of science on a large measure of autonomy be reconciled with the constitutional requirement that elected officials of government are accountable for the expenditure of public funds, and the persistent view of the Bureau of the Budget that the president was more qualified to define public interests than any single federal agency or any external constituency group? The compromise that resolved this issue appeared, for a time, to grant science a sufficient degree of autonomy, while assuring accountability to the Congress, the president, and his Bureau of the Budget.

The first issue was joined in July 1945, a few days after the proposal to establish Bush's National Research Foundation was introduced into the Congress by Sen. Warren Magnuson of Washington.[15] The Magnuson Bill would have modeled the new agency on existing private philanthropic foundations by vesting ultimate management authority, as well as authority for determining priorities for dispersing funds, in an independent, part-time, presidentially-appointed board of distinguished scientists and educators. Bush and his congressional supporters argued that such a National Research Foundation would guarantee a maximum degree of autonomy to science and insulate it almost completely from interest-group or pork-barrel politics. A relatively narrow spectrum of groups with direct interests in scientific research would set its agenda.[16]

Within days Sen. Harley Kilgore of West Virginia, who had waited patiently since 1943 to implement his own vision of how government should support science, introduced a competitive bill for a National Science Foundation that also would have been administered by a presidentially-appointed, nongovernment board. But the Kilgore Bill would have broadened the range of interests represented on the board by defining the latter in decidedly New Deal terms. To be sure, the Kilgore board would have included distinguished scientists. But, reflecting a mid-1945 liberal Democratic perspective about the social groups that best articulated public interests, there would also have been representatives of small business, labor, and agriculture, for example. Clearly, such a board would have been a threat to the traditional construct of autonomy for science.

Ultimately, the more conservative Magnuson Bill, which accepted the Bush thesis that self-governing activities of science best served the public interest, prevailed in both houses of Congress. That bill, however, was vetoed in August 1947 by President Truman, on the advice of the Bureau of the Budget. Truman's veto message accepted with enthusiasm the legitimacy of public support for basic research in universities and the need for a reasonable level of scientific autonomy. But it emphatically rejected the claim that the president could delegate ultimate authority for the use of public funds to an independent, part-time board representing the interests of those who would use those funds and to a director who would serve at the pleasure of the board and not the president.

Three years later, in May 1950, President Truman signed into law a compromise measure to create a National Science Foundation (NSF). That law reserves to the president (and to the Congress that appropriates funds for the agency) ultimate authority over the ways in which the NSF disperses its funds. For the law provides that the director of the agency is not appointed by the foundation's National Science Board, but by the president, and is therefore responsible to the president.

The law also vests overall policy guidance and responsibility for providing advice at the highest levels of government to the National Science Board, to be composed mostly of eminent scientists and people with "distinguished records of public service."[17] As time has passed, this requirement has meant that the board has come to be comprised of people with strong scientific and management backgrounds, from academic institutions, business, and industry. The board has generally accepted the traditional assumption that scientists themselves are best qualified to determine the detailed research priorities that will best serve public interests. Since scientists and engineers have traditionally been employed by a relatively narrow spectrum of institutions, however, this formulation has meant that the board itself has generally represented a narrow spectrum of societal interests. Such a group may be predisposed to overlook value issues associated either with ostensibly scientific choices or with questions raised by scientists' affiliations with institutions whose priorities may not always be purely scientific or always emphasize public interests.

One consequence of the long debate over the creation of the NSF was that, when the agency was finally established, it could not aspire to become the comprehensive federal agency for the support of basic scientific research that Vannevar Bush had envisioned in 1945. During the three years between August 1947, when President Truman vetoed the Magnuson Bill, and May 1950, when he signed the compromise act into law, several other agencies—most notably the Department of Defense, the Atomic Energy Commission, and the National Institutes of Health—had established themselves as supporters of basic research in universities in areas broadly related to their missions. Thus a pluralistic, decentralized system of basic research support, in which individual investigators could seek funding from more than one agency, began to evolve. This result has often been taken as a positive outcome.

Additionally, the growth of basic research support within the so-called mission agencies encouraged the development of institutional links between the basic research conducted within university communities and the predominantly applied research and development programs of these agencies. This outcome has also been regarded as positive, since it facilitates the transfer of basic research results into tangible products and processes. On the other hand, this trend has also had some influence in blurring the boundaries between basic research and other types of science and engineering activities, which blurring in turn strains the relationship between government and independent scientific institutions in the United States.

RENEWAL OF THE DEBATE

Given the unprecedented nature of the concept of a substantial, mutually-beneficial, continuing dependence of science and government on each other; and given the novelty and complexity of the issues associated with translating that concept into workable, institutionalized reality, it is remarkable that a viable set of policies for linking government and science managed to emerge at all. That a compact was reached that has provided a more or less satisfactory framework for the relationships between science and government for four decades was due both to the considerable political skill of the scientists who participated in those protracted negotiations, and to the conviction on the part of influential factions within both science and the executive and legislative branches of government that close working relationships had become essential.

Four sets of incompletely articulated assumptions or expectations underlay the post-World War II policy framework negotiated between science and government:

First, the expectation that specific problems associated with differing stances on issues of accountability and autonomy could be resolved on a case-by-case basis by means of continued, good-faith negotiations between the interested parties.

Second, the tacit expectation that the interested parties in the evolving relationship would not change significantly, but rather that negotiations would continue to be managed primarily by an identifiable group of leaders of the U.S. basic research communities on the one hand, and on the other, by representatives of the federal R&D agencies, the Bureau of the Budget, and a few members of Congress who largely supported the views of accountability and autonomy inherent in the compact between government and science.

Third, the assumption that there was no need to develop specific institutional mechanisms to translate the results of the basic research conducted in universities into social benefits. Rather, government accepted the three-centuries-old presumption that a "magic hand" would ensure that the translation would occur in the best interests of the public, and that any well-meaning attempts to intrude upon the autonomy of science to facilitate that translation would be counterproductive.

Fourth, the expectation that it would remain possible to make a clean separation between longterm, non-mission-oriented research conducted in universities, and other mission-oriented research and development activities (related to national defense, atomic energy, health, and agriculture, for example) supported by, or engaged in directly by, the federal government; that basic research support would remain a microscopic part of the federal budget; and that those engaged in the conduct of basic research could remain aloof from questions of social responsibility and interest group politics.

Corollary to the third and fourth of these expectations was the implicit assumption that there was no need to negotiate a comprehensive or complex set of policies to link the country's basic research efforts either with a variety of goal-oriented research and development activities, or with more broadly conceived social and economic goals. Rather, the only requirement was for a minimum set of essentially non-interventionist policy guidelines that would assure autonomy for science within an accountability framework acceptable to the Bureau of the Budget. The National Institutes of Health (NIH) and NSF institutionalized this presumption in the form of peer review. The mission-oriented agencies behaved similarly, often supporting "science-driven" research while trusting that it would somehow help them meet their specific, nonscientific goals.[18]

84

In the late 1940s development of a comprehensive policy framework would have been difficult. It would have implied a need for longrange planning of the nation's basic research effort to try to meet national goals. It would have entailed explicit recognition of the conflicting societal agendas held by different groups of American citizens — conflicts that existed even within subsets of particular groups — and among scientists themselves. It would have conflicted with American antipathies toward centralized or governmental social planning and challenged the deeply rooted aversion of U.S. scientists to the idea that scientific activity, particularly basic research activity, can be planned in the aggregate. For planning smacks of centralization, the denial of free choice to individual scientists, and the attenuation of the ability of a scientist to follow up unanticipated breakthroughs that may occur in the course of research.

The erosion of this quiet compact over the past thirty-five years has led in turn to renewed debate over issues of autonomy and accountability, as well as to suggestions that the minimalist policy framework of the late 1940s may be incommensurate both with the augmented scale of science today and with the heightened public perception of the significance of science to all aspects of life.

Any expectation that science and government could negotiate as roughly equal partners began to erode within a year of NSF's creation, and at the initiative of science rather than government. In a February 15, 1951, memorandum to F.J. Lawton, director of the Bureau of the Budget, William T. Golden (a special consultant to the White House) described the National Science Board as the principal adviser to the president and Congress on the uses and directions of basic research in pursuit of longterm national objectives. He also envisioned a planning and coordinating function for the NSF.[19] Lawton passed the memorandum on without comment to Harvard President James B. Conant, chairman of the National Science Board. However, the board and NSF rejected the bureau's invitation to play such a limited but still important planning and coordinating role. Indeed, they rejected the position of the bureau that the Act of Congress that created the NSF gave it the *responsibility* to play that role.[20] This continued rebuff was due in large measure to the conviction that NSF would not be allowed to fulfill its central mission, to support basic research and graduate education, unless it remained insulated from political controversy and from political negotiations within the federal government.

In itself, this was a political decision. In retrospect, its wisdom seems

85

problematical. It may well be true that this novel idea — that government should provide direct support for basic research in universities, for no immediate end save the advancement of knowledge — could only take root if the search for knowledge remained aloof not only from political negotiations within government, but also from natural or potential allies both within and outside of government. Nevertheless, by declining to play even the limited policy-advisory role envisioned by both Congress and the Bureau of the Budget, the National Science Board abdicated a good deal of the political authority it might have had to negotiate with more powerful actors in government — including the Bureau of the Budget and the mission agencies — on behalf of the basic research communities it claimed to represent. Scientific interests have never been clearly identified or articulated. Science continues to play a role subsidiary to government and, save for relatively brief periods of "crisis" such as followed the launching of Sputnik by the Soviet Union in 1957, science has not been the formidable negotiator it was in the aftermath of World War II.

The expectation that the legitimate stakeholders in negotiations about the public support of science would not change appreciably has also been eroded both by the expansion and consequent fragmentation of the scientific community, and by the closely related heightening in the perception of the social relevance of science — in both positive and negative senses. As early as 1946 there were warnings that the interested stakeholders could not be defined realistically as a small group of leaders in the basic research communities and their supporters in industry and the executive and legislative branches of government. Debate over civilian vs. military control of atomic energy, and the almost concurrent debate over the Kilgore versus the Magnuson versions of the National Science Foundation, should have suggested that other stakeholders in the larger society, who took a different view of the science-government relationship, might one day reassert their right to a voice in the negotiations. Scientists involved in those debates took differing positions on political issues related both to the longterm health of science and the relations between science and society, suggesting that the "scientific community," if indeed it existed at all, did not always speak with one voice. Indeed the questions, Who speaks for science? and, For whom does science speak?, which were scarcely articulated forty years ago, have now become central to the problems of science, technology, and their governance.

Certainly today the "metastasis" of science, in William D. Carey's words, "into all of our institutions, choices and dilemmas"[21] has made it clear that the range of stakeholders extends well beyond those defined by the Bush-Magnuson version of the National Science Foundation. It has also made less tenable the myth that there is a single monolithic scientific community, led by a small handful of respected elders who are empowered to negotiate on its behalf. As in the prototypical case of atomic scientists in the immediate aftermath of World War II, scientists during the past two decades have been involved on both sides of numerous public controversies concerning the applications of research results and even the directions of basic research itself, and have allied themselves with various other groups to press their case. This, too, has eroded the myth that those directions of applications are, or can remain, insulated from politics in the broadest sense of the term.

Who, then, speaks for science? The National Academy of Sciences? senior faculty in a handful of prestigious research universities? employees of high-technology industries who are constantly exhorted to greater efforts to meet the competitive threat of Japan? scientists in Defense Department laboratories who have committed their talents to the maintenance of the security of the United States? scientists working in less-developed countries under Agency for International Development auspices to discover means of allieviating parasitic diseases?

And for whom does science speak? For U.S. universities? U.S. industry? the U.S. defense establishment? broader segments of the U.S. population? the international scientific community? Clearly these questions cannot be answered by singling out any one of these groups.

Similarly, faith in the third expectation—that reliance on a "magic hand" would remain the best policy to assure the translation of basic research results into social benefits—has also eroded. Ironically, the scientific communities may have been too successful in convincing the U.S. public that technology is centrally important to the resolution of significant national problems such as maintaining national security, improving economic competitiveness, and protecting the environment; and that public support for basic research underlies essential technologies. Dollars allocated to one basic research area in preference to another are increasingly seen to influence whether and how these problems will be solved. Thus, the final expectation—that basic research would remain relatively cheap and cleanly separable from mission-oriented research and development—has also proved illusory. It is not surprising, then, that the public, and its representatives in Congress, have become increasingly skeptical about the proposition that no better policy can be found than reliance on a "magic hand" to insure rapid, optimal returns on public investments in basic research.

Since the late 1940s there has been an immense increase in government supported research and development (R&D). This item now approximates 25 percent of the controllable federal budget, inviting close scrutiny from the Office of Management and Budget[22] (OMB) and Congress. High costs and a need for coordination are strong arguments for longrange planning (and for a policy framework to define such planning) to make the most effective use of limited resources. Furthermore, the types and sites of the activities supported by the overwhelming bulk of the federal R&D budget are very different from the types of activities that lay at the center of the post-World War II debate between science and government. Yet the present institutional structure for the support and conduct of science is such that those activities intrude heavily upon the conduct of basic research in universities.[23]

The Department of Defense (DOD) dominates the *total* federal R&D budget but is a relatively minor recipient of funds for the support of basic research in universities. In fiscal year (FY) 1984 (which began on October 1, 1983), the total amount appropriated for R&D by Congress was $43.2 billion, of which $26.4 billion, or 61.1 percent, was earmarked for defense and military purposes. (See Table 3.1.) Basic research funds appropriated for DOD during FY 1984 were, however, only $847 million, or 3.2 percent of all defense-related R&D. (See Table 3.2) In his FY 1986 budget (effective beginning October 1, 1985), President Reagan proposed obligations of $39.4 billion for defense- and military-related R&D, or 68.4 percent of the total proposed R&D budget of $57.6 billion. Of this total, $934 million, or 2.4 percent of defense R&D, was earmarked for basic research.

By comparison, a total of $10.7 billion, or 24.7 percent of the total federal R&D budget, was appropriated for basic research (both civilian and military) in FY 1984. Proposed obligations in the president's FY 1986 budget were $12.0 billion, or 21.0 percent of the total requested for R&D. In FY 1984, $3.9 billion was appropriated for the two federal agencies that support most civilian basic research — the Department of Health and Human Services (HHS) and NSF. For FY 1986, the president proposed obligations of $4.4 billion for basic research in HHS and NSF. Research grants awarded to independent investigators and institutions by these agencies are dispersed according to procedures very much in accord with the post–World War II compact that assigns decisions about detailed research priorities to the scientific communities. The goal

TABLE 3.1. Fiscal Year 1984 Total R&D Appropriations for the Six Federal Agencies Accounting for Over 90 Percent of the R&D Budget, and Obligations Requested for Those Agencies in President Reagan's Fiscal Year 1986 Budget (in Billions of Dollars)

Agency	FY 1984	FY 1986
Department of Defense	$26.4	$39.4
Department of Health and Human Services	4.8	5.2
Department of Energy	4.6	4.7
National Aeronautics and Space Administration	2.9	3.7
National Science Foundation	1.2	1.5
Department of Agriculture	0.9	0.9

Source: Office of Management and Budget, *Budget of the United States Government, Fiscal Year 1986* (Washington, D.C.: Government Printing Office, Feb. 1985), K5.

of such research — publication in the open scientific literature — is generally viewed as unproblematical.

Even though money available from the Department of Defense for basic research in universities is relatively modest compared with funds available from the civilian agencies and has remained substantially constant, universities have increased their competition for it. Accountability requirements can be more onerous in defense-related research, and questions arise concerning publication in the open literature and communication with scientists and engineers in foreign countries.[24]

Further strains in the science-government relationship originate from the growing capital requirements in different fields of basic research. Decentralized and uncoordinated research has become economically unfeasible in many cases. Recognizing that slices of the pie, while bigger, may be fewer, individual institutions compete more and more intensely for their share.[25] The high cost and consequent need to centralize large-scale facilities for basic research, such as particle accelerators and radio telescopes, has made possession of such facilities an economic plum, subject to competition in the political arena beyond the control of the scientific communities. Scientists and engineers themselves have institutional loyalties and are not above lobbying against one another when representing those institutional interests.

All these arrangements blur further the lines between basic research and other types of R&D activities, justifying added public skepticism

TABLE 3.2. Fiscal Year 1984 Appropriations for Basic Research, and Obligations Requested for Basic Research in President Reagan's Fiscal Year 1986 Budget, for the Six Agencies Listed in Table 3.1 (in Millions of Dollars)

Agency	FY 1984	FY 1986
Department of Defense	$847	$962
Department of Health and Human Services	2812	3049
Department of Energy	827	934
National Aeronautics and Space Administration	713	834
National Science Foundation	1132	1366
Department of Agriculture	393	418

Source: Office of Management and Budget, *Budget of the United States Government, Fiscal Year 1986,* K6.

of scientific claims to value-neutrality. Once again we face the question, Who speaks for science?

FACING UP TO POLITICAL CHOICES

In summary, strains in the post-World War II system of government support for science have arisen largely because of the decreasing viability of the centuries-old assumption that scientific autonomy would in itself suffice to bring social benefits to king and pauper alike. Paradoxical as this assumption appears, there is ample anecdotal evidence that the results of undirected basic research conducted by relatively autonomous scientific communities have yielded a long stream of such benefits. A central problem, then, is how to modify the post-World War II compact between science and government to take account of the present realities of increased scale and augmented social relevance of science, while preserving sufficient autonomy for truly creative scientific work—creative work that will very likely continue to underlie a great deal of social progress.

We would begin by recognizing that science, as an important social activity conducted in large measure with public resources, is necessarily conducted in the political arena. We would recognize as a myth the idea that any part of scientific activity can be insulated from political processes. Basic research has not remained relatively insulated from interest-group politics because the apolitical nature of that small but centrally significant component of scientific activity was universally conceded in advance. Rather, its insulation was negotiated between scientific and other interest groups as part of the political compact of the late 1940s and thus became a cornerstone of U.S. science policy.

In recent years, even that presumably insulated component of science has been subject to increasingly political definition, as contending groups have begun to recognize the significance of science to their short-term interests. So science itself has become politicized. But the myth of insulation has prevented science from developing a strong overt negotiating stance as it did in the late 1940s, and the terms of its politicization are not necessarily in the best interests of science or society. The myth may still be useful, but to whom?

How, then, can science participate as a strong actor in the political process, while maintaining or even improving its internal governance structure and autonomy? First, science will probably have to abandon the myth that it is and must remain totally insulated from political influences. Scientists, engineers, and their organizations surely recognize that they can and do play important roles in negotiating directions and priorities for research. They realize that their interests may conflict even with one another and even within a discipline. Even though it is no longer possible to identify a small handful of elders who can speak for science, most scientists recognize and can agree about the essential linkages between science and various other aspects of national life. Most also agree about the need for science to maintain a reasonable degree of autonomy if it is to maintain a viable relationship with other social sectors, although there is often disagreement about what the nature of such relationships can or should be.

General directions and priorities for dollars for research are clearly politically negotiated, and scientists, engineers, and their organizations can and should play important roles in those negotiations. Judgments about the scientific value of particular research efforts should continue to be vested in scientific peers, although it is sometimes difficult to identify those peers or the best mechanisms through which to engage their services. In addition, it is sometimes difficult to determine the nature and limits of scientific value. Nor is it clear how choices between widely different research areas should be made.[26] Nonetheless, accountability legitimately demands intelligent and intelligible explanations. At times, accountability will raise important issues, overlooked by a narrowly defined group of scientific peers, that should be considered before final judgments are made.

Science will also have to consider the necessity for aggregated long-range planning, since the cost of research, even in many basic research disciplines, requires planning to make the most effective use of limited financial resources. Indeed, despite the persistence of the autonomous governance model and a corollary distaste for planning, U.S. scientific communities do engage in considerable planning, and do so increasingly as the cost and scale of basic research escalates. For example, basic research activity in several disciplines requires extensive capital investments in costly, centralized facilities, such as optical and radio telescopes, particle accelerators, or oceanographic vessels. A decade or more may be required to design, construct, and test such facilities, dictating the need for longrange planning and decisions about the allocation of financial and human resources. Once constructed, such unique, centralized facilities are expensive to operate. Moreover, they rarely have the capacity to satisfy requests for their use by qualified scientists from all over the country—and from many foreign countries. Therefore planning for the optimum, equitable use of research facilities is necessary, as is delegation of a large measure of authority to those who manage the facilities.

Long-range planning is not limited to the construction and operation of facilities in the "big-science" disciplines such as astronomy, particle physics, or oceanography. It must also take usage into account. For the resources allocated by the president's annual budget to the federal agencies that support basic research in universities—principally the Departments of Defense and Energy, the National Aeronautics and Space Administration, the National Institutes of Health (within the Department of Health and Human Services), and the National Science Foundation—are insufficient to satisfy the claims of all qualified scientists. Therefore, these agencies, working in concert with their scientific constituents, must necessarily plan on how to make the best use of those limited resources. And that planning process must inevitably address the questions, Who speaks for science? and, For whom does science speak?

Current planning is, in most instances, carried out in an *ad hoc*, piecemeal fashion. There is little coordination among agencies except for that which the Office of Management and Budget imposes in preparation for the president's annual budget. Planning remains piecemeal in part because of an aversion to centralization, but even more because the United States—unlike other industrialized countries—still lacks an explicit, comprehensive national science policy that would provide an agreed-upon framework for such planning. That is, the United States has never attempted to develop a coherent statement of goals for science and engineering.

In one sense, however, this chapter *has* described current U.S. science policy—a policy based on a tradition of American faith in scientific progress. Harking back to the post–World War II compact, that faith requires, first, that public funds be expended to support the basic research that scientists themselves decide is important, and, second, that the university-based scientific community enjoy the greatest possible measure of autonomy in the conduct of that research. It assumes that science policy should consist of little more than a reasonable assurance that funds appropriated for the conduct of basic research be more or less adequate, and a set of guidelines for targeting resources to meet explicit and usually short-term science- and technology-related objectives of the federal government.

Such a policy and the faith that underlies it carry the corollary assumption that science best serves broad social purposes when it speaks primarily for itself. Finally, as we have already noted, they require the subsidiary notion that scientific research — particularly basic research — can be insulated from politics and that a magic hand can be relied upon to facilitate the transfer of research results into tangible benefits for each and every one of us. The compact can also accommodate other subsidiary objectives — for example, directing ample scientific resources to meet defense requirements or supporting science education largely as a spinoff of basic research support in universities. It has the advantage of appearing to take the politics out of science, and it satisfies powerful political forces both inside and outside of science.

This view is perhaps most appropriate, pragmatically speaking, when federal budgets for the civilian science agencies are expanding. In such times, even those agencies with strong mission orientations can afford to support "science-driven" science that is only peripherally related to their specific objectives. They can afford to accommodate, quietly, the goals of groups that do not dominate in the process. In lean years, however, federal agencies — particularly the mission agencies — are forced to retrench and focus more narrowly on their objectives. This process may be labeled apolitical because it occurs administratively for the most part and does not involve specific discussions in the political estate.[27] Nevertheless, such refocusing constitutes *de facto* policy making.

A broader view than what we have grown accustomed to during the past forty years would envision national science policy as including, in addition to most of the pieces that comprise this existing minimalist policy, explicit provisions and strategies for incorporating scientific information and insights into decision making on a wide range of national issues that may not relate directly to the conduct of research — for example, the assessment and management of the hazards of toxic chemicals in the environment, or the problem of making effective use of science and technology as adjuncts to U.S. foreign policy.

Implementing a broad policy of this sort would require political negotiations of the kind that may have begun with an extensive series of special hearings scheduled during 1985 and 1986 by a House of Representatives task force under the chairmanship of Rep. Don Fuqua of Florida.[28] Certainly the formulation and implementation of a broader science policy would require scientists and engineers to develop clearer ideas of the appropriate roles for their expertise in democratic decision making. It would also require the development of initiatives well beyond those appropriate to the federal government. Such a policy — or set of policies — would have to include, at a minimum, strategies to stimulate and focus research and development activities elsewhere than in the federal government and in the institutions that rely heavily upon federal support. Such policies would have explicitly to articulate distinctions between the roles of the federal government, universities, private industry, and state governments, for example, in realizing national science- and technology-related objectives. They would also have to specify areas in which the federal government would depend primarily upon universities and industry to attain national objectives, and areas in which it would not intervene in university and industry activities.

But of course no new science policy could be implemented prior to its formulation. And formulation of a comprehensive science policy — or, alternatively, forging a new, more comprehensive compact between government and science — would require undertaking a wide-ranging political discussion and achieving a broad political consensus on a number of difficult issues, many of them only peripherally related to the conduct of research and many involving constituencies that are not presently regarded as natural allies of university-based scientific research communities. A more comprehensive policy need not imply more centralized control. On the contrary, negotiations leading to a more comprehensive compact between government and science would have to involve interests presently without a substantial voice in establishing priorities for federal support of scientific research. These interests would include, but not be limited to, those to which the Kilgore version of a National Science Foundation might have given a voice in the late 1940s. In other words, reopening serious negotiations would require facing the question, For whom does science speak?

Since a comprehensive national science policy would subject the basic research component of the annual federal R&D budget to considerably more political negotiation than it faces at present, it can be and has been argued that support for scientific research in universities might be subject to changing political fashions. However, despite this very real risk, there is by now a longstanding consensus about the desirability of stable basic research support at reasonable levels. That consensus is likely to persist, despite negotiations about other, closely related components of the federal R&D budget.

A converse argument can also be made, namely that the process of negotiating a more comprehensive science policy could actually foster the autonomy of science within universities and even increase the resources devoted to scientific activities in those settings. For at present, science negotiates with government for resources and preservation of autonomy from a relatively weak position. However, if science were to seek and forge alliances with other groups with a strong interest if a less direct stake in the outcome of scientific activity, then science might be able to convince those groups of the longrange value of its vision of human knowledge and of its governance mechanisms, such as the peer review process. Science might then come to enjoy a much stronger negotiating position with respect to its core values, even though it might have to accept more realistic limits on the political uses of scientific knowledge. Science cannot and does not solve political problems, although it can help define, illuminate, and even partially resolve such problems within a well-defined political structure and set of political procedures.

A comprehensive, negotiated science policy, then, might help to improve the political position of university-based research communities. In addition, it could direct science and engineering activities more purposefully toward the illumination and resolution of a broader range of national problems, as perceived by a wider range of social groups, than at present. But formulation and implementation of such a policy would require that science accept Bacon's vision of science as an integral component of the larger society and larger culture. Then a broad spectrum of stakeholders might speak for science, and the answer to the question, For whom does science speak? would be almost self-evident.

95

NOTES

1. See, for example, Jerome Ravetz, " . . . Et Augebitur Scientia," in *Problems of Scientific Revolution: Progress and Obstacles to Progress in the Sciences,* ed. Rom Harre, (Oxford: Clarendon Press, 1975), 42–57.

2. Ibid.

3. Vannevar Bush, *Science—The Endless Frontier* (Washington, D.C.: U.S. Government Printing Office, 1945). First issued as a report to the president of the U.S. on July 5, 1945, the book was reprinted in 1980 by the National Science Foundation.

4. Ibid., 5.

5. Ibid., 12.

6. "It has been basic United States policy that Government should foster the opening of new frontiers. It opened the sea to clipper ships and furnished land for pioneers. Although these frontiers have more or less disappeared, the frontier of science remains. It is in keeping with the American tradition—one which has made the United States great—that new frontiers shall be made accessible for development by all American citizens." Ibid., 11.

7. A. Hunter Dupree, "The Great Instauration of 1940," in *The Twentieth-Century Sciences,* ed. Gerald Holton (New York: Norton, 1972), 433–67.

8. Thomas Sprat, *History of the Royal Society*, ed. Jackson Cope and Harold Jones (London: Routledge and Kegan Paul, 1958), 61.

9. The early development of the peer review system that was destined to become central to the internal governance of science has been traced by Harriet Zuckerman and Robert K. Merton, "Patterns of Evaluation in Science: Institutionalization, Structure, and Functions of the Referee System," *Minerva* 9 (Jan. 1971): 66–100.

10. Sprat, *History of the Royal Society.*

11. Alexandra Oleson and Sanborn C. Brown, *The Pursuit of Knowledge in the Early American Republic* (Baltimore: Johns Hopkins Univ. Press, 1976), xvi.

12. A. Hunter Dupree, *Science in the Federal Government: A History of Policies and Activities to 1940* (Cambridge: Harvard Univ. Press, Belknap Press, 1957), 3–6.

13. Bush, *Science—The Endless Frontier,* 31–40.

14. Alice K. Smith, *A Peril and a Hope.*

15. Daniel J. Kevles, "The National Science Foundation and the Debate Over Postwar Research Policy, 1942-1945: A Political Interpretation of *Science—The Endless Frontier,*" *Isis* 68 (Mar. 1977): 5–26. J. Merton England, "Dr. Bush Writes a Report: *Science—The Endless Frontier,*" *Science* 191 (9 Jan. 1976): 41–46.

16. The phrase "interest group politics," as we use it here, refers to processes through which interest groups such as organized labor, business, minority groups, and educational associations, for example, negotiate within the political arena in attempting to achieve their aims. William Carey has remarked on the absence of this sort of political negotiation for science policy, noting, "When policies for science do emerge, they are not negotiated policies. The customary bargaining, the give-and-take, and the negotiating that shape economic and fiscal policies, foreign and defense policies, or policies for energy or tariffs or trade, do not occur when policies for science are involved." William D. Carey, "Science and Public Policy," 12.

17. National Science Foundation Act of 1950. Public Law 81-507 (64 Stat. 149), Sec. 4.

18. W. Henry Lambright, *Governing Science and Technology,* 154–55.

19. William T. Golden, "Memorandum on Program for the National Science Foundation," 13 Feb. 1951. National Archives, RG 51, Series 39.33, File Unit 94–NSF General Administration.

20. Milton Lomask, *A Minor Miracle: An Informal History of the National Science Foundation* (Washington, D.C.: National Science Foundation, 1976), 91–110.

21. William D. Carey, "Science and Public Policy."

22. The Bureau of the Budget was reorganized, and its oversight functions broadened, as the Office of Management and Budget (OMB) in 1972. See, for example, Larry Berman, *The Office of Management and Budget and the Presidency, 1921–1979* (Princeton: Princeton Univ. Press, 1979).

23. For another view of changes in the political economy of science, see Donald Kennedy, "Government Policies and the Cost of Doing Research," *Science* 227 (1 Feb. 1985): 480–84.

24. See, for example, National Academy of Sciences, *Scientific Communication and National Security.*

25. The economic advantage in having specialized research facilities has led, since 1983, to a number of so-called "pork barrel" incidents in which universities, often with the assistance of professional lobbying firms, have taken their case for funding such facilities directly to congressional committees or the floor of Congress, thus circumventing — some would say subverting — established peer review procedures for determining the need and the location of such facilities. See Colin Norman, "Pork Barrel Scorecard," *Science* 226 (2 Nov. 1984): 519; Richard C. Atkinson and William A. Blanpied, "Peer Review and the Public Interest," *Issues in Science and Technology* 1:4 (Summer 1985): 101–14; and *Congressional Record*, 25 Sept. 1984, pp. E4002–3, and 3 Jan. 1985, pp. E108–9.

26. See Richard C. Atkinson and William A. Blanpied, "Peer Review and the Public Interest."

27. W. Henry Lambright, *Governing Science and Technology*, 9–10.

28. U.S. Congress, House, Committee on Science and Technology, *An Agenda for a Study of Government Science Policy* (Washington, D.C.: Government Printing Office, Dec. 1984).

4. The Scientist-Entrepreneur and the Paths of Technological Development

DENNIS FLORIG

Consider just some of the more dramatic triumphs of contemporary medical science: wonder drugs which cure dread diseases, intricate new operations which save lives once lost, transplants of human and animal hearts to replace failing organs, implantation of artificial hearts, the creation of entirely new organisms in the laboratory. Similar prodigies have been achieved in computer technology, physics, petrochemicals, and other fields of science and technology. It has become a background assumption of life in the twentieth century that accelerating technical advance will produce ever more benefits to society.

PORTRAIT OF THE SCIENTIST-ENTREPRENEUR

The men and women behind these advances have become a new kind of folk hero. While the human drama of a William Schroeder, Barney Clark, or Baby Fae may take center stage, the pioneers of our new technology bask in the glow as well. With their artificial hearts, the William DeVries, Robert Jarviks, and Wilhelm Kolffs join the Christian Barnards and Michael DeBakeys as legendary pathbreakers in the treatment of heart disease. Not all technological innovations become instant front-page news, but their creators and sponsors gain recognition among their peers and reap potentially vast material rewards. Technology, after all, is the god that works—that has brought ever more blessings on its devotees. And those who have the special knowledge to command the machinery are its high priests. The very designation of scientist or engineer commands respect and reward. Direct association with some new triumph of technology lends further authority to its creators' pronouncements, whether they deal with the scientific or nonscientific aspects of the technology.

One measure of the social value attached to technological advance is the financial gain that goes to the creators and sponsors of new techniques which yield marketable products. If knowledge is power, then marketable knowledge is economic power. The corporate world is ever aware that getting in early on a new wave of technical innovation is a sure way to make money. Entire scientific and engineering disciplines have been influenced by this reality as well. The scientific professions and the corporate world have become ever more intertwined in the quest for profitable technologies. The individual scientist-entrepreneur who bursts on the public scene with some awesome new technology is only the most visible manifestation of a whole complex web of scientific, corporate, and governmental relations which tie the practice of science to external political and economic forces.

This chapter examines the role of the scientist-entrepreneur in science and technology policy making. The focus is on the political economy of technological development — on those ties between science and the corporate world which shape technological innovation, on the difficulties of social direction of technological development under current institutions of governance, and on strategies for reform. In contrast to Wofsy's essay (Chapter 5), this discussion centers not so much on the particular linkages between universities, individual scientists, and corporations, as on the larger system dynamics which orient the political economy to particular forms of technological development. The individual scientist-entrepreneur symbolizes the wider interpenetration of science and the corporate world which is increasingly evident in capitalist societies. To see so clearly in the individual scientist turned entrepreneur the potential conflicts of interest, the compromising of the ideal of a socially neutral science, crystallizes the even more fundamental social conflict between democratic choice about paths of technological development and private investment in particular technologies. This essay traces how the scientist-entrepreneur exercises disproportionate influence over science and technology policy; it then sketches some ideas about how more effective democratic control can be brought to bear on the process of technological development.

ALTERNATIVE PATHS OF TECHNOLOGICAL DEVELOPMENT

Science and technology have brought us all great blessings. But the blessings have not been unmixed. Recent history is replete with examples of technological advances that have had serious negative consequences for our quality of life. The prodigious growth of the petrochemical industry has brought in its wake occupational and environmental exposure to numerous toxic chemicals, which has increased cancer rates, birth defects, and other maladies in millions of chemical workers and citizens of exposed communities. Technically fascinating but costly medical techniques such as CAT scanners, heart transplants, and artificial heart implants have entailed astronomical direct costs and have diverted health care resources from more cost-effective investments in preventive medicine and health care delivery to underserviced rural and inner-city populations. Advances in agricultural technology have placed ever more pesticides in the environment and increased dependence on remote sources of material inputs. And the massive arms competition between the United States and the Soviet Union continues to consume roughly one-third of all the scientific and technological capacity of the American economy, inhibiting civilian economic development while increasing our gruesome capacities for destruction.

So while the benefits of technological development are great, they do not come without costs and risks. Governance of science and technology rests on assessing the tradeoffs among the benefits, costs, and risks of technological innovation; the social purpose of governance is to guide scientific and technological development into the most socially beneficial routes and away from those studded with the most serious costs and potential costs. In discussing energy policy options, Amory Lovins uses the metaphor of alternative paths to illustrate the choices implicit and explicit in energy policy making.[1] Lovins contrasts two sets of policies—the actual energy policies that emerged following the mid-1970s OPEC oil-cutoff crisis, which relied on rapid expansion of nuclear power generation and longer-term expansion of coal-generated electricity; and a second strategy that would rely primarily on conservation and the development of renewable energy sources such as solar, biomass, etc. Lovins characterizes this choice as between hard energy paths which encourage waste, generate heavy environmental costs, and increase the risk of environmental catastrophe and even war in the Middle East; and soft energy paths which foster decentralized energy generation, minimum environmental damage, and community control of resources.

The relative merits of hard or soft energy development is less the point here than that the metaphor of alternative paths provides a useful way of conceptualizing issues in the governance of science and technology. Lovins' imagery emphasizes that public policy choices, and only public policy choices, can consciously guide future forms of technological development into democratically chosen paths. At an even deeper level, Lovins notes that particular political institutional relationships can predispose policy to certain paths rather than others. He argues that past hard energy path choices have made it ever more difficult to turn back to a soft energy strategy.

> A hard path can make the attainment of a soft path prohibitively difficult in three ways: by starving its components into garbled and incoherent fragments; by changing social values and perceptions in a way that makes the innovations of a soft path painful to envisage; and by evolving institutions, policy actions, and political commitments in a way that inhibits those same innovations.[2]

PUBLIC POLICY AND THE SCIENTIST-ENTREPRENEUR

If the task of science and technology governance is to direct research and development into the most socially beneficial paths, the material interest of the scientist-entrepreneur can conflict with this aim. The scientist, eager to develop new knowledge, has an intellectual commitment to move knowledge forward and thus may be predisposed to underestimate the costs and risks associated with her or his work. But the scientist-entrepreneur who seeks to gain substantial profits from full development of new technical processes and new marketable products has not only an intellectual commitment, but also a very real material commitment, to press forward to profitability despite social costs and risks. He or she has a vested interest in overestimating the social and economic benefit that will flow from current research and underestimating the costs and risks associated with further development of the field.

This interest in overestimating benefits and underestimating costs and risks is no more, but no less, than that shown by a Pentagon contractor trying to sell a new weapons system to the military, a highway contractor proposing a new project to a state highway commission, or a chemical company assessing the effect of toxic chemicals on its workers, the local water supply, and the local community. Consciously or unconsciously, those who plan to profit from technical innovation will inflate their estimates of the benefits which will flow from their research, in order to sell their work to government agency sponsors, corporate investors, and the general public. Similarly, they will be biased toward underestimating direct costs, portraying serious risks to society as remote, and assessing remote risks as of zero probability.

Unlike the highway contractor, who operates in a field in which at least some of the cost and benefit parameters are well known to public officials, the scientist-entrepreneur can largely shape public perception of the costs, risks, and benefits of new research and development. Like the individual patient facing a physician who holds a near monopoly on advanced medical knowledge, members of the mass public, and often government bureaucrats, have limited ability to assess the validity of the claims of the expert scientist-entrepreneur. But while the scientist-enterpreneur, because of her or his special knowledge, is in a position to shape public perception of benefits, costs, and risks, it will be members of the public (as individuals and as taxpayers) who will likely bear most of the direct costs of R&D and the social costs of poor risks.

The overestimation of benefits and the underestimation of direct and indirect costs is illustrated by the case of the Artificial Heart Program. In the mid-1960s, prominent scientists testified before congressional committees and claimed in the mass media that a usable, workable artificial heart was on the immediate horizon, awaiting only a government program to spur R&D.[3] In 1966, early in the history of the resultant program, a space program contractor conducted evaluation studies concerning the introduction of artificial hearts into general medical use, pegging the probable date of such an event as the early 1970s.[4] These projections proved wildly optimistic, but at the time they surely seemed to non-expert government officials, journalists, and citizens as credible as any other claim of technology's high priests.

Cases also abound of underestimation of the risks of technological development by those who stood to profit from it. Assurances by the nuclear power industry that accidents on the scale of Three Mile Island were of near zero likelihood or by chemical companies that workers exposed to particular chemicals would not suffer increased cancer deaths or birth defects are perhaps the most salient examples.

Science is big business and getting bigger. Not a week goes by without mass circulation business or general news magazines hailing the profits to be made from the marriage of science and economics.[5] What is less often recognized is that high technology is particularly favored by the giant multinational corporations whose advantages over smaller

102

competitors in economic productivity are based primarily on greater complexity of technical processes. But high tech does not always represent greater economic rationality. More and more military analysts are lamenting how the "gold plating" of unnecessarily complex technology weighs down U.S. military procurement by making the unit cost of acquisitions prohibitive. Fewer, more sensitive weapons do not assure greater efficiency. Oligopolistic advantages do, however, accrue to large firms using complex technologies.[6] Many firms can manufacture a rifle, but there are only a few that could be prime contractors for "Star Wars" systems, that could coordinate such a technically complex, capital-intensive project. While the situation is not exactly the same in non-military technology, the general advantage that Fortune 500 companies have in high technology does obtain in many areas of technological development. Commoner, like Lovins, argues that "hard" energy paths are irrationally selected in large part because of the nonmarket advantages that fall to particular marriages of scientific knowledge and big capital.[7] While the public image of the scientist-entrepreneur may be that of a "lone wolf" using his genius to blaze new trails, much of the political muscle that drives public and private investment in technology comes from the corporate backers of particular high-tech products.

The relationship between capital and science is not without friction. Many scientists are concerned about the differences in norms of conduct in the scientific and corporate worlds.[8] For example, the corporate desire for secrecy and those quasi-monopolistic advantages conferred by patents and trade secrets runs counter to the scientists' desire to build knowledge through open access to new information; and the scientific tradition of open dissemination of new knowledge and cooperative endeavor run counter to the corporate norms of competition and protection of proprietary information. Particularly when large public subsidies go into creating entire fields of scientific activity, corporate appropriation of the material fruits of the collective effort by patenting its products represents a questionable privatization of knowledge. There is also a tension between scientists' desire for research funding that gives priority to investigation of the most scientifically interesting and significant problems, and the corporate priority on projects with the most likely short-term applicability to innovation in productive processes — a conflict over the balance between basic and applied research. The problem scientists perceive in generating support for basic research is exacerbated by the increasing dependence of science on corporate support in an era of governmental austerity.

The scientist-entrepreneur increasingly functions as the institutional mechanism for muting potential conflict between the corporate agenda for technological development and competing social values such as support for basic research, environmental protection, and public guidance of technological development. By conferring the mantle of scientific legitimacy on priorities driven by corporate wants, the scientist-entrepreneur helps hide these value conflicts behind the facade of a universally shared goal of technological advance.

THE MASS MEDIA AND THE SCIENTIST-ENTREPRENEUR

The scientist-entrepreneur would have only limited influence on science and technology policy if she or he stood alone in decision-making councils. But the scientist-entrepreneur has allies in influencing public opinion and persuading others within the complex set of institutions that make science and technology policy. The relationship between the scientist-entrepreneur and the media is particularly important in shaping both general public opinion and the context in which policy makers think about issues. Thus, this relationship bears scrutiny.

Thinking of the news media as allies of those they cover runs counter to the media's self-portrayal as watchdogs vigilant of public figures. Certainly the media can play a key role in the policy process by publicizing information which contradicts that presented by public officials and prominent scientists. The ordinary citizen is largely dependent upon the media to alert her or him to issues in technological development. And certainly many public figures, including some leading scientists, have felt that the media were against them.

But while the media prefer to be seen as watchdogs, they have also acted as advocates for numerous scientist-entrepreneurs urging particular paths of technological development. Access to the popular press and special readership journals gives the scientist-entrepreneur a chance to play on the fears, anxieties, hopes, and dreams of ordinary citizens, opinion leaders, and even policy makers. In selling their research agendas, scientist-entrepreneurs often offer the mass public a twentieth-century version of pie-in-the-sky. Since modern technology has delivered on many promises that may have seemed like pie-in-the-sky at the time they were made, it is difficult for the non-expert to distinguish plausible claims from implausible ones. Because, within their own lifetimes, most people have seen technological advances that they had never imagined possible, many people tend to believe any authoritative pro-nouncement that bears an aura of scientific legitimacy. While credibility gaps have on occasion caught up with politicians and even with high-tech industries, the norm has been acceptance rather than skepticism toward most promises bearing the imprint of scientific authority.

In fact, the public seems to believe that science can solve any problem, even ones that are primarily social and political in nature. From "Star Wars" antimissile systems to put the nuclear-war genie back in the bottle, through magic-bullet cures for cancers generated by occupational and environmental exposure to carcinogens, to artificial hearts and heart transplants to replace organs damaged by smoking, diet, and other lifestyle factors, people find it easier to hope for a simple technological "fix" than to face up to difficult social realities.

The media prove valuable allies to the scientist-entrepreneur who wishes to encourage this process of mystification. It is easier for journalists to write a gushing piece on the coming of new technological miracles, and on the men and women behind them — simply to relay the optimistic perspective of the scientist-entrepreneur — than to become educated to the full implications of a new technology and seriously to discuss costs and risks as well. The media both feed on and reinforce the aura of knowledge, authority, and beneficence projected by the scientist foretelling new technological wonders. And as extra glue for this bond, the media, ever zealous in pressing their own claims to First Amendment protection, are particularly sensitive to the scientists' claim that "freedom of inquiry" is trampled upon in any attempt by society to regulate or shape paths of technological development.

THE POLITICAL ECONOMY OF TECHNOLOGY POLICY

One might expect that the institutions of governance designated to make science and technology policy might systematically incorporate challenges to the perspective of the scientist-entrepreneur on technological innovation. However, instead of acting as a check on the peculiar view of technological development characteristic of the scientist-entrepreneur, the political institutions which govern science and technology tend to amplify it. Wofsy (in Chapter 5) documents the impact of the scientist-entrepreneur on the university, one key locus of science and technology policy making. Elected officials and science and technology bureaucracies also affect patterns of development through decisions on such issues

105

as level and form of public subsidies and regulatory processes. And, like universities, elected officials and bureaucracies are also susceptible to the influence of the scientist-entrepreneur.[9]

Elected officials often have great incentive for receptivity to the agenda of corporate science. For example, state and local officials are in fierce competition to lure industry to meet municipal needs for a commercial tax base. Just as spinoff benefits are often promised as a result of public investment in space technology, direct and indirect benefits for overall local industrial development are promised by high-tech industries to state and local governments. Beyond the ordinary multiplier of service, business and employment that is generated by any new industrial plant, high-tech industries promise that rapid economic growth will inevitably follow from being on the leading edge of a new technology soon to be in great demand. State and local officials seeking heavy industry have engaged in what has been called "smokestack chasing," although as Wright has pointed out regarding environmental and labor regulation, a better term might be "competition in laxity."[10]

A new part of the sales pitch is that high-tech industry has replaced smokestack pollution with "clean" industries. But toxic wastes seeping into people's water supply did not come from low-tech industries. State and local officials bidding to develop the next "Silicon Valley" are predisposed to screen out the pricetags hidden on the dream. Even if opposition to new technologies which pose particular environmental risks appears in some communities, as resistance to recombinant DNA research did in Cambridge and Berkeley, there will be local officials somewhere among the tens of thousands of municipalities who will believe industry officials' claims.

National elected officials are also susceptible to the influence of corporate science. Members of Congress, like local officials, benefit from economic development in their districts and often aid local corporations and universities in gaining access to national R&D funds. Even American presidents engage in this behavior. It was no accident that the new space command center built during Lyndon Johnson's presidency was located in Houston, in his home state of Texas.

Federal R&D bureaucracies have their own reasons for joining scientist-entrepreneurs in proclaiming new horizons of painless technological development. Even when national coffers are relatively full, agencies must justify proposed increases in their shares of public largesse. In periods of austerity, R&D bureaucracies must proclaim more strenuously than ever the future benefits that will flow to the ordinary citizen and voter from their work. The more dramatically compelling these benefits seem to the Office of Management and Budget, congressional committees, and the public imagination, the more support the bureaucracy can ask for. For example, the National Institute of Microbiology became the National Institute of Allergies and Infectious Diseases when it was discovered that a new name would lead to larger appropriations from Congress. No-one had ever died from "microbiology," and thus research appeals lacked dramatic force.[11] The "sexier" the innovation, the better for an agency's longterm budgetary health. And dwelling on costs and "low probability" risks can only harm an agency's case.

It is more than ironic that corporate and conservative ideologues, so quick to point out how political relations influence social spending, are largely silent concerning the way government R&D expenditures represent subsidies for capital. Instead of being the target of "welfare Cadillac" anecdotes, the scientist-entrepreneur is viewed as evidence of the beneficence of technological innovation and the special powers attributed to capitalist economies as a result of such advances. The overall contribution of public expenditures in providing many of the key prerequisites for technical innovation — including not only direct R&D funds but also most of the infrastructure of organized scientific activity — is downplayed, as the glories of the innovative individual entrepreneur and private sector are sung. In corporate mythology it is the entrepreneurial spirit of beneficent but bold risktakers that blazes new trails of technological advance in productivity and consumption. While government is assigned a responsibility to support this process, corporate ideology focuses on the negative effects government regulation will have on the work of the entrepreneurs, and on how raising fears about environmental and social costs only puts obstacles between us and a cornucopia of innovative new products.

MARKETS, POLITICS, AND TECHNOLOGICAL DEVELOPMENT

One social mechanism which plays a role in mediating technological development and which might be expected to check the selection of costly or risky paths of development is the economic marketplace. According to a conventional view of economic markets, the costs and risks that go into product development are born by the firms that ultimately market the products, and thus are reflected in the price of new products. Since the direct and indirect costs of the product are signaled by the

107

price of the product, consumers who choose to buy the product would be demonstrating that, at least to them, the benefits they receive from these products are greater than the costs involved.

But in fact market forces do little to limit the social risks of revolutionary technological developments. No one firm or even one industry could ever pay for the social costs associated with releasing genetically altered microorganisms into the environment and so setting off a chain of ecological disturbances in the microscopic world. Those who press for artificial heart technology assume that government will subsidize not only the development of the device but also the much greater potential expense of using this costly technique as many as tens of thousands of times a year. Even the current attempt of the "superfund" to internalize the costs of environmental damage caused by the chemical industry shows how inadequate even billions of earmarked tax dollars are to meet the social costs imposed by this one industry. While the superfund finally has mandated that the chemical industry bear some of the environmental costs of its activities, most of these costs have been borne by uncompensated individuals who have already been exposed and by government medical and environmental budgets. High-tech industries also often can win government decisions blunting the impact on their own finances of any environmental damage they cause. The Price-Anderson Act explicitly limits the legal liability of the nuclear power industry in the case of a major accident, thus socializing the risks associated with the development of nuclear power. Even when courts have imposed penalties for harm done, individuals have not always been fully compensated. In the case of Johns-Manville, for example, the firm declared bankrupcy rather than pay the victims of exposure to asbestos.

The moral of these stories is that direct and indirect subsidization of the costs and risks of corporate technological development is being built into the system as it operates. Therefore major new technologies are not subject to valid market determination of the balance of costs, risks, and benefits. The political economy of technological development is not so much one of market competition as of differential influence of government decision making. Since markets cannot be relied upon mechanically and neutrally to regulate technological development, the importance of direct political decisions on these issues is heightened. If there is to be social guidance of scientific and technological development, it will have to be done through the complex set of political institutions that make public policy. Yet these institutions as currently constituted have shown a pronounced tendency to amplify rather than to correct the biases of the scientist-entrepreneur.

THE ILLUSION OF SOCIAL CONTROL

What has been outlined is the range of economic and political forces which are predisposed to reinforce rather than to challenge the view of technological innovation presented by the scientist-entrepreneur. This does not mean that challenges to the perspective of the scientist-entrepreneur never occur, only that the balance of economic and political forces as currently constituted favors the position of the scientist-entrepreneurs over critics of particular paths of technological innovation. Occasionally, projects that are advanced by scientist-entrepreneurs as important to technological innovation have been subject to regulatory constraints, changes in funding priorities, and even termination. But there are many cases where social control clearly has been exerted only on the margins of technological development.

The most common mechanism by which society attempts to influence technological development are regulatory policies which seek to protect the public against specific adverse events. Yet a substantial body of political science and economics literature argues that government regulation of economic activity often gives the illusion of social restraint while in reality allowing industries to use public power for private purposes.[12] The regulatory process has even been described as a series of rituals which provide symbolic reassurance of protection to poorly-organized mass publics while legitimizing a system which actually favors organized economic interests.[13] Not all regulatory processes are "captured" by entrenched interests, but many are.

One example of an area in which organized interests dominate self-regulatory systems that reassure the public but do not really control is NIH regulation of recombinant DNA (rDNA) research. More detailed accounts of this case can be found elsewhere in this volume; my point here is simply the limited nature of this regulatory process. Reflecting scientific and public fears about the consequences of inadvertently releasing genetically altered microorganisms into the environment, NIH developed guidelines for physical containment of the products of all rDNA research under their sponsorship. While this response allayed public fears, NIH continued to sponsor projects whose logical consequences would be deliberately to introduce new life forms into the ecosphere. In addition, by placing regulation in the framework of NIH-sponsored projects, NIH exempted private industrial use of the new technology from the same restrictions, despite the fact that once this technology enters commercial application in manufacture and agriculture, risks from such use of altered organisms will drawf the risks involved in small-scale academic projects. As for the composition of the committees that were to implement the regulations on a local level, NIH opted for self-regulation over external control. While the committees were required to include public members not in fields connected with the research, members of the disciplines conducting research were to dominate the committee. And at an even more fundamental level, NIH set an agenda focused on *how* to do research rather than on *whether* to do it.

Even when the national science bureaucracy provides for review of research funding priorities by public members not predisposed by disciplinary ties to favor subsidies, the review often comes too late for any fundamental judgments about basic paths of scientific and technological development. The Artificial Heart Assessment Panel (AHAP) was a case in point. Nearly a decade of funding had shaped the direction of research before AHAP was even created to evaluate the philosophical and social issues involved in artificial heart development.

In one sense, AHAP could be seen as a potential model for public participation in decision making regarding technology. Its ostensible purpose was to examine the moral, social, and economic implications of ongoing research in the field and to make recommendations to the agency supporting artificial heart research. Yet AHAP falls far short of being an adequate model of social choice among paths of technological development. The work of AHAP focused on what forms of artificial heart development were desirable, rather than on whether the path of artificial heart development should be traveled and whether a government program should be dedicated to spurring artificial heart development at all.

Just as with local biohazard committees in rDNA research, so AHAP's agenda was specifically limited to steering down a path of development already chosen. This agenda was defined by an administrative agency which was not bound to follow any of AHAP's recommendations. AHAP was operating in a predefined context which restricted its consideration of alternatives to one particular set of issues regarding how to spur development of this technology. The range of issues it was charged to consider did include broader philosophical and social questions as well as technical issues. But AHAP faced severe limitations on time and resources in carrying out its mission. It met only a handful of times. Members expressed frustration over the superficiality of briefings they received and even over the limitations of their official agenda, reflecting their sense that their work fell short of any genuine exercise of social control over technological development.[14]

SUMMARY OF ANALYSIS

To the extent that the expansion of scientific knowledge in a particular field affects technical and economic processes and thus has environmental and social impacts, pursuit of research represents implicit or explicit social choices. While science strives for neutrality in interpreting research findings, the very act of choosing certain research priorities over others can never be neutral in its impact on society. Even the scientist in the laboratory pursuing questions of pure knowledge needs to have her or his desire to know tempered by social guidance of scientific and technological development. But the scientist-entrepreneur has a special motivation to pursue particular lines of research — namely, the pursuit of profit. Under these circumstances, it is inevitable that the stamp of scientific legitimacy will be attached to the overestimation of potential benefits and the underestimation of social costs and risks of particular forms of technological innovation.

Further, existing institutions which provide the appearance of social control of technological development are in actuality predisposed to accept and even to advocate the scientist-entrepreneur's characteristic perspective on particular innovations. External review of funding priorities and regulation of laboratory and economic processes is more often a system of self-governance rather than of external guidance. Economic commitments to particular paths of technological development are rarely consciously evaluated in comparison with alternative paths of development, although commitment to one path may preclude alternative paths from emerging. All scientific and technological development requires forging ahead into the unknown and thus entails possible social costs and risks. But the current structures of science and technology governance encourage distorted public subsidies and excessive risks to the environment and society.

Since certain forms of external guidance over scientific and technological development represent less than real social control over events, they serve more as warnings of how external review can be co-opted rather than as positive models for emulation.[15] American society, faced with particular risks from technological innovation, tends to react more to the symptom than to the deeper causes that produced it. Regulation often takes the form of self-regulation, where economic actors and their allies in government steer public policy along their preferred paths of development. The regulatory apparatus which emerged in the case of rDNA research is typical of the *modus operandi* of much of the regulatory process. It expresses an implicit political decision to allow members of affected disciplines to make the most fundamental decisions, while assuring the general public that social control is being exerted. Even when broader issues of social choice are formally on the agenda, as in the case of AHAP, those committed to particular paths of development have ways of co-opting the external review and using it to legitimize their choices. Clearly, external review alone is not enough to ensure real social guidance of science and technology policy. Real governance requires real power to make basic choices.

THINKING ABOUT REFORM

The foregoing has sought to establish that a certain set of interests — corporate and scientific elites — dominate the making of science and technology policy. What follows is an attempt to draw prescriptive implications which are loosely based on this analysis. In essence, I have argued that corporate and scientific elites have disproportionate power and that this imbalance often results in policies either oblivious to, or in direct opposition to, the broader public interest. The dominance of corporate and scientific elites means that the claims of other social interest groups are effectively suppressed; so policy cannot reflect either the needs of the broad majority or the rights of particular individuals who are harmed by particular technologies.[16] Scientific and technological development is predisposed to travel the paths dictated by corporate needs and wants, which may or may not be the most socially beneficial paths. Improper disposal of radioactive and other toxic wastes, technically sophisticated but poorly distributed health care, the possibility that artificially created organisms may upset the microecology — all these are products of the predisposition to particular paths of technological development evinced by corporate and scientific elites. The only way public interest in environmental, distributive, and ethical concerns can become integral dimensions of technological development is through new mechanisms and institutions of policy making which overcome the power of the forces currently dominant.

Because one set of interests has a history of dominating policy making, democratic policy making needs to focus largely on redressing these imbalances. The only way public policy can reflect suppressed public needs and wants is to empower suppressed interests. This, to be straightforward, means lessening the relative power of corporate and scientific elites. When there is a consistent pattern in which dominant interests prevail over other societal interests, then government must recognize a positive obligation to redress the imbalance, particularly when this situation largely was created and maintained by past government policies.

What would such a positive governmental obligation to empower suppressed social interests require, and what would it entail in terms of concrete policies? First, it would require a change in the "political nonpolitics" of science and technology policy making. On the ideological plane, the mythology of scientific autonomy would have to be replaced by recognition that alternative social and economic futures are shaped by today's public and private decisions about R&D funding. A whole series of widely held myths impede emergence of the political will to control development: that science follows its own internal, predetermined logic of development and cannot be shaped by social action, that all social participation in selecting forms of technological development interferes with an absolute "freedom of inquiry," that any exercise of social control of science and technology is based on irrational sentiments like those that drove the Church to repress the findings of Galileo and Copernicus. Such myths provide the ideological legitimation for unrestricted development of particular profitable technologies favored by entrenched economic interests despite the known or potential environmental or social costs.

On the directly political plane, social groups which might represent suppressed interests need to mobilize and press their cases more vigorously. Such latent forces might manifest themselves in a number of forms: 1) mass-based political organizations (trade unions, environmental groups, ideological groups, etc.) that recognize the importance of R&D decisions to their constituencies, 2) elites whose professional predispositions run counter to dominant corporate interests (the environmental sciences, public interest lawyers, etc.), and 3) elites within the scientific establishment who become aware of the negative impact of current institutions of governance and of the desirability of much greater social responsibility in science (groups like Physicians for Social Responsibility, the Federation of Atomic Scientists, and Science for the People).

Certainly, if one set of elites is dominating a particular policy domain, one plausible prescription for securing more democratic and more just public policy is to broaden the base of public participation in decision making. The fundamental problem is how. Without pretending to answer this question fully, I will suggest one basic point. The undifferentiated mass public — the "silent majority" — may be an effective rhetorical object, but it is rarely an effective political subject, particularly in a policy arena as complex as science and technology. Despite the tendency of political theory to see participatory democracy and representative democracy as polar opposites, the key to effective participation is systematic representation of mass-based political organizations in councils of decision making. Thus range of interests factored into the policy process is broadened. Empowering suppressed social interests in a large and complex society requires empowering mass-based political organizations which will speak for large segments of the public who would otherwise remain without effective representation. In the case of toxic chemicals, it was the unions and the local homeowners who bore the costs of exposure that mobilized to press for more vigorous public policy. The result was the creation of the Occupational Safety and Health Administration and the superfund, the latter using earmarked taxes to require those who profit from a technology to bear some of the costs of its negative environmental and social impacts.

Another set of potential representatives of suppressed social interests are professions which develop general or case-specific knowledge of the actual costs and risks of particular technologies. For example, epidemiologists and other environmental scientists are professionally committed to searching for the health costs and risks associated with particular technologies. Public interest law firms are another professional group that often gains from public exposure of particular costs of technology and which can at least in some cases, secure compensation for individual victims.

Compensation of individual victims or internalization of some environmental costs via mechanisms like the superfund are *post hoc* attempts to grapple with mounting costs, rather than full social direction of technological development. Real governance of science and technology requires more than simply compensating indentifiable victims or smoothing over social dislocations by side payments to those disadvantaged by new technologies. But these examples do show the impact on policy that can occur when popularly based political forces or counter-elites are mobilized to confront those committed to a given technology.

Another potential avenue of expression for suppressed social interests lies within the scientific establishment itself. Given the quasi-monopoly of specialized knowledge inherent in science and technology issues and the entrenchment of existing institutional forms, scientists are inevitably going to have great power in making science policy. There have been times when scientists have raised a collective voice against corporate and bureaucratic priorities which they felt ran counter to the public good. The cases of civilian control of atomic energy and the emergence of the environmental movement are prime examples. The official norms of science often do come into conflict with corporate and governmental pressures, creating the possibility of movements within scientific communities for greater social responsibility. The rise of the scientist-entrepreneur is disturbing exactly because it so effectively subordinates scientific activity to corporate and bureaucratic values—that is, it subordinates leading scientists to the dominant value of the corporate world, cold cash.

Finding means of representing suppressed interests in institutions that make science and technology policy is only part of the problem. It still remains to effect substantive reforms. Which tools and mechanisms, then, are capable of directing technological development into more socially beneficial paths? Let us examine two key tools—funding and regulation; or, promotion and prescription.

In our society, it is money that really talks. Technological development is not so simple that if we either want something to come into being or want to keep it from doing so, that outcome can be assured simply by public funding decisions. But as Lovins points out in the case of energy R&D, differential public funding for competing technologies can have massive effects on the forms of technological change over the long term. Politics already drives R&D funding priorities—witness the militarization of ever-increasing sectors of science and technology, due to the simple availability of funding from military sources. But for R&D funding decisions to reflect systematic democratic choice about paths of technological development, social as well as scientific factors must be incorporated into decision making about funding. This would require at least two innovative administrative forms: 1) broad-based panels to study the social effects of scientific and technological development options and to develop explicit guidelines to shape R&D funding decisions, and 2) greater nonscientific representation on the bodies that make actual decisions on particular projects, to ensure implementation of democratically determined priorities.

If public R&D funding is a carrot to lead technology down socially desirable paths, then regulation is a stick to impede certain particular outcomes. Despite the problems outlined earlier that hinder successful social control via regulation, the regulatory process when properly constituted can proscribe particularly dangerous activities. For example, once public pressure mounted and the regulatory apparatus was reformed, more vigilant regulatory efforts had a significant impact on the nuclear power industry. Regulation can also heighten the probability that particular social values will be enforced within ongoing technological development, as the ever more careful protocols concerning research on human subjects demonstrates.

There are certainly risks involved in calling for greater politicization of science and technology policy. In any political process, there is no guarantee that the good guys (however you define them) will win. More open politicization could lead to even more effective domination by entrenched economic interests. It could also encourage the mobilization of political forces that would shape science and technology in ways that would do more harm than good to society. But the alternative to opening up the process is to leave fundamental decisions about our future in the hands of a narrow set of elites whose perspectives and interests do not reflect the needs and wants of the larger society. That risk is the truly intolerable one.

NOTES

1. Amory Lovins, *Soft Energy Paths* (New York: Harper & Row, 1979).

2. Ibid., 59.

3. Joshua Lederberg, testimony before Senate Labor-Health Education and Welfare Appropriations Subcommittee (1965) and Senate Government Operations Committee — Subcommittee on Government Research (1968). Also "The 'Heart Gap' Will Cause Soul Ache," *Washington Post*, 24 July 1966.

4. Hittman Associates, *Final Summary Report of Six Studies Basic to Consideration of the Artificial Heart Program* (report to the National Heart Institute, NIH contract PH 43–66–90, 1966).

5. See, for example, recent issues of *Readers Guide to Periodicals* (New York: H.W. Wilson) under the heading of genetic engineering.

6. See, for example, James O'Connor, *The Fiscal Crisis of the State* (New York: St. Martin's, 1973).

7. Barry Commoner, *The Politics of Energy* (New York: Knopf, 1979).

8. Philip Siekevitz, "The Scientist-Enterpreneur," *Nature* 101 (1979): 100.

9. See, for example, Robert Cowen, "Grant Awards Should Be Based on Merit," *Christian Science Monitor,* 16 Aug. 1984; Colin Norman, "Pork Barrel Scorecard"; and Colin Norman, "How to Win Buildings and Influence Congress," *Science* 222 (16 Dec. 1983): 1211–13. For a more general treatment of close relations between high-tech interest groups, Congress, and the bureaucracy, see Gordon Adams, *The Iron Triangle* (New York: Council on Economic Priorities, 1981).

10. Deil Wright, *Understanding Intergovernmental Relations* (Monterey, Calif.: Brooks-Cole, 1981).

11. Harold Seidman, *Politics, Position, and Power* (New York: Oxford Univ. Press, 1970).

12. See, for example, Marver Bernstein, *Regulating Business by Independent Commission* (Princeton: Princeton Univ. Press, 1955) and Theodore Lowi, *The End of Liberalism* (New York: Norton, 1979).

13. Murray Edelman, *The Symbolic Uses of Politics* (Urbana: Univ. of Illinois Press, 1964).

14. U.S. Department of Health, Education, and Welfare, National Heart and Lung Institute, Artificial Heart Assessment Panel, *The Totally Implantable Artificial Heart* (Washington: Government Printing Office, NIH 74-191, 1973).

15. Malcolm Goggin, "Commission Government."

16. For discussion of the concepts of suppressed and dominant interests, see Robert Alford, *Health Care Politics* (Chicago: Univ. of Chicago Press, 1975), and Charles Lindblom, *Politics and Markets* (New York: Basic, 1977).

5.   *Biotechnology and the University*

LEON WOFSY

A surge of industrial and military interest in the university's bioscience community signaled the start of the new age of biotechnology.

In some ways this was a familiar script. The university's partnership with industry and the military is well established in engineering and the physical sciences. President Eisenhower's recognition of the "military-industrial complex" could well have encompassed the university. The resources of academia have contributed indispensibly to the waves of new technologies that fill life with miracles even as they have given humanity the capacity for self-extinction.

Yet biotechnology, born of revolutionary advances in university molecular biology laboratories, is not quite the story witnessed before — neither for the university nor for society. At least some of the events and issues are distinct, despite parallels in electronics and computer fields, and a history of academic involvements with agriculture and the chemical and pharmaceutical industries.

We consider in this chapter the changes and challenges that the rise of biotechnology brings to the university — problems in the educational environment and the conduct of research, issues not only of internal regulation but also of the university's relationship to social policy and to the public interest.

The role and problems of the university are central to the relationship between science and society and to the formulation of policies for science governance. That the university is the primary source of the golden egg need hardly be argued, but it is necessary (though often futile) to remind politicians, administrators, trustees, and sundry others of the university's special vulnerability. In fact, the pressures generated by the technology boom make it appropriate for those of us who are scientists and educators to look hard at dilemmas that are integral to the university's place in society.

118

The university is required to provide the continuous flow of knowledge and new leadership needed to maintain prevailing social structures and institutions. But new knowledge, fresh minds, innovative cultural expression, and good science arise in an atmosphere of challenge and skepticism, of unwillingness to be controlled by external pressures and interests. The social responsibility of the scientist and educator is indeed great, but it is not fulfilled, as some suggest, by availability in the marketplace or by conformity to the expectations of political or military agencies. These issues are strikingly presented by the transformations in biology whose import for science, society, and the university is still emerging.

TURBULENT BEGINNINGS

What is special about the encounter between biotechnology and the university? Why did it initially attract so much attention and generate so much heat? Why did previous experience in other fields not suffice to cover matters of policy?

We can summarize some of the ways in which things are different, some of the features that require fuller consideration.

1. One factor is the suddenness and speed with which the new domain emerged. There has been an unprecedented rush of major, often unusual, financial arrangements with the rising biotechnology industry by individual faculty members as well as by university and medical school administrations.
2. Adding to the tension is the sharp before-and-after contrast in prevailing values among academics in biology, due to their rapid adaptation to a market-oriented environment once regarded as alien by most of those committed to basic research in the life sciences.
3. Recombinant DNA techniques and the feasibility of genetic engineering inevitably brought forward new issues of morality, ethics, social priorities, and public policy. Some heated debate took place among biologists at an early stage, but the areas of concern have been narrow. As for the general public, there has been no significant involvement except as a target of sensational media treatment of the new biology.
4. There is a unique aspect to the long-term public investment in the university research that led to biotechnology. Alone among revolutionary technological advances of recent times, biotechnology is not a

119

spinoff from research and development in weapons and space. Rather it resulted directly from decades of public funding of basic biomedical research predicated on an ultimate commitment to improved public health.

5. The university's interaction with biotechnology is taking shape in a social and political climate that differs significantly from that in which the foundations of the new biology were built. In the 1980s, the thrust is toward replacing government's social responsibility for education, health, and welfare with free rein for the private sector. The only federal government priority designated as sacrosanct by the present administration is the expanding military budget.

BIOMEDICAL RESEARCH IN THE MARKETPLACE

Already in 1981, Barbara Culliton, news editor of *Science*, described "a virtual explosion of 'technology transfer' as researchers and industrialists have moved with unprecedented speed and determination to exploit molecular biology in a search for useful and profitable products based on recombinant DNA and monoclonal antibodies — technologies whose conceptual roots are in university-based science. . . ." She commented: "Biomedical research itself has entered the marketplace; molecular biology has become big business. Concern increases that this development will result in fundamental changes in the way in which research is conducted, that new ties between the academy and industry will strain the fabric of the university, and that the public perception of science will be altered."[1]

The most publicized phenomenon in the commercialization of biology has been the emergence of the professor-entrepreneur,[2] but university administrations have actively competed for contractual arrangements with biotechnology industries. The first of a series of such agreements was established between Harvard and the Monsanto Corporation in 1974. For $23.5 million Harvard sold Monsanto patent rights and access to an outstanding biomedical research group over a period of twelve years. Analyzing the contract, Wayne Biddle points out[3] that Harvard changed its patent policy, which simply had been: "No patents primarily concerned with therapeutics or public health may be taken out . . . except for dedication to the public." "Apparently," Biddle says, "the Monsanto arrangement hinged on discarding this traditional guideline. And the

120

standard practice of peer review through faculty committees and public comment was avoided during the year and a half of negotiations that preceded final agreement."

From 1980 on, there has been a rush of such contracts, varying in form and amounts of money involved, but similar in character. The university gives the corporation privileged access to outstanding academic personnel, their laboratories, and their students; it grants favored, sometimes exclusive, patent or licensing rights; it often agrees that the company is to review and approve research manuscripts before they can be submitted to journals.

A few of the universities entering such contracts are MIT (Exxon, W.R. Grace), Yale (Celanese, Bristol-Meyers), Cornell (General Foods, Union Carbide, Kodak), Illinois (Sohio), Rockefeller (Monsanto), and Columbia (Bristol-Meyers).[4] Washington University at St. Louis has been one of the most enterprising, contracting with Monsanto for $23.5 million and with Mallinckrodt for $3.8 million, both grants for five years duration.

One of the largest such direct grants, for $70 million, binds Massachusetts General Hospital, Harvard's main teaching hospital, to the Hoechst firm of West Germany. The *The New York Times* reported: "Under the terms of the 10-year contract, Hoechst is creating a new department of molecular biology at the hospital. In return, the company can capitalize on the department's research findings before others learn of the results and obtain exclusive licenses to develop related commercial procedures . . . The Hoechst grant raises a new issue, since so large a grant forces an entire department to be financially dependent on one company."[5] On the size of the grant, the *Boston Globe* commented: "It surpasses the total endowments of either Boston University or Tufts University and the total endowment income of all U.S. medical schools in 1978–79."[6]

A different form of financial tie, but a far larger private investment, is represented by the Whitehead Institute, established at MIT after some faculty controversy.[7] Edwin Whitehead, founder of Technicon and presently the largest shareholder of Revlon, gave MIT $7.5 million for teaching and research in institute-related academic departments, financed the building and equipping of a 130,000-square-foot research facility, and agreed to contribute $5 million annually until the year 2003 and a bequest of $100 million upon his death. The institute, whose board of directors includes Whitehead's three children, is to have up to twenty

121

faculty members who also share appointments in regular MIT departments. It owns all inventions and other intellectual property created by personnel it funds.

Of course not many universities can attract deals of such magnitude regardless of the accomodations they may be prepared to make. The State University of New York and the University of Michigan have initiated more limited institutes or research centers supported by industrial consortia.[8] Similarly, Stanford and the University of California, Berkeley, formed the Center for Biotechnology Research in conjunction with the establishment of a new company, Engenics, with six corporate sponsors.[9]

The university-industrial arrangements cited here are only a sampling. To picture how pervasive a transformation has occurred, one would have to consider the multiplicity of commercial connections that now involve many faculty members in almost all departments with active research programs in molecular and cellular biology. A study now underway of "formal, long term ties between scientists and biotechnology firms"[10] establishes the prevalence of dual academic-business affiliations among leading biologists—those who are members of the National Academy of Sciences and/or serve on study panels of the National Institutes of Health and/or review grant applications for the National Science Foundation or the U.S. Department of Agriculture.

NEW CRITERION OF ACADEMIC SUCCESS

Some culture shock was bound to accompany the link-up between academic bioscience and the new world of commercial biotechnology. The milieu in biology had been distinguished in some ways from that prevailing in other areas of science and engineering. The dominant culture among biologists was one of emphasis on basic rather than applied research and of hostility toward mercenary ambitions and patent seekers. Nevertheless, such ideological and psychological barriers seemed to collapse when opportunity's knock became persistent.

Competition among biotechnology firms for the vital resource of prestigious academic talent, along with fears that government support for basic biomedical research may be eroding, have generated very powerful pressure on individual scientists and on the university itself. A new criterion of academic success in the life sciences has emerged, the ability to attract commercial offers, to swing deals, and to make money.

As one writer comments: "Publish or perish was once the popular admonition to the young academic scientist. Now, with federal research funding dropping, scientists fear that while they publish they will also perish — unless they can find ways to patent through some industrial benefactor."[11] Another article[12] quotes Cesar Milstein, who has since been awarded the Nobel Prize for co-discovery of monoclonal antibodies: "In this society you're made to feel stupid if you can't make money." The writer notes that the inventors of monoclonal antibodies, true to the ethic of earlier days, sought no patent protection. He continues, "Plenty of researchers now are reeling from pressure, some of it applied by their immediate colleagues, to show that they can make money."

To ascribe the changed atmosphere and attitudes primarily to individuals who see a chance to become wealthy[13] would be to overlook the main problems before the university. The university itself is a much bigger part of the problem than the temptations experienced by individual faculty. If Harvard contracts with Hoechst and MIT makes a deal with the Whitehead family, other universities must scramble for comparable coups — at stake is the ability to compete, claims to academic status and ranking. Increasingly university deans and administrators are themselves the conveyors of the connection between progress in an academic career and skill at developing commercial ties.

CONFLICT OF INTEREST?

There is no shortage of advocates, enthusiasts in fact, for the new academic-industrial connection in biotechnology.[14] Leaving aside the entrepreneurial motivations of some, the case for greater support by industry to the university and to research in biosciences is surely strong. Few if any who express concern about the way things are going would want the university not to encourage expanded interest from private as well as public sources.

Why then the concern?

At the most basic level, there is the need to distinguish some of the essential drives, goals, and values of the commercial boom in biology from those of academic research. Quite simply, the business of business is to make money, to beat the competition, and the mode is secrecy, a proprietary control of information and the fruits of research. Ideally, the motive force of the university is education and the pursuit of knowledge, and the mode is open exchange of ideas and unrestricted publication of the results of research.

These very different missions call for a necessary separation between the university and the marketplace. One may make a crude analogy to the relationship between other elements in our society that have different missions, for example religion and public education. Experience indicates that respect for the democratic "separation" principle should apply if the mission of the university is not to be diverted to the motivations and practices of the business world. Safeguards are needed to keep research and education in biology from being submerged in the entrepreneurial tide.

A conference on "Commercialism and University Research" was convened at Pajaro Dunes, California, in March 1982 by President Donald Kennedy of Stanford and cohosted by the presidents of Harvard, MIT, Cal Tech, and the University of California. The list of those attending the meeting was both impressive and exclusive: in addition to the university presidents, there were top executives (including six presidents) of nine leading biotechnology corporations (Genentech, Dupont, Gillette, Damon, Applied Biosystems, Cabot, Cetus, Syntex, and Beckman); ten professors, several of whom are founders and/or top executives of additional biotechnology firms; eleven other top administrators and two general counsels from the host universities; and, completing the list, one Harvard Fellow and the president of the Henry J. Kaiser Family Foundation, which funded the meeting with a $50,000 grant.[15]

Prior to the conference, Kennedy had warned in testimony before a congressional committee that with "the introduction of strong commercial motivations and conflicts of interest on the part of faculty members . . . there is the prospect of the significant contamination of the university's basic research enterprises."[16]

Following the conference, nothing noteworthy was claimed for its deliberations either by the conferees or in commentaries in the press and scientific journals (reporters were excluded from the sessions). Unfortunately the Pajaro Dunes meeting was more significant as evidence of the seriousness of the problems than as a contribution to their analysis or amelioration.

There is no reason to question the concern or the intentions of the convenor, yet the very structure of the meeting — a restricted conclave of highest-level executives of select universities and corporations — blurred boundaries between commercial and academic interests. Symptomatic was the prevalence of dual affiliations not only among the faculty chosen to attend, but in each of the participating contingents. At least three of the university presidential hosts are on boards of directors or are highly-paid consultants of several corporations, including one (Cabot) represented at the meeting by its president; at least four of the chief executive officers who were the direct representatives of industry are trustees of Cal Tech, MIT, or MIT-sponsored enterprises.

Pajaro Dunes distilled to its essence the problem of conflict of interest: what is usually discussed as a matter of individual faculty behavior is shown to be first and foremost an institutional problem.

More indicative than who was at Pajaro Dunes is who was not. The challenges presented by the great revolution in biology — the opportunities even much more than the difficulties — are of profound general interest. The many dimensions of its potential significance for society, as well as its impact on education and research, certainly require new thinking and deliberation in all quarters. Yet there is no extraordinary initiative by the university in reaching out to stimulate minds and involve others beyond the business world. Nor is there much reaching inward to enlist student and faculty opinion on the changes wrought within the university or on the larger societal issues.

CAN BASIC RESEARCH BE DEPENDENT ON INDUSTRY FUNDING?

A condition for affording some protection to the integrity of the university's program for education and basic research in the biological sciences is to discount illusions that industry will take over major responsibility for its support.

Commenting on proposed federal cutbacks in biomedical research, a *New York Times* editorial pointed to "the rich flow of venture capital into biotechnology" and observed: "There are also times when a field of research no longer needs the Government as nursemaid . . . "[17] However, the prospectus circulated to the Pajaro Dunes invitees offered a different and more telling observation: "Ever since Herbert Hoover's energetic but frustrating effort to raise funds for 'pure science' from corporations in the mid-1920's universities and the government have sought to make the commercial sector a fuller partner in the basic re-

125

search venture. It is still the case, however, that less than 4% of the support of all university research is derived from this source. And about two-thirds of all basic research is located in universities."[18]

It is true that a major consequence of the remarkable progress in biology is to bring basic and applied research into closer contact. Laboratories that investigate riddles of cell function and of development may now generate "practical" information and ideas leading to possible applications in medicine, agriculture, or manufacture. While this university resource is recognized and eagerly tapped by the biotechnology industry, the highly competitive character of the industry precludes farsighted general funding of basic research and training. The several university-industrial contractual arrangements discussed earlier show a typically directed character, targeted to particular laboratories or departments and often to defined projects that offer hope of commercial returns. The latter feature may not always be quite so explicit as in Yale's contract with the Celanese Corporation, as reported by the *New York Times:* "Last week, Yale University and Celanese Corporation, a chemical and fabric manufacturer, tied the knot. . . . Yale will conduct basic research for Celanese on enzymes, particularly enzymes useful to chemical and fabric production."[19]

As a matter of fact, the scramble by commercial interests for favored status within the university distorts and weakens the commitment to basic research. It changes especially the circumstances in which a new generation of aspirants to creative careers in biology must approach its training and goals. Abuses of the faculty-student relationship have drawn attention at several universities: neglect of pre- and post-doctoral trainees by "two-hat" advisers busy with commercial involvements, increasing pressure for secrecy that inhibits communication and regards colleagues as competitors, fear that thesis and research ideas will be transferred to the commercial sector and exploited.[20]

Yet there is a question more fundamental than any specific areas of abuse. Young investigators must now feel an almost irresistable pressure, indeed a logic, to go into so-called "hot" areas if they want to develop their careers. Whereas hot problems in biology previously have been those where a breakthrough in scientific understanding appeared possible, hot projects now may more often be those with an implied promise of marketable results. In this kind of process, a young scientist may pay a much bigger price than a more established scientist. That price may well be the sacrifice of independence and creativity, because most

126

researchers entering the new venture sphere will be operating with priorities set by others, generally on the basis of short-term considerations.

SAFEGUARDS

With the biology boom, many universities have felt compelled to review and revise guidelines on avoidance of conflicts of interest. Corrective action has been taken in isolated cases.[21]

Although administrative safeguards are hardly an adequate solution to complex educational and social issues, it is worth projecting measures that might have some positive influence. It is also instructive to consider the difficulties in applying such regulation. Three recommendations discussed and generally favored at a conference of immunologists in 1982[22] may serve as reference points. The immunologists' proposals are clearly not exhaustive, but they relate problems within the university to issues of integrity in the conduct of research and in interaction with the public.

Proposition One states: "Faculty members who receive research support from any agency, public or private, should be willing to disclose the source and amount of personal income derived from private enterprises in areas related to their research."

Despite traditional resistance in the academic community to such disclosure, the matter is one of credibility. Once commercial attachments abound, a scientist cannot assume automatic public trust. Especially as scientists are called on for expert guidance to the public on the regulation of new technologies, on applications of genetic engineering, and on the sensitive areas of genetic screening and gene therapy, there should be no privileged immunity from questions about conflicting interests. There are already far too many cases where the expert status of scientists is compromised by commercial ties — the list runs the gamut from chemical pollution to vaccines, pesticides, nutrition, and drug evaluation.

The second proposition presents serious difficulties, even though it is based squarely on fairness and common sense: "Peer review processes of granting agencies and journals which require access to confidential grant applications or the refereeing of manuscripts should not involve the participation of individuals who have a financial or commercial interest in the research areas under review."

The principle here seems beyond challenge. The problem is that the

127

invasion of biology by the business world has been so sweeping. If this proposition were to be applied without reservation, it would probably knock out a heavy proportion of the experts from every important review body.

Nevertheless, it is important to consider the principle, no matter how it might be interpreted ultimately in practical terms. As long as the fruition of all academic research achievements has remained publication, there has been a brake on the abuse of peer review. True, there has been no guarantee against plagiarism or taking advantage of confidential material. Yet there is a restraining influence on unethical practices when results and claims have to be presented in public before one's colleagues. In contrast, if in one's day-to-day activity the premium is on commercial development, secrecy must take over. There is no strong inhibition on cheating, deliberate or subconscious, where there is a rationale for *not* publishing so that you can beat your business competitor.

The third principle says: "Acceptance by the university of support from any source for a faculty member's research should always be contingent on assurance of adequate provisions for peer review and the absence of conflicts of interest that compromise educational standards and commitment. A standing faculty committee should verify that acceptable standards of review have been met and should, where there is doubt, initiate an appropriate *ad hoc* review procedure."

The intent of the latter proposition is that the quality of research and the nature of commitments involving graduate students and postdoctoral trainees would be evaluated, whether the support money came through a deal negotiated on the marketplace or was awarded on the basis of established review procedures of non-profit granting agencies such as the National Institutes of Health, the National Science Foundation, or the American Cancer Society.

There are numerous other areas in which safeguards might curb inequity and restrain abuse. One critical need is for procedures that guarantee students and university employees effective means of registering and getting action on complaints without fear of direct or indirect retribution.[23] Outside the university, some journals have opposed the trend toward restricting scientific communication for proprietary reasons by refusing to publish manuscripts that withhold information or access to reagents needed for validating the reported research.[24] The imposition of such a sanction by a few journals, while surely desirable, will hardly compensate for the depressing effect of patent wars that have become "biotech's battlefront," especially since the Supreme Court's decision that life forms can be patented.[25]

THE MILITARY—THE OTHER PARTNER IN BIOTECHNOLOGY

Biotechnology has not only created commercial interest in the bioscience resources of the university, it has brought on new military intervention as well. At the 1984 annual meeting of the American Association for the Advancement of Science (AAAS), it was reported that "the Department of Defense (DOD) now sponsors more than 30 research projects involving recombinant-DNA techniques, including 11 at in-house laboratories and 25 major universities."[26] On August 31, 1984, the AAAS journal, *Science*, carried three full-page advertisements from the Fort Detrick headquarters of the U.S. Army Medical Research Acquisition Agency inviting proposals for research in "Bacterial Diseases of Military Importance," "Low Molecular Weight Toxins of Military Importance," and "Parasitic Diseases of Military Importance."

Three major features of policy of the Reagan administration combine to force a serious distortion of academic research in the life sciences.

First, analysis of the proposed federal budget for fiscal year 1986[27] shows that military research and development "would climb by $7.2 billion, while total spending on all other R&D would drop by more than $500 million." In basic research, the military would receive an increase of 16 percent, while the life sciences would be reduced by 4.9 percent.

Second, there is a dramatically increased investment in chemical and biological weapons research.[28] In other words, while biologists seeking research support from the National Institutes of Health will have a harder time, there is a place to turn—the military is ready to fund appropriate projects involving the latest developments in genetic engineering and monoclonal antibodies.

Third, there is an unprecedented effort to increase federal intervention in the conduct of academic research, to impose restraints that, according to a recent document from Harvard University, threaten "to erode the American tradition of academic freedom." "The Harvard report," commented the *New York Times*,[29] "has appeared just as the Pentagon is making its most forceful push into university research since secret military work was all but banished from campuses in the Vietnam War."

As grants from the military attract a growing number of life science researchers, the issues identified by the Harvard report — secrecy, security investigations, censorship, pressure to conform — will become more difficult to avoid even at universities that have rules against classified research. So will public suspicions about what may be going on in campus laboratories.

Acute contradictions are presented by the jointly sponsored university-military institutes for research and development, one of which is the Naval Biosciences Laboratory (NBL) affiliated with the School of Public Health at the University of California, Berkeley. Established in the later 1940s as part of the university, "the NBL was discreetly camouflaged, but was in reality an agency of bacteriological warfare until 1969,"[30] when the Nixon administration entered negotiations toward the Biological and Toxin Weapons Convention signed in 1972. The laboratory continued under contracts requiring conformity to UC regulations prohibiting classified research on campus, but it fared poorly, and its termination was being considered until a major revival occurred with the advent of biotechnology and the new attitudes of the Reagan administration.

The ways in which NBL's fortunes have now changed are interesting. It has attracted some first-class molecular biologists. From direct conversations which this author has had with faculty involved with NBL, the basis for the attraction is clear: equivalent facilities and support are not available elsewhere for their research, much of which relates to parasitic infections and potential vaccines that could be of particular value in the Third World. Some other faculty who are not a part of NBL, but who have access to it, are anxious to keep UC sponsorship of NBL because it has one of the best containment facilities for experiments with pathogenic organisms or forms of recombinant DNA. Most of these investigators would want nothing to do with a renewal of preparations for germ warfare, and they rely on the effectiveness of UC's ban on secret research to prevent that from happening at NBL. Yet it wasn't until 1976, as a result of a lawsuit, that the public learned what NBL (then called the Naval Biological Laboratory) had been doing in the early 1950s when it conducted tests spreading a supposedly harmless microorganism over San Francisco and surrounding areas.[31]

In general, credibility is strained by arguments often heard among academics that sponsorship of a military research unit gives the university ultimate power of governance and, moreover, curbs the influence of the military establishment. That is the rationale that permits the Los

Alamos and Lawrence Livermore Laboratories, which conduct almost all national research and development of nuclear weapons, to be designated affiliates of the University of California. The NBL is, of course, minuscule in comparison to the nuclear weapons laboratories, and its contract does not now sanction classified research. Yet past experience and present directions in national policy present valid cause for concern.

What sponsorship of military research institutions gives to the university, omitting monetary considerations, is inevitable conflicts of interest. What it gives the military is greater academic access, respectability, and influence. Again there is the issue of contradictory missions that ought to be kept separate: military secrecy and authority are incompatible with the norms and values one should expect in the university.

THE PUBLIC – ON THE OUTSIDE

Probably no technological advance has as much longrange potential for benefit to humankind as the revolution in biology. As with other technologies, society is challenged as to how priorities are formed, how hazards are limited, how moral issues are met. The challenge is all the more intense since biology is about the nature of life.

While the scientific and technical advances are awesome, little is inspiring in the way the university and the bioscience research community are relating to the new social issues, to matters of public interest, education, and policy. The only excitement, other than in celebration of new discoveries and claims, seems to be in discounting warnings from environmentalists and countering any notion that biotechnology needs regulation.

Scientists, offended by perceived exaggerations of potential hazards, fear that misconceptions and anti-intellectual prejudices may interfere with their freedom of inquiry. The anomaly, however, is the low level of concern over the intrusions by commercial and military interests which actually are distorting research directions and values. More often than not, representatives of the university and of the biotechnology industry appear to be sending a common message to the public: stay out of the way, leave it to the experts, await the blessings of the new biology.

Concern about the growing involvement of the university bioscience community with commercial interests is sometimes dismissed with the observation that technology transfer can only be accomplished via the marketplace — that is "the American way" of making the benefits of sci-

131

ence available to the public. This is, to say the least, a most limited representation of the social and political context in which matters of public interest are to be considered and contested.

The potential impact of biology is not confined to matters of "technology transfer" from the university to the private sector. It is indeed a matter of public policy and social responsibility—more emphatically now that the fruits of the heavy public investment in biomedical research are beginning appear.

Just what and how much must be left to the marketplace? our priorities as a society? our values as educators? Do we really have no options other than to adjust, as if it were inevitable and eternal, to the current emphasis in Washington on deregulation, rolling back social benefits, and colossal military expenditure?

What we do with biology will be shaped by policy and goals in public health, education, nutrition, and agriculture; by attitudes toward the environment, relations with other nations, and problems of the Third World. What biotechnology does for humankind will depend less on what can be done in the laboratory than on society's values—and a most critical test will be whether we permit it to be developed for germ warfare. The need is for more public involvement, not less; for hearings, discussion, and research on how developments in the life sciences relate to broad areas of public policy.

Both the intellectual and the social significance of the new biology should make it more, especially for the university, than another "hot property" to be offered on the marketplace.

NOTES

1. Barbara J. Culliton, "Biomedical Research Enters the Marketplace," *New England Journal of Medicine* 304 (14 May 1981): 1195.

2. This subject is treated by Dennis Florig in ch. 4 of this volume.

3. Wayne Biddle, "A Patent on Knowledge," *Harper's*, July 1981, p. 22.

4. Thorough review and analysis of university-industrial links in biotechnology are contained in Martin F. Kenney, "Biotechnology: From University to Industry," (Ph.D. diss. Cornell Univ., 1984); and Kenney, *Biotechnology: The University-Industrial Complex* (New Haven: Yale Univ. Press, forthcoming).

5. David E. Sanger, "Business Rents a Lab Coat and Academia Hopes for the Best," *New York Times*, 21 Mar. 1982.

6. Richard A. Knox, "German Firm, MGH in $50M Research Pact," *Boston Globe*, 20 May 1981.

7. Colin Norman, "MIT Agonizes Over Links with Research Unit," *Science* 214 (23 Oct. 1981): 416–17.

8. See Note 4. Kenney, "Biotechnology," 74–82.

9. *Berkeley Gazette*, 14 Sept. 1981.

10. Sheldon Krimsky, "Corporate Academic Ties in Biotechnology," *Genewatch* 1 (Sept.–Dec. 1984): 3–5.

11. Will Lepkowski, "Research Universities Face New Fiscal Realities," *Chemical and Engineering News*, 23 Nov. 1981, p. 23.

12. Jeffrey L. Fox, "Can Academia Adapt to Biotechnology's Lure?", *Chemical and Engineering News*, 12 Oct. 1981, p. 44.

13. The rapid rise in the financial fortunes of biotechnology's scientist-entrepreneurs is described by William Boly, "The Gene Merchants," *California Magazine* 7 (Sept. 1982): 76–79.

14. Ronald E. Cape, "Academic and Corporate Values and Goals—Are They Really in Conflict?" *Professional Relations Bulletin* (American Chemical Society) 30 (Oct. 1982); Marilyn Bach and Ray Thornton, "Inevitable and Desirable," *Immunology Today* 4 (1983): 125–27.

15. Stanford University, *Campus Report*, 14:26 (31 Mar. 1982).

16. Testimony of Donald Kennedy on 8 June 1981 before the Subcommittee on Investigations and Oversight and the Subcommittee on Science, Research, and Technology, in U.S., Congress, House, Committee on Science and Technology, *Hearings on the Commercialization of Academic Research,* 97th Cong., 1st sess., 8 and 9 June 1981 (Washington, D.C.: Government Printing Office, 1981), 6–28.

17. *New York Times*, 28 Jan. 1985.

18. The *Conference Prospectus* was not a public document. It was made available by the National Resources Defense Council, Inc., San Francisco, Calif.

19. Sanger, "Business Rents a Lab Coat."

20. Fox, "Can Academia Adapt to Biotechnology's Lure?"

21. One of the more significant cases of corrective action is described in "The Evolution of Calgene, a Potential Conflict of Interest and Its Resolution—From a Dean's Perspective," testimony presented 16 June 1982 by Charles E. Hess, Dean, College of Agricultural and Environmental Sciences, Univ. of California, Davis. In U.S., Congress, House, Committee on Science and Technology, Subcommittee on Investigations and Oversight, *Hearings on University/Industry Cooperation in Biotechnology*, 97th Cong., 1st sess., 16 and 17 June 1982 (Washington, D.C.: Government Printing Office, 1982), 49–88.

22. A session at the Midwinter Conference of Immunologists, Asilomar, Calif., on 24 Jan. 1982, was devoted to discussion on commercialism in biology. The three recommendations quoted in the text were approved in a sense vote by the assemblage.

23. At Stanford, the Graduate Student Association addressed this problem in a letter to the Academic Council Committee on Research, 8 Apr. 1982. In a campus announcement, Stanford students were invited to "contact the Ombudsman's Office" if they experienced "research directed toward capital gain rather than scientific advancement."

24. This issue is the subject of a communication by Martin Raff, *Nature* 295 (25 Feb. 1982): 642.

25. Gail E. Shares, "Patents are Biotech's Battlefront," *San Francisco Chronicle*, 7 June 1984.

26. R. Jeffrey Smith, "The Dark Side of Biotechnology," *Science* 224 (15 June 1984): 1215.

27. Colin Norman, "The Science Budget: A Dose of Austerity," *Science* 227 (15 Feb. 1985): 726.

28. Susan Wright, "The Military and the New Biology," *Bulletin of the Atomic Scientists* 41 (May 1985): 10–16.

29. David E. Sanger, "Campuses Fear Federal Control Over Research," *New York Times*, 18 Dec. 1984.

30. Roger Y. Stanier, "The Journey, Not the Arrival, Matters," *Annual Review of Microbiology* 34 (1980): 14–19.

31. "The Army's Secret" (editorial), *San Francisco Chronicle*, 12 Dec. 1976.

PART II

RESPONSES TO THE CRISIS OF GOVERNANCE

The chapters in Part I addressed questions relating to the effects of recent developments in science, technology and society, changes that have created some of the most perplexing problems confronting government, the university, industry, and the general public in the 1980s. Taken together, these changes in science and technology underscore the need for democratic governance. The organizing theme of Part II is *institutional responses* that have been stimulated by the need to control modern science and technology. The essays analyze the nature of several types of responses and assess the extent to which they have worked. In this sense, the contributors in Part II turn from problems of governance to solutions to them.

Part II begins with Leon Trachtman's inventory of the many challenges — fraud, abuse of human subjects, first and second order risks from hazardous technologies — that a changing science, technology, and society have created for existing governing institutions. Other chapters in this section analyze a particular kind of conflict that arises over the control of modern science and technology.

In Chapter 6, Trachtman asks the question, Who *does* govern science and technology? In recognizing the pluralistic and representative nature of American democracy in the 1980s, Trachtman makes clear from the outset that it would be both undemocratic and politically infeasible to allow a single group exclusive control of science and technology. In fact, he accepts as a given that science and technology are now subject to external controls and goes on to describe the many institutions, processes, and behaviors that limit both basic and applied research. In the first part of the chapter he discusses the many ways in which the cur-

135

rent system of external controls is working and identifies breakdowns in the system of governance.

Following up the treatment of this issue in Chapter 1, Trachtman also raises important questions about which scientific activities should be regulated, in what ways, by whom, under what circumstances, and to what ends. But then Trachtman returns to his major concern by describing both the many actors who press their claims against the government on matters scientific and technological and the ways in which these actors make their preferences known.

What Trachtman concludes from this analysis is that the system is messy — a tangled web of institutional relationships that leads to a fragmented, often contradictory set of national policies for science and for technology, policies frequently subject to the whims of changing political administrations. He concludes by examining the alternative — a centrally coordinated state plan for the rational use of scarce resources for research and development. He rejects this alternative to partisan mutual adjustment on grounds that central planning is politically impractical. Instead, Trachtman recommends that improvements can be made by strengthening the existing institutions of governance.

The other original essays in this section are case studies of how a federal, state, or municipal agency of government has managed and directed particular scientific or technological activities within its jurisdiction boundaries. What these case studies illustrate is that scientific inquiry is not a single process; nor is there a single solution to the problems of governance that were described in the chapters in Part I. Indeed, the manner in which institutions have responded to the crisis of governance varies considerably. And those variations depend on the nature of the problem and whether the problem challenges institutions in the private or public sector. If the challenge occurs primarily in the public sector, then the response depends upon which branch and at what level of government the problem arises. What these chapters show is that variations can occur, for example, in institutional arrangements, legal remedies, and mode of citizen participation.

Although each represents a case of an institutional means of resolving a controversy in science, the chapters by Harold Green, Helen Leskovac, and Sheldon Krimsky illustrate the variety of institutional responses that are available. Harold Green's Chapter 7 examines the government's response to a potentially risky research technique (rDNA). His analysis of the strengths and weaknesses of the current structures for regulating research and development in the field of biotechnology focuses on the federal level of government but clearly involves other levels of government as well. After asserting that industry-based recombinant DNA research is essentially unregulated and after defending the constitutionality of the National Institutes of Health's guidelines for regulating publicly-funded gene splicing research in the university laboratory, Green questions the appropriateness of NIH as the locus of rDNA research and technology regulation.

In light of proposals to alter human genes as therapy for lethal diseases and scientific experiments to release genetically-altered genes into the environment, and in view of the inevitability of large-scale industrial manufacturing of the products of gene splicing research and technology, this essay is extremely timely. It illustrates several possible institutional responses to problems plaguing genetic engineering. Two new regulatory formats have already been adopted by the federal government. The first is NIH's new Working Group on Human Gene Therapy, a subcommittee of the Recombinant DNA Advisory Committee (RAC), chaired by Leroy Walters of the Center for Bioethics at Georgetown University. The second—a Department of Health and Human Services-coordinated network of advisory committees in several federal agencies —is currently being put in place by the White House Office of Science and Technology Policy. This attempt at central coordination represents a new regulatory structure, the mission of which would be to review all biotechnology products and research. Green investigates these and other alternatives to the existing NIH system, which he believes is inappropriate for regulation of *industry* research and development: NIH lacks regulatory experience and, because its mission has traditionally been to promote biomedical research rather than protect the public, may be subject to conflicts of interest.

Following a discussion of the pros and cons of these and alternative federal regulatory structures, Green concludes that the optimum locus of regulatory authority over aspects of gene splicing research that are unique and therefore not now subject to regulation is in both NIH and the Environmental Protection Agency (EPA). His prescription for regulatory reform? Leave academic research as it is, namely, under the regulatory eye of the RAC; and create a firmer and more positive structure for regulating science and biotechnology in the private sector. The optimal agent for federal regulation of industry, according to Green, is the EPA.

If Green's chapter shows the *federal* government taking the lead to solve a regulatory problem by creating a new structure that institution-

137

alizes input from people with a variety of backgrounds and interests, Helen Leskovac's Chapter 8 is a case study of what *state* governments are doing both to promote science and technology and to contend with some of the costs and risks as well as benefits of new high-technology industries. Her locus is the state, especially the state university system; her focus is California's attempts to use the state's existing Fair Political Practices Commission and its regulations to curb conflicts of interest of university researchers.

At issue are the changes in relationships between state government and members of the public university research faculty that have resulted from more private funding of university research. Leskovac reviews how an existing California law, originally passed to curb conflicts of interest of public officials, was interpreted broadly to include professors employed by a state agency, in this case the university. As public officials, university researchers are subject to state-mandated requirements that under certain circumstances they must disclose any financial interests that they might have in the corporation that is sponsoring their research. The history of actual or potential conflicts of interest in the university setting is reviewed in order to illustrate the nature and extent of the problem, defined as any situation in which private interests appear to clash with public responsibilities. Ultimately, a review committee at each university is empowered to decide what to do about cases of conflict of interest on the campus, but this does not negate the fact that the state's intrusion into the areas of financial privacy or academic freedom of university faculty is unprecedented.

In concluding, Leskovac recognizes the importance of science and technology as an *instrument*, as well as an *object*, of policy and emphasizes the social responsibility of the university and its faculty members. In this regard, regulatory structures to deter conflicts of interest, whether administered by the federal government, the state, or the university, are portrayed as being in the larger public interest.

Sheldon Krimsky also writes about efforts — this time by a *municipal* government — to protect the public interest. And, like the other chapters in this section, his Chapter 9 revolves around a conflict. The locus of the conflict is Cambridge, Massachusetts. The focus is the authority of a municipal government to regulate federally-sponsored research that is potentially hazardous to the health and safety of residents of a local community and its environs. He gives us a unique participant-observer's account of how a local governing body made its decisions, and compares and contrasts the case with that of the Cambridge Experimention

Review Board (CERB), a "citizen court" that was convened by the Cambridge City Council to resolve another local science and technology controversy in 1976.

At issue in this chapter is the City of Cambridge's right to protect the public from potentially hazardous experiments in the laboratory versus the right of a private corporation to complete a contract with the Department of Defense to conduct chemical weapons experiments in a laboratory located within the city limits. What Sheldon Krimsky explores is the controversy surrounding supremacy, an issue that was also raised in the mid-1970s in Cambridge in connection with the recombinant DNA controversy. A second issue is the reasonableness of the city ordinance preventing a private company from conducting chemical weapons research of a hazardous nature. Hence, the outcome of the controversy hinges on two separate but related questions. First, does the city's regulation prohibiting Arthur D. Little from conducting nerve and blister gas experiments in its Philip L. Levins Laboratory constitute a clear conflict with federal interests? And second, is the city ordinance to regulate, restrict, and proscribe scientific research and technological development reasonable?

The controversy, which began in 1982, reached a crisis point in March 1984 when Arthur D. Little filed a suit petitioning the City of Cambridge to cease and desist from its moratorium on hazardous chemical weapons research within the city limits of Cambridge. The court sided with the consulting firm, issuing a temporary restraining order, but Cambridge went ahead with its plans to convene a commission of Cambridge residents, the Scientific Advisory Committee (SAC). Krimsky, a member of SAC, devotes much of the chapter to an insider's account of the workings of the committee, which completed its task in September 1984. SAC's final report concluded (1) that an accident was probable; (2) that since the risks of supertoxins research outweighed the benefits to Cambridge residents and to society, storage and testing was inappropriate; and (3) that a risk management plan should be prepared. In December, the Superior Court of Massachusetts ruled that the Cambridge city ordinance to restrict research with hazardous materials is not preempted by federal law. More recently, the Supreme Judicial Court in Massachusetts upheld the ban on Arthur D. Little's chemical weapons research.

6. Science and Technology: Who Governs?

LEON E. TRACHTMAN

The reasons typically cited for external regulation of science and technology in our society are both obvious and compelling. Science and technology are pervasive forces in modern western society and it is impossible to read the daily newspaper without encountering articles documenting both their benefits and risks. No society should or would be willing to put into the hands of a small group of scientists and technologists unchecked and unrestrained power to affect its environment and the lives of all its members.

A second reason for some form of external regulation lies in the character of democratic society. We accept the principle that all power in a democracy flows from the people to and through their elected representatives. The people of a democratic society reserve to themselves the power, both directly and through their representatives, to influence public policy decisions and ultimately to govern the conduct of all social institutions which impinge on their lives.

Finally, since a major share of science and technology is either directly or indirectly supported with public funds, the simple principle of accountability demands that those engaged in publicly-funded enterprises be responsible and accountable for their actions to those who pay the bill.

Because of the virtually unanimous acceptance of these principles, we have already created a wide variety of both formal and informal mechanisms which regulate and restrain science and technology. The real question we must face, therefore, is not so much whether or not there should be external regulation and governance of science as whether or not the present mechanisms of regulation work for the most part, and if they do not, what modifications are necessary to make them work.

141

It is basic, in launching this whole discussion, to understand and accept the premise that, by its very nature, scientific research is an essay into the unknown, and that some of the generally used principles of risk assessment and evaluation are less effectively applied to this sort of activity than to such technologies as automotive or air transportation, in which both the character and the extent of risk can more easily be defined and measured.

As might be expected, the existing mechanisms for governing science and technology in our society share some of the *ad hoc*, improvisational and unintegrated qualities of many of our political institutions. For more than twenty-five years political scientists have been writing articles with titles like "Ten (or Twenty or Thirty) Billion Dollars in Search of a Policy." Well-organized scholars have sometimes found it difficult to accept the decentralized, fragmented, sometimes adversarial, free-marketplace approach to support of science that has characterized many of the agencies of our government since the end of World War II. Many have advocated tighter, more centralized, more rational, more highly organized, more coherent, and more effectively integrated longrange plans for public support of research, conceived and implemented by a more efficiently institutionalized planning structure.

Since our mechanisms for governing, regulating, and restraining science resemble our science funding mechanisms, they too seem both redundant and inefficient by organizational standards. This paper will, therefore, be concerned, among other issues, with the following question: Would a better-designed set of formal and institutionalized regulatory mechanisms be likely to confer greater costs or benefits on our society, compared with the unsystematically developed machinery now in existence?

TYPES OF REGULATORY MECHANISMS

Basically, there are five types of restraining and regulatory mechanisms which can be imposed at various stages of the research and development process.

1. *The legislative power of appropriation.* The Congress has the power to control appropriations to the various mission-oriented and other scientific agencies of government. While withholding funds does not necessarily mean cessation of research, the lack of public funding for

any program or specialized area of research or development has a profoundly inhibiting effect upon work in the area.

2. *The power of a variety of federal, state, and local statutes* designed to limit or check the negative impacts of technology.

3. *The investigatory and enforcement power of a variety of federal and state regulatory agencies*, many of them established by these statutes. Among these agencies are the Environmental Protection Agency, the Nuclear Regulatory Commission, the Food and Drug Administration, the Federal Communications Commission, the Occupational Safety and Health Administration, state environmental protection agencies, and a number of others.

4. *The power of committees and boards of approval* in research institutions themselves. These Institutional Review Boards and Committees on the Use of Human Subjects must give administrative approval to protocols of proposed research which makes use of human subjects. In addition, most institutions oversee the facilities in which research animals are housed and the experimental procedures in which they are used.

5. *The power of the judicial system* at every level to issue injunctions restraining activities perceived to violate statutes or the rights of individuals, and to hear cases, judge compliance with the law, and impose penalties.

The very considerable influence of all these restraining and regulatory mechanisms seems sometimes to be overlooked by proponents both of scientific self-regulation and of more highly institutionalized external control. The nature and extent of this influence will be explored later in this chapter; an evaluation first should be made, however, of the expressed fears of some scientists that *any* external regulation poses the threat of extinguishing freedom of scientific inquiry and imposing on the scientific community the dogmas of particular civil authorities. The cases of Galileo and the Roman Catholic Church and of Soviet genetics during the Lysenko period are commonly invoked to illustrate the dangers of this sort of external governance. Leonard Cole analyzes these cases in the context of their times and cultures and argues convincingly that the ecclestical and political institutions and precedents responsible for these suppressions of free scientific inquiry are simply not present in contemporary American life and that, therefore, we run virtually no risk of this sort of repressive control. Further, he asserts that careless analogy which blurs the distinctions between appropriate social controls on science and technology and heavy-handed political or theological domination of science creates risk for both science and the general public. [1]

This argument, coupled with the accepted influence of a variety of existing regulatory mechanisms, makes irrelevant or purely theoretical the case for completely untrammeled and unconstrained freedom of the researcher. The real issue, therefore, is not one of simplistic contrast between scientific autonomy and a smothering blanket of external control. Rather, consideration of both historical and contemporary science demands answers to a more complicated set of questions, namely, Just what scientific activities are regulated, in what ways, by whom, under what circumstances, and to what ends?

THE RELATIONS OF SCIENCE AND TECHNOLOGY

Many discussions of this set of questions use the terms science and technology in tandem, appearing to recognize no significant distinction between the two. The fact that two separate terms are used, however, suggests that there is a difference between them and that it should be understood. Weingart makes the case that despite their apparently disparate roots in prehistory — science being grounded in the explanatory role of the priest and the magician, and technology in the accidental and trial-and-error empiricism of the craftsman and artisan — the two had become virtually indistinguishable in the pre-paradigmatic period of modern science. [2] The amateurs who belonged to the newly established scientific societies of the seventeenth century were equally concerned with theory and practice, and were as avid to discover how mechanisms worked in practice as to understand more fundamental scientific principles. [3] According to the charter of the Royal Society, it was the business of the society to "improve the knowledge of natural things and all useful Arts, Manufacture, Mechanic practices, Engynes and Inventions by Experiment . . . for explication (of) all phenomena produced by nature or art . . ." [4] The absence of any institutional separation between science and technology, as illustrated by these words of the charter, persisted for the better part of a century. With the gradual development in the late eighteenth and the nineteenth centuries of paradigmatic science, however, especially as conceived and practiced in the German universities, the streams of science and technology began to diverge, with science seeking to develop conceptual principles and fundamental understanding of nature, and technology both reducing these principles and this understanding to practice and operating independently of science, in traditional empirical fashion. University science, which became concerned with methods of learning and with creation of general principles of knowledge, viewed technology as subsequent to science and concerned only with specialized application of scientific concepts to production of useful mechanisms, devices, and practices.

Although this period of divergence between science and technology extended into the early years of the twentieth century, the greater part of this century has witnessed a reconvergence of the two. The causes of this reconvergence are several: the exhaustion of possibilities of further basic research in certain scientific areas, the obviousness of technological applications in others, and, because of the continuing accumulation of theoretical knowledge, the scientification of many areas of technology. Illustrating the first cause, Weingart points out that the National Academy of Science's 1973 evaluation of eight subfields of physics characterized such areas of optics and acoustics as "high in their potential for contribution to technology" rather than having potential for discovery of fundamental laws. An example of the second cause is recombinant DNA research which, while still extraordinarily rich in potential for further fundamental research, has such obvious applicability to a variety of applied and technological biomedical issues that the simultaneous conduct of basic research and technological application is almost inevitable.

Finally, the accumulation of fundamental physical, chemical, and biological theory has been so great that there is great impetus to scientize and rationalize many areas of applied technology.[5] In other words, rather than following more traditional trial-and-error empirical techniques in developing new technologies, there is an increasing tendency to refer technological problems to a context of theoretical understanding for solution. For example, a cancer chemotherapy program, involving routine trial-and-error testing of vast numbers of chemicals, in today's more theoretical and "scientific" environment yields inevitably to an approach in which our conceptual understanding of chemical-biological system interactions increasingly directs and controls experimental rationale and procedures. In the same way, Ziman points out that, in doing research on the phenomenon of "fatigue" in metals, "we are almost forced into the position of saying that on Monday, Wednesday, and Friday we are just honest seekers after the truth, adding to our understanding of the natural world, etc., while on Tuesday, Thursday, and Saturday we are

145

practical chaps trying to stop aeroplanes from falling to pieces,"[6] so intimately related to basic physical and chemical theory are many contemporary issues of technological investigation.

As a result of this reconvergence of science and technology, the most important contemporary distinction between science and technology may involve their social context, rather than the subjects of their research or their experimental methods.[7] It is the character and the organization of those to whom the investigator directs his communications which increasingly determine whether what is done should be called science or technology. If the communication is directed to an invisible college of peers, if few or no constraints are imposed on the dissemination of this information, if the typical medium of communication is first the scientific meeting and then the scientific journal, we can judge that it is science which is being done. If, on the other hand, the audience for the investigator's communications exists at another level in an organizational hierarchy of which the investigator is part, if reports must be reviewed and cleared before being released, if limits on communication must be imposed to protect the information and permit its exploitation, we can call what is being done technology. Even in the university, the traditional sanctum of "pure" research, the interest in patents and copyrights and their licenses, in spinoff companies, and in university-industry joint ventures is causing a change (though so far, a relatively modest one) in traditional scientific communication patterns.

Technological Basis of Most Risk.   When we consider the issue of the social costs and risks of research in the light of this new developing relationship between science and technology, virtually all of them seem rooted in technological rather than scientific enterprises. The problems of siting nuclear power plants; of handling and disposing of radioactive and toxic chemical wastes; of dealing with acid rain; of air, water and land pollution; of energy generation and its environmental impact; of human nutrition; of carcinogenesis; and a host of others — all relate to activities most vigorously pursued in what we define as technological organizations. The only widely identified potentially high-risk activity which is at least as strongly pursued in basic research environments as in technological institutions is recombinant DNA research, and even that is moving at an increasing pace into a more technological mode.

To elaborate on this issue, we may examine Cole's illustrations of scientific abuse in the Tuskegee syphilis study, CIA mind-control experiments, and Army germ warfare tests.[8] While the argument is certainly valid that the scientists engaged in these experiments should have protested against the unethical treatment of research subjects and against the unwarranted risk to which nonconsenting members of the public were exposed, the fact is that all of these programs—as well as other similar risk-engendering research—were sponsored by agencies of government in pursuit of their institutional goals rather than the goals of disinterested, independent scientific inquiry. In other words, these ethical breaches were committed by what are, in terms of our definition, technological organizations. It is true, of course, that these experiments were not all necessarily statements of national policy nor parts of a national scheme condoning abuse of research subjects (as, for instance, were the Nazi experiments of human subjects), but they certainly did not stem from the pure scientific curiosity of the investigators alone.

RISKS AND ABUSES OF SCIENCE AND TECHNOLOGY

Accepting this distinction between science and technology, and freely granting the general principle of accountability of scientists, whether functioning in basic scientific or technological organizations, let us more systematically explore the range of scientific abuse that societal oversight should identify, characterize the controls imposed by existing mechanisms of regulation, and judge what, if anything, might be accomplished by the creation of additional echelons of governing mechanisms. All abuses and risks engendered by science appear to fit into one of the following five categories:

1. *Incompetent science:* inadequacy of design, ignorance of the literature, inappropriateness of methods to the problem, and similar faults.
2. *Fraud:* deliberate theft of information, plagiarism, distortion, misrepresentation, or fabrication of results.
3. *Abuse of research subjects:* deception, failure to obtain informed consent, or withholding proper care from subjects.
4. *Imposing first-order risks on the public:* for example, creating new pathogens or chemicals for which adequate safeguards do not exist and which could directly harm the public.
5. *Imposing second-order risks on the public:* doing research which, though presenting no immediate risks, may introduce technologies which could have significant negative impacts on social, economic, political, or ethical institutions or norms.

147

What protections against these abuses are already offered by existing regulatory institutions and procedures? Can additional constructive safeguards be anticipated by creating new governing mechanisms? Let us consider each category by itself.

The first area of abuse — incompetence — does not really pose a significant risk to the public except insofar as it may waste funds better expended elsewhere. Furthermore, there appears to be no way in which nonspecialists can effectively identify it. It is in this area that peer review functions to prevent incompetent research from being funded and, if it is performed, to prevent its results from appearing in the scientifically sanctioned archival literature.

The second area of abuse — fraud — is likewise not identifiable in advance. No prior announcement is made of the intent to fabricate, misrepresent, or steal results, and only those acquainted with the research area and capable of replicating suspicious studies can identify fraud. Once more, peer review is the means most likely to identify fraud. Recent disclosures of fraud suggest that the scientific establishment is reasonably effective at policing this kind of abuse and, further, that scientists find it very much in their interest to detect and expose it.[9]

The third kind of abuse of science and technology is indeed a serious public concern, and a sufficient number of horrible examples exists to give us pause. On the other hand, wide public discussion of the use of human and animal subjects has clearly sensitized the scientific community to the potential for abuse. While it is true that external pressures have been important in improving the situation, the extent of abuse, even in the past, is probably not very great. Further, as has been pointed out, the most widely cited examples of the abuse of human subjects have occurred, not merely in programs supported or directed by government agencies, but specifically in those programs in which government agencies have had a distinct policy interest: nuclear testing in Utah by the Atomic Energy Commission, Army germ warfare tests, CIA mind-control experiments. In all of these, to be sure, the involved scientists have been compliant and have tended to acquiesce in the methods employed, but this compliance has been premised on an overriding concern for policy issues of national security and the like. If the abuses stemmed from the policy goals of government agencies rather than from the pure scientific curiosity of the investigators, and if government is to be the watchdog of science, who is to be the watchdog of government in such cases? *Quis custodiet ipsos custodes?*

In spite of the notoriety of a few specific cases, the fourth area of potential abuse actually occurs relatively rarely in basic scientific research. It happens only when a conceptual or methodological breakthrough opens a new general area of investigation. In recent decades, recombinant DNA research in the life sciences and nuclear fission research in the physical sciences are the paramount examples. By now, of course, the issue of nuclear fission has become almost entirely a technological one, and a number of the potential hazards attributed to DNA research are at least as likely to be associated with its technological applications as with fundamental laboratory investigations.

Other research programs creating first-order risks for society are far more likely to be the result of technological development or application in already well-established areas than of scientific laboratory research. Such work is likely to deal with agricultural or industrial chemicals, pharmaceuticals, or energy generation and is not characterized by the imponderability of risk related to genuinely new areas of fundamental research.

The fifth area — creation of second order risks — seems almost too massive and unknowable even to consider in this context, and yet it is impacts in this broad area which seem responsible for much of the increasing ambivalence in public attitudes towards science.[10] If concern over these impacts should prompt development of governing mechanisms, it would be almost impossible to set limits on control. Even accepting the general principle of accountability, it is hard to think that basic science, expecially life science, is in any way unique in requiring a kind of control not normally applied to the wide range of enterprises which possess comparable potential for affecting our lives.

Two problems beset us in trying to impose regulation on this sort of research. First, the character of second-order impacts is almost completely imponderable. One hundred years ago, for example, it would have been impossible to predict to any close approximation the enormous social, economic, political, and environmental impact of the invention of the automobile on the life of modern man. In view of the inadequacy of our attempts to assess first-order impacts of technology, our second-order impact predictions are surely virtually worthless.

Even specifically in the life sciences, consideration of second-order impacts could probably not be permitted to precipitate decisions on what research to do and what to reject. For example, life-extending research for septuagenarians and octogenarians, while certainly not directly threatening to the rest of the society in a biological sense, might certainly, if highly successful, be socially and economically disastrous.

Imagine the impact on the economy of having a large proportion of the population over eighty years of age, forcing a productive minority to bear the upwardly-spiraling cost of their subsistence and health care. Yet who would suggest that life-extending or maintaining research should be controlled or halted because of these possible results?

It seems clear that our judgments about the gravity of second-order consequences of research and our decisions about whether or not, and to what degree, to control it are based on a confusing blend of precedent, custom, habit, social preference, economic interest, and political power, and that no single system of assessment and evaluation can or should be permitted to limit choices based upon these shaky estimates of long-range consequences.

HOW SCIENCE AND TECHNOLOGY ARE GOVERNED

Now, having enumerated the five categories of risk, let us examine two questions: Who governs science and technology? And what are some of the implications of this governance? The principal mechanisms of regulation lie in the powers of appropriation, of peer review, of statute, of regulatory agencies, of institutional review boards, and of judicial review.

Regulation by Appropriation.   The first of the regulating, stimulating, or inhibiting mechanisms is the power of appropriation. In general, the role of appropriation is to stimulate rather than to inhibit research. It is largely because of administrative commitment to specific scientific goals (space exploration, national security, elimination of specific diseases, etc.) as reflected in legislation, that the impact of appropriations decisions tends to be positive and productive.[11] The negative impact of appropriations decisions appears normally to come by default rather than by conscious decisions to limit or inhibit research in a given area. In other words, low-priority goals simply get leftover dribbles of support. The exception occurs, of course, when a specific project or program of research or development is singled out for reduction or elimination. Congressional refusal to subsidize the design and construction of an American supersonic transport is one of the rare occurrences of this sort.

When administrative proposals are forwarded to the Congress for review and action, many pressures and forces are unleashed. Although

Congress seeks to acquire independent expert information and advice, its record of doing so is at best uneven. The mission-oriented agencies and the experts they supply provide vigorous defenses of agency activities and decisions, and frequently their only antagonists are self-appointed science and technology critics who, whatever their "bona fides," are frequently viewed as outsiders, incompetents, or single-interest lobbyists.

To improve its ability to get solid and responsible technical and fiscal advice, the Congress in the 1970s created two agencies, the Congressional Budget Office (CBO) and the Office of Technology Assessment (OTA). While the adequacy of these two, especially the OTA, is still open to question,[12] the move is clearly in the direction of balancing special interest and agency testimony with unbiased evaluations of technological issues and their economic and other impacts.

One characteristic of the legislative appropriation process is that even the relatively modest changes from session to session in the makeup of congressional committees may limit somewhat our longterm planning abilities. Another characteristic is that since chairpersons tend to work closely with agency heads to guide budget authorizations and appropriations, many appropriations decisions seem to rest on personal politics and the economic climate, and that the role of purely technical advice is strictly circumscribed by political necessity and strategy. Further, timetables for congressional elections and for R&D planning and performance have little in common, putting the legislative calendar "out of sync" with the normal research and development process. Finally, the criteria for independent technology assessment are really unknown, and there are no guarantees concerning the competence, honesty, objectivity, and impartiality of technology assessors.[13]

Since federal policy decisions are in many cases carried out under contract by private enterprise, significant sectors of the private economy are affected by public policy decisions concerning directions and funding of scientific and technological enterprises. Threat of major economic or social consequences of appropriations decisions — for example, labor dislocation at large space or defense installations — can have as great an influence on funding policy as does the intrinsic character of the research itself.[14] This may well be among the causes of the complaint, widespread over the past twenty years, that, because it is widely dispersed and relatively weak politically, the basic research community has consistently failed to receive from the federal government its appropriate share of research funds.

In sum, the appropriation process has tended to be a highly politicized, decentralized, fragmented, and entrepreneurial activity. On the face of it, less political and more highly centralized, coherent, and goal-based administrative planning procedures would seem a far more attractive alternative. On the other hand, a more highly structured and formalized science and technology review and appropriation procedure might well ultimately put too much governing and controlling power into the hands of technology czars whose institutionalized delegation of power would put them a step further removed from the people and their elected representatives. These mandarins would, therefore, be less responsive to public attitudes and pressure. Ultimately, the source of expert advice under any governing and regulatory system would be the same, but it may be that the "pulling and hauling" of adversarial free-marketplace politics is a more sensitive and salutary, if less efficient, mechanism of control than would be a more highly organized and more centralized system of planning and appropriation.[15] This competitive and adversarial process may well permit more sensitive shortrun responses to real-world issues than would a deliberately and consciously forged, well-developed, centralized, and more efficient longterm plan for resource allocation. For example, the refusal of the Congress to support funding for an American SST reflects a responsiveness to economic and environmental issues that were raised by a variety of interest groups. If development of an SST had been part of a well-developed longterm research and development plan, it would have been much more difficult for policy members to be responsive to these demands.

While this approach may seem like tacking into the wind, taking a long and indirect way to achieve goals, and making the science and technology establishment subject to every vagary of popular opinion and unable to count on longterm sustained support, it may also offer optimal opportunities for oversight of activities perceived to pose risks to society.

Obviously, however, cutting off or limiting resources is at best an indirect form of external control for all but the most expensive research — that which depends absolutely upon such costly equipment as particle accelerators, mohole-type seagoing vessels, and the like, which are available only through government appropriation. More modest programs of research in other areas can be carried out with local and far more limited sources of funding and not be dependent upon the approval of the federal legislature. Many of these day-to-day decisions about funding are made on the basis of peer review procedures. The character and extent of peer review differ from agency to agency, with the National Science Foundation and the National Institutes of Health having the most formalized and extensively developed systems, and various units of the Department of Defense and other agencies depending to a far greater degree on in-house evaluations of responses to requests for proposals. While the agencies using in-house evaluations are, in some sense, using peer review, their reviews are not provided by disinterested experts but rather by those who are part of and have a stake in the programs of research being supported. In general, the agencies involved in support of more basic research tend to depend more on peer review; those involved in technological development on in-house evaluation.

Although peer review is the traditional and esteemed method of maintaining standards of scientific performance, a number of questions have been raised in recent years about its efficiency. The charge is made that some reviewers are unduly influenced by the professional standing of authors or proposals and articles or by the eminence of their institutions. Hence, some advocate more widespread use of blind reviews, in which the identity of the author is unknown. On the other hand, some commentators believe that a track record of high performance in an eminent institution is evidence of value to reviewers.[16]

Whether or not peer review is more objective than and superior to in-house review as a system of evaluating the quality of proposals, it is clear that many of the specific decisions concerning which proposals to fund or not fund are made, not on the basis of legislative appropriation but as a result of a highly diffuse and decentralized process involving the judgments of many independent referees. In general, however, these judgments are made on the basis of perceived scientific quality of the proposals and not for the purpose of limiting scientific work thought to involve risk. A number of mechanisms exist, however, which *are* specifically designed for the purposes of restraint and regulation, chiefly of risk-posing technologies.

Regulation by Statute.   At the federal, state, and local levels there exists a fabric of statutes governing a wide variety of science- and technology-related activities. Examples are environmental protection laws; pure food and drug laws; food and chemical labeling laws; laws governing nuclear power plant siting, toxic chemical and nuclear waste transportation and disposal, pesticide use, asbestos use, and tobacco product labeling; and many more. As in any layered federal system, the character of the laws

153

and the integrity and intensity with which they are enforced may vary from jurisdiction to jurisdiction, but the statutory basis for protecting the public from identified technological hazards does exist.

In addition to this body of statutes, there are several types of administrative regulation which are binding upon recipients of federal grants and contracts for research. Where the statutes are designed primarily to protect the general public from risks associated with applications of technology (the fourth category of risk), the administrative regulations are more specifically oriented to the conduct of research in the laboratory itself and are designed to assure ethical treatment of human subjects of research and humane treatment of animals. Again, abuses and violations occur; but failure to identify and correct them is typically a fault of inspection and enforcement rather than of absence of regulatory mechanisms themselves.

It is rare that a new thrust in science will create a hazard, either within the laboratory or to the public at large, which is so novel that it does not fall under general protective provisions of the body to statutes and regulation or within the jurisdiction of the bodies established to enforce the rules. Once more, the emergence of recombinant DNA techniques is the only significant such development in recent years.

Regulatory Agencies. A third mechanism for governing scientific and technological activities is intimately related to the body of regulatory statutes. Legislation designed to impose controls on technological applications in areas of risk frequently establishes governmental agencies or bureaus charged with the responsibility of overseeing the area, enforcing the provisions of the law, and developing administrative regulations to facilitate this oversight and enforcement. Among these agencies are the Nuclear Regulatory Commission, the Food and Drug Administration, the Environmental Protection Agency, the Occupational Safety and Health Administration, and the Federal Communications Commission, as well as a variety of state and municipal agencies responsible for surveillance and enforcement at these levels. Once more, the overwhelming majority of activities regulated by this network of agencies consists of technological applications in nuclear, chemical, and other areas which are institutionally far removed from the basic research laboratory.

There are, of course, numerous reports of inadequacies, incompetence, and malfeasance in regulatory agencies. Whatever the reasons for these breakdowns in regulatory activities, the solution would appear to be a shoring up of their authority, the appointment of more competent, more disinterested or less corruptible members, and, when necessary, statutory modification of their charges in order to cover areas which may have been inadvertently excluded from their areas of jurisdiction, rather than creation of yet another review echelon.

Local Review Boards and Committees.   While these various agencies of government are designed principally to cope with hazards to the general population which stem from a variety of scientific and technological activities, another group of mandated boards has been established within scientific research institutions to deal with the issue of risk to subjects of experimentation (the third category of risk). These Institutional Review Boards and Committees on the Use of Human Subjects exist in every institution which receives National Institutes of Health and National Science Foundation support for programs of research. For practical purposes, this includes every significant research university in the United States. These bodies are empowered to demand and routinely review detailed research protocols from investigators proposing to perform research involving human subjects. In general, the term "use of human subjects" is construed so broadly as to include populations being asked to complete questionnaires and take standardized psychological and other tests, so that every possible risk of damage — emotional and psychological as well as physical — is taken into account. These boards have the power to recommend modification in protocols in the interest of protecting human subjects of research and may withhold approval from programs of research which fail to meet appropriate standards.

The Role of the Judicial System.   The final existing mechanism for controlling and regulating risks engendered by scientific and technological activities is the judicial system itself. The judiciary is equipped both to enjoin the performance of activities which it contemplates may pose substantial or unwarranted risks and to hear cases brought by parties alleging that they have incurred harm from scientific and technological activities. Judge David L. Bazelon has incisively explained the role of the courts as well as that of other governing and regulatory bodies. The central issue, he points out, is not whether or not society shall accept some level of risk associated with developments in science and tech-

155

nology (it shall), but rather how much risk is acceptable, what individuals or groups should be exposed to this risk, and who is finally empowered to make society's decisions concerning acceptability of risk.[17]

Quite clearly, society has a variety of ways, formal and informal, by omission and commission, of making decisions concerning risk, without ever having the issues adjudicated in the courts. The American public has emphatically decided in the marketplace, for example, that 50,000 deaths a year is not an exorbitant price to pay for the benefits of automotive transportation. Yet it has on occasion fairly compliantly accepted the banning of one artificial sweetener or another, which arguably causes no deaths a year, undoubtedly because a different benefit-cost calculus is involved.

Many disputes involving risk, however, are ultimately referred to the courts because the agencies responsible for appropriation, legislation, and regulation decisions are faced with conflicting expert advice, frequently offered in the context of different value systems. In many cases, equally reputable experts will draw from the same body of data widely differing inferences concerning level and acceptability of risk. Even in those cases where there is consensus on technical data, diverse political, economic, and ethical contexts and standards can lead to different conclusions concerning the risk's acceptability. Value systems—those of experts and the general public alike—which determine their assessments of acceptability of risk, are rooted in grounds far removed from the scientific and technological issues themselves. For example, even if technical experts agreed on the certainty of radiation at certain levels reaching a certain proportion of the population if nuclear power plant development continued, judgment on the acceptability of that risk would very likely be quite different for someone convinced that the future of the nation was absolutely dependent upon development of nuclear resources and for someone whose political and economic values create a commitment to soft-energy development. An individual's vision of the ends of human existence, of man's place in the world, of the proper role of this nation in the international community, and of the way it should wield its economic, political, and moral influence obviously affect technological judgment in a variety of ways.

Although the courts cannot change or make uniform the individual and group contexts of values in which disputes develop, they can at least help make sure that decision makers articulate the basis for their decisions in terms of both data and value systems. They can insist that ignorance be confessed where it exists, that arguments for acceptability or unacceptability of certain risks be explained in terms of tradeoffs for society, and that all this be done in language comprehensible to the general public.[18]

Since "common law is one means to control the consequences of technological development,"[19] the role of courts is of special importance. They are equipped both to adjudicate scientific and technological disputes between private parties and to counteract the actions of executive agencies which are outside the law. To these roles may be added the enjoining power of the courts to prohibit scientific and technological activities which appear to pose unwarranted threats. Further, "by dramatizing injustices and reflecting public values a lawsuit can also cause the public to exert pressure for more responsible technology." One serious problem is that the courts, in spite of their power of injunction, can generally only respond to complaints and cannot really anticipate them.[20]

The experience of recent years suggests that torts cases dealing with product liability, nuclear risk, recombinant DNA, experimentation with human subjects, environmental protection and a host of other science- and technology-related issues will demand ever-increasing scientific sophistication on the part of the courts. To deal with issues of this sort, Kuehn and Porter suggest the possibility of establishing within the context of the legal system special appeals courts, on the model of the U.S. Patent or Maritime Courts.[21]

For those individuals or classes who believe that scientists and technologists are engendering unacceptable risks or that responsible regulatory agencies are failing properly to evaluate and control risk-producing conditions and activities, the courts are the logical and appropriate ultimate forum for adjudication. One particular advantage which existing judicial structures and remedies offer is that they have constitutional and statutory authority which is clearly superior to any which would be possessed by constitutionally unsanctioned science and technology courts and other proposed *ad hoc* mechanisms of regulation.

THE UNSYSTEMATIC SYSTEM OF GOVERNMENT

The complex web of social, political, and economic institutions and procedures available for evaluating and controling risk-producing scientific and technological activities is nothing less than a microcosm of the

American governmental system itself. It operates at many levels, in both formal and informal ways. It has a variety of overlapping areas of jurisdiction. It is certainly more disorderly than any system established by an authoritarian and centralized government. On the other hand, its openness, its many pressure points, and the opportunities it offers for both deliberative and adversarial proceedings at many levels makes it perhaps more sensitive and more responsive to a variety of public imputs than would be a highly more institutionalized and hierarchical set of structures.

This complex system of legislative, administrative, and judical machinery, while perhaps largely reactive in exercising control, has developed certain patterns by which potential or actual risks are brought to its attention for appropriate action. If any novel regulatory machinery should be created, the question would have to be addressed of how such machinery should be used. Should it be employed routinely to review and monitor all scientific and technological activities for potential risk? Should it be used when its personnel have some prior perception of risk? Or should it be called into action only upon complaint of a victim or class of victims, a whistle blower or a public interest group? If the first of these is true, we might be launching an enormously cumbersome, complex, and time- and effort-consuming system which would slow or inhibit the conduct of all research, the greatest share of which poses no conceivable risk. If the second were true, its use might well depend on the intuitive, idiosyncratic, or biased perceptions of its members. If the third were true, it would have no function different from the existing judicial system.

The nature of the relatively unsystematic body of controls which we possess inevitably results in some ambiguity concerning the scope and function of the various levels of governance as well as some inconsistency in interpretation and enforcement of statute from agency to agency and institution to institution. Even so, the redundancy of the system offers a reasonable measure of protection to society. More important, the risk of unethical and socially hazardous behavior on the part of science must be balanced against the risk of having tighter, more cumbersome, more time-consuming, more elaborate, and more inhibiting rules and regulations. In general, it has not been demonstrated that the overwhelming majority of practicing scientists is so devoid of basic ethical concern and a sense of social responsibility that they would deliberately and malevolently undertake research patently dangerous to society.

158

ROLE OF THE PRESS

One final protective mechanism must be mentioned: the press. It must be acknowledged that press coverage of science and technology over the years has been at best uneven. Accused of sensationalism and over-simplification in dealing with complex materials, press treatments of science and technology have been specifically criticized because of their tendency:

1. To be highly selective in choice of materials and to use a variety of questionable selection criteria.
2. To oversimplify, and hence to misrepresent, the methods and the character of scientific inquiry.
3. To treat scientific news as discrete events and hence to create another false conception of science.
4. To draw undue inferences about the meaning and significance of particular lines of research.
5. To report on inadequate, incomplete, and poorly designed research as readily as on competent research, as long as the subject matter is relevant to immediate popular concerns.
6. To raise false expectations of what science is capable of doing.
7. On occasion, to create stress among readers more damaging than the real risks being reported on.[22]

Even if we accept the validity of this list of criticisms and grant that it has a frequent tendency to "cry wolf," the press does play one absolutely crucial role: it publicly calls society's attention to the possibility of scientific and technological risk. Many of these calls will be exaggerations; a few will not. In a political democracy which is at the same time the most technologically sophisticated society in the world, it is probably worth having several false alarms registered for every one that signals genuine risk to subjects of research or to the general public.

Without the press to signal the existence of probable risk and without the knowledge by the scientific and technological community that the press is always prepared to perform this warning function, the probability of abusive actions and the likelihood of their going undetected might well be greatly increased.

As with other protective mechanisms, the behavior of the press is, of course, flawed. Like the legislative and executive bodies responsible for appropriation and regulation, the press is susceptible to improper pressure and can be misled by incompetent or biased "expert" advice.

In addition, like many other institutions in our society, the press is moving toward greater centralization in administration, with decreasing opportunity for individual initiative to identify and develop stories. This is especially true in science, where the pressroom agenda can be controled by scientific societies[23] and where a small inner circle of science writers tends to set the pattern for selection of items for coverage.[24] In spite of these flaws, the press remains a most valuable informational and signaling resource for the Congress and for regulatory agencies, as well as for the general public.

In some sense, the press's greatest contribution is its service as a watchdog of government science itself. It should be reemphasized that some of the most flagrant documented abuses of science have been perpetrated in pursuit of political and governmental policies rather than as a result of the disinterested curiosity of scientists themselves. The whole issue of nuclear policy, for example, has been bound up with a broadbased federal policy toward atomic energy. It is certainly true that scientists are involved with federal agencies in pursuit of both their scientific and the government's political and economic goals, but the abuse seems to originate chiefly in policy rather than in science. For example, Cole points out "how single minded and duplicitious"[25] the Atomic Energy Commission had become when it publicly announced that radioactive fallout from nuclear tests in Nevada posed no threat to people in the area. It was the imperative of national policy rather than of scientific curiosity which caused AEC Commissioner Thomas Murray to say in 1955, "We must not let anything interfere with this series of tests — nothing," and which prompted Commissioner Willard Libby to decide that "people would have to 'learn to live with . . . fallout,' even if they did not know they were receiving it."[26]

The ability of the press to identify and focus on issues of this sort probably represents its most positive contribution to the protection of the public from unethical and dangerous scientific and technological practices.

THE ROLE OF PUBLIC OPINION

A final informal control of science and technology is public opinion. Obviously, as an instrument of stimulation or restraint of research, the role of public opinion is closely related to that of the press, with which it functions reciprocally. In its reporting and editorializing about scientific and technological subjects, the press is highly instrumental in shaping public opinion. At the same time, the press reports on various expressions of public opinion and so, in addition to shaping opinion, reflects and sometimes amplifies attitudes held by specific attentive and interested publics. In this reciprocal relationship, the two make mutual use of one another. Interested publics try to use the columns of the paper in order to broadcast their views more widely, while the newspaper, in its search for stories which are interesting and novel or which report on conflict, use these groups as sources of information. The entire issue of the relations between the press and public opinion is, however, not one which can be explored at this time. Suffice it to say that the combination of the voices of the public and the press plays a significant role in affecting both the attitudes and the behavior of the individuals and institutions charged with more formal responsibility for the governance of science.

Specifically, legislative bodies responsible for appropriations decisions, especially in areas about which there is public controversy, have developed a variety of hearing procedures in order to permit interested publics to express their views as they try to affect levels of support for research and development enterprises. While federal regulatory agencies, various national and state commissions, and institutional review committees and control boards are typically more insulated from public opinion than are legislative bodies, there is no question that the intensity with which these bodies enforce regulations is related to public and journalistic expressions of concern about such issues as environmental pollution, nuclear risk, hazards related to use of various foods and drugs, etc.

CONCLUSION

This survey of the kinds of risk imposed on society by scientific and technological activities and the response to these perceived risks by a variety of formal and informal political and social institutions yields a picture of widespread but decentralized restraining mechanisms. Our society's approach to governance and restraint of science and technology is characterized by a relatively high degree of redundancy and overlapping authority and a low level of coherence and coordination. Nonetheless, all of this rather cumbersome and unwieldly machinery seems to be able to respond reasonably effectively to the emergence of major new risks and to public attitudes concerning these risks. The adversarial

161

character of much of the deliberation concerning these risks seems to guarantee that our society is unlikely either to underreact or overreact in any major way to perceived risks over an extended time, although disproportionate responses may well emerge in the short run. While the case can be made that a much more highly centralized, hierarchical, and coordinated structure might be a desirable alternative to the present system, there is simply no chance that such a major overhaul of our political institutions will take place. If this assumption is accepted, we should probably entertain serious doubts about creating and developing yet additional mechanisms of governance and control which will almost inevitably complicate the already overlapping jurisdictional structure of the existing machinery. A better course might well be to attempt to clarify and strengthen the authority of the mechanisms we have.

NOTES

1. Leonard A. Cole, *Politics and the Restraint of Science*, 61–79.

2. This is the early period of modern science, when the Baconian quest for empirical knowledge prompted a largely atheoretical search for descriptive information about the whole range of natural and manmade phenomena which lent themselves to this sort of investigation. Such a search is typically not directed and limited by a set of general principles expressed in the form of a controling theory or paradigm.

3. Peter Weingart, "The Relation Between Science and Technology—A Sociological Explanation," in *The Dynamics of Science and Technology*, ed. Wolfgang Krohn, Edwin T. Layton, and Peter Weingart (Dordrecht, Holland and Boston: D. Reidel, 1978), 257–64.

4. F. Sprat, as cited in A.R.J.P. Ubbelode, "The Beginnings of the Change from Craft Ministry to Science as a Basis for Technology," in *A History of Technology*, v. 4, ed. C. Sinclair et al. (Oxford: Oxford Univ. Press, 1958), quoted in Weingart, "The Relation Between Science and Technology," 261.

5. Weingart, "The Relation Between Science and Technology," 276–79.

6. John Ziman, *Public Knowledge* (Cambridge: Cambridge Univ. Press, 1968), 23.

7. M.J. Mulkay, "Sociology of the Scientific Research Community," in *Science, Technology and Society*, ed. Ina Spiegel-Rösing and Derek de Solla Price, (Beverly Hills: Sage, 1977), 95–96.

8. Cole, *Politics and the Restraint of Science*, 109–18.

9. Patricia Woolf, "Fraud in Science: How Much, How Serious?", *Hastings Center Report* 11 (Oct. 1981): 9–14.

10. Both subjective and objective evidence exists to suggest this ambivalence. For one thing, compared with two or three decades ago, when much of the literature emphasized the concepts of progress, growth, and human betterment as the consequences of research, today we see an increasing number of publications concerned with assessing the costs as well as the benefits of science and technology. For example, Robert S. Morison, in the Introduction to the "Limits of Scientific Inquiry" special issue, *Daedalus*, 107 (Spring, 1978): vii, writes:

In the last few years, several different kinds of unease have led to a questioning of the status of new knowledge and the effectiveness of society's arrangements for encouraging or restraining the growth of knowledge. In practice, the controversy changes rapidly from one level to another, and it is often difficult to be sure of the particular concerns and motivations of the principal protagonists. For purposes of preliminary analysis, however, several sources for this new anxiety may usefully be distinguished. The most elementary, perhaps, is a concern for the harm that may be done to individuals in the simple pursuit of knowledge. Closely related is the concern for the possible damaging effects of new technologies that may result from new knowledge. Next, come the long-term hazards, hard to foresee except rather dimly, that carry some finite possibility of serious perturbations in our current way of doing things. . . . The fourth source of anxiety is somewhat more remote from everyday affairs and concerns the possibly unsettling effects of new knowledge on man's concept of his relations to society or the rest of the natural world. This last concern may take the form of a deep-seated and not always clearly verbalized anxiety about the possible limitations and bases of scientific knowledge itself.

Similarly, Philip Handler, "Public Doubts About Science," *Science* 208 (6 June 1980): 1093, recently called for scientists to reverse the trend of increasing public skepticism toward science.

The results of a number of public opinion polls confirm this sense of unease or ambivalence. For example, one poll showed 56% of the respondents agreeing that "science and technology do as much harm as good," and 77% agreeing that "science and technology often got out of hand, threatening society instead of serving it." Research and Forecasts, Inc., survey performed for the Continental Group, Inc., unpublished data cited in National Science Board, *Science Indicators, 1982*, 146–47. And compared with only 2% of respondents in 1957–58, 7% of respondents in 1976 felt the world was worse off because of science, while those who believed the world was better off decreased from 83% in 1957–58 to 71% in 1976. The number feeling ambivalent increased from 8% to 15%. Pion and Lipsey, "Public Attitudes Toward Science and Technology."

Many other public statements and opinion polls confirm this modest but consistent trend toward increasing ambivalence about the social impact and consequences of science and technology.

11. American Association for the Advancement of Science, "Organization for Science and Technology in the Executive Branch," in *Science, Technology, and National Policy* ed. Thomas J. Kuehn and Alan L. Porter (Ithaca: Cornell Univ. Press, 1981), 257–59.

12. Kuehn and Porter, "Introduction: The Agenda for Science and Technology Policy," in Kuehn and Porter, *Science, Technology, and National Policy*, 21.

13. Kuehn and Porter, *Science, Technology, and National Policy*, 21–22.

14. James L. McCamy, "The New American Government of Science and Technology," in *Science and Policy Issues*, ed. Paul J. Piccard (Itasca, Ill.: F.E. Peacock, 1969), 42–43.

15. For thoughtful comparisons between these two contrasting approaches to political decison making, see Charles E. Lindblom, *The Intelligence of Democracy* (New York: Free Press, 1965), and Lindblom, *Politics and Markets*.

16. For a discussion of this issue, see the symposium in *Behavioral and Brain Sciences* 5 (June 1982): 187–255. In the key article of this symposium, Douglas Peters and Stephen

163

Ceci offer experimental evidence that changing the name and institutional affiliation of authors of articles dramatically affected their acceptance rate. But in an accompanying article Rosalyn Yalow defends the practice of "rejecting papers from unknown authors working in unknown institutions." See Donald P. Peters and Stephen J. Ceci, "Peer Review Practices of Psychological Journals: The Fate of Published Articles Submitted Again," *Behavioral and Brain Sciences* 5 (June 1982): 187–95, and Rosalyn Yalow, "Competency Testing for Reviewers and Editors," *Behavioral and Brain Sciences* 5 (June 1982): 244–45.

17. David L. Bazelon, "Risk and Responsibility," in Kuehn and Porter, *Science, Technology and National Policy*, 356–57.

18. Ibid., 361.

19. Kuehn and Porter, "Introduction," 22.

20. Ibid., 22–24.

21. Ibid., 23.

22. Leon E. Trachtman, "The Public Understanding of Science Efforts: A Critique," *Science, Technology, and Human Values* 6 (Summer 1981): 14.

23. Sharon Dunwoody, "Science Writing Study Finds: AAAS is Master of What Makes News at its Sessions," *Newsletter—National Association of Science Writers* 28 (Nov. 1979): 1–3.

24. Sharon Dunwoody, "The Science Writing Inner Club: A Communication Link Between Science and the Lay Public," *Science, Technology, and Human Values* 5 (Winter 1980): 14–21.

25. Cole, *Politics and the Restraint of Science*, 124.

26. Ibid.

7. *Federal Regulation of Biotechnology*

HAROLD P. GREEN

THE REGULATORY BACKGROUND

Ever since the emergence in the mid-1970s of recombinant DNA (rDNA) research as a major element in biotechnology, there has been a strong undercurrent of interest in whether and how the research and resulting technology should be regulated. For a time there was intense activity at the state and municipal levels to impose various forms of regulation. At the same time, Congress was considering proposed legislation that would create a federal regulatory structure. Congressional interest was temporarily diminished when the scientific community presented evidence that the hazards of rDNA research were substantially less than had originally been thought. More recently, however, interest in regulation has revived in reaction to proposed experiments that would release genetically engineered microorganisms into the open environment. It is useful, therefore, to consider the events of the first decade of gene splicing as an example of how social, legal, and political institutions respond to the emergence of an important new technology.

The regulatory history of biotechnology began with a call by a number of the scientists most involved in rDNA research for a moratorium on further experiments in this area, pending an international conference on rDNA research.[1] Such a conference, it was asserted, would consider the possible hazards of the rDNA technology and decide whether the moratorium should be continued, modified, or abandoned. The international conference, held at Asilomar in February 1975, concluded that the moratorium should be continued with respect to certain kinds of experiments, while other experiments might be conducted subject to appropriate levels of physical and biological containment.[2] The fact

165

that the call for the moratorium emanated from the scientists working in the gene-splicing area is in itself a notable model of public influence. Beyond this, the fact that the proceedings at Asilomar were widely reported by several members of the press who were present and witnessed all of the deliberations adds to the significance of this model.

At the time of the Asilomar Conference, almost all rDNA research in the United States was funded by federal agencies, primarily the National Institutes of Health. Shortly after Asilomar, NIH promulgated its Guidelines for Recombinant DNA Research, which essentially implemented the conclusions and recommendations reached at Asilomar.[3]

The point of this is that only ten years ago, the leading scientists in rDNA research and the primary funding source both had genuine concerns that the results of such research could have quite detrimental impacts on life, health, environmental, and ecological values, and the moral fiber of the community.

NIH and its parent organization, the Public Health Service, had a statutory charter primarily to *promote* the public health, with only limited authority to regulate to *protect* the public health. Accordingly, the NIH guidelines have been applicable only to institutions which receive research funding from NIH (although other federal agencies have also made the guidelines applicable to recipients of research funded by them). An institution that performed research in violation of the guidelines would become ineligible for further government funding. Entities that were not recipients of such government research funds were urged to comply voluntarily with the guidelines, and, so far as is known, all have done so.

Promulgation of the guidelines, which was accompanied by an Environmental Impact Statement[4] in compliance with the National Environmental Policy Act, provoked two diametrically opposed reactions. First, a number of scientists and lawyers argued that the guidelines' restrictions violated a constitutional right to scientific freedom—that is, the right to do science—and these arguments found some support from legal scholars.[5] At the other extreme, two states (New York and Maryland) enacted legislation directed towards regulation of rDNA activities, and a number of municipalities (e.g., Cambridge, Massachusetts) considered ordinances that scientists feared would severely restrict rDNA research within the city limits. Indeed, perhaps a dozen municipalities actually enacted regulatory ordinances, although none of these seems to have had a really inhibiting effect.

The Constitutional Issue. The argument that the NIH guidelines unconstitutionally restricted scientific freedom had little substance. To begin with, the guidelines were not regulatory in nature, but merely established conditions for the expenditure of public funds. It is well established constitutionally that the government may spend its money as it chooses and may establish nondiscriminatory conditions for receipt of government funds.[6] Moreover, even if NIH had, as a matter of outright regulation, prohibited certain kinds of experiments (assuming that statutory authority existed), there seems to be no doubt that such regulation would be constitutionally permissible if there were a rational basis for the regulation. The mere fact of the moratorium, the Asilomar Conference, and that conference's conclusions clearly established a rational basis for such regulation. The guidelines in no way interfered with the freedom of scientists to think, to put their ideas on paper (or into computers), and to communicate their ideas freely. All that was prohibited were certain actions, specifically experiments, where there was a rational basis for belief that these actions could be harmful to the public health and safety. Surely the asserted implied constitutional right to scientific freedom could have no greater dignity than the explicit constitutional right to freedom of speech, and constitutional doctrine has long recognized a basic distinction between pure speech, which is constitutionally protected, and action (for example, picketing, demonstrating, and flag burning), which may not be constitutionally protected.

Moreover, there have been many precedents of overt federal regulation of scientific activities far more restrictive of scientific research than the NIH guidelines — the food and drug laws, the Atomic Energy Act, and antivivisection laws, to mention only a few.

State and Local Regulation. The interest of state and municipal governments in regulating rDNA technology was generally stimulated by intense political activity on the part of concerned members of the public. The prospect of such regulation was thoroughly disconcerting to the scientific community, which visualized a "scientific checkerboard" that would make the conduct of rDNA research dependent upon purely geographical considerations. Moreover, no rDNA researcher could be certain that her or his research activities would not be abruptly interfered with by new state or municipal regulations. Researchers argued in favor of federal preemption of the area, so that all rDNA research would be subject only to regulation imposed by the federal government.

Such an argument against state and local regulation cuts across the grain of American federalism, under which protection of the health and safety of the public is essentially a state function unless and until the federal government adopts a regulatory scheme that so comprehensively occupies the field as to leave no latitude for state regulation. Obviously, the scientists who opposed state and local regulation were also opposed to a comprehensive federal regulatory scheme—which they believed was totally unnecessary.

The above considerations are now largely matters of historical significance, although, to be sure, the issue of violation of a constitutional right to scientific freedom has not been completely laid to rest. Two circumstances have contributed to the changed situation.

First, the NIH guidelines have been substantially relaxed in a series of amendments, as a result of a revisionist proposition that has gained general scientific acceptance—that rDNA activities involve far less hazard than was speculated about the mid-1970s. Scientists today have much greater latitude and flexibility than they had under the original guidelines. Accordingly, there has been less cause to complain about restraints on scientific freedom.

Second, since the late 1970s a biotechnology/genetic engineering industry has emerged. Paradoxically, the NIH guidelines have applied on a mandatory basis only to research in the academic area, while the profit-seeking industrial entities have complied with the guidelines only on a voluntary basis.

Not surprisingly, this anomaly has shifted attention from the question of the guidelines' impairment of scientific freedom to the question of how the biotechnology industry should be regulated. If gene splicing indeed involves risk to the health and safety of the public, the risk is presumably more likely to be found in the industrial than in the academic arena. On the other hand, the new forms of academic-industrial consortia that have evolved in the last five years or so leave the academic scientific community with an acute interest in the regulatory fate of the industry.

The New Era of Regulatory Concern.   Many of the products of the biotechnology industry are clearly subject to one or more forms of conventional regulation. For example, food additives, pharmaceuticals, and biologicals are subject to regulation by the Food and Drug Administration (FDA); and other products may be subject to regulation by the Department of Agriculture (USDA). Activities within industrial facilities that may affect employees are subject to regulation by the Occupational Safety and Health Administration. But activities within the facility that may impact on the outside environment and experiments conducted in the open environment have had no clear regulatory locus. There has been a growing belief that rDNA activities, at least those conducted by industry, should be subject to affirmative regulation.

There are at least two reasons why NIH is not the appropriate agency to regulate the industry or, indeed, to regulate academic rDNA research. NIH has never had any regulatory authority and therefore has no regulatory competence or experience. Its principal function has been to promote and support biomedical research. Aside from the question of its regulatory competence, an attempt to vest it with real regulatory responsibility would lead to the same kind of conflicting promotional and regulatory responsibilities that detracted so severely from the regulatory credibility of the Atomic Energy Commission before it was abolished in 1974. Since almost by definition regulation operates to slow development of the regulated activity, it seems clear, particularly after the atomic energy experience, that Congress will not be disposed to place important regulatory responsibilities in the hands of an agency whose primary mission is to accelerate the development of the technologies it is also regulating. (See Chapter 9 of this volume for a critique of the Department of Defense as both sponsor and regulator of chemical weapons research.)

It is useful at this point to recall some wisdom expressed by one of the twentieth century's most important technologists, Adm. Hyman Rickover, father of the nuclear Navy, in 1965. In his Guildhall Lecture before the British Association for the Advancement of Science, entitled "A Humanist Technology,"[7] Rickover called attention to the tendency "to treat every attempt by society to regulate . . . [technology] in the public interest as if it were a modern repetition of the persecution of Galileo." This reminds one of the attack on the NIH guidelines as a suppression of scientific freedom. Rickover went on to discuss what he termed the pattern of opposition to regulation:

I have mentioned efforts to confuse the issue by arguing as if a law of science were at issue when in fact the proposed legislation deals with technology, not science. If this argument fails, the need for the proposed law is then categorically denied. Warnings of scientists are rejected as "unproven" and "exaggerated." Later, when these prove to have been entirely correct, the argument shifts from the substantive question of whether a technology is harmful to an attack on the legitimacy of any kind of protective legislation. Such legislation would violate basic liberties, it is claimed; it would establish government tyranny and subvert free democratic institutions. If all this proves futile and legislation is imminent, there will be urgent demands it be postponed until "more research" can be undertaken to establish the appositness of the proposed law.

Rickover's plea was that no technology be used until "reliable tests . . . have been made to prove it will be useful *and* safe" [emphasis added].

The general trend of federal laws relating to technology has been to require previous clearance to establish efficacy and safety before products may be used. Of course, it is never possible to demonstrate complete safety, and each regulatory agency has its own approach, derived from statutory language, legislative history, and judicial decisions, to the question of how safe is safe enough. We find the concept of safety preclearance in the Food and Drug Act, and more recently in many of the environmental laws enacted in the past fifteen years. Under such laws, a technology or product is deemed unsafe unless and until it has been demonstrated to be safe. For example, food is deemed to be adulterated if it contains a chemical additive that has not been approved by FDA.

On the other hand, in the atomic energy area, we see exactly the opposite approach—a virtual presumption that a piece of technology is safe unless there is evidence that it is harmful. Indeed, this departure from the prevailing regulatory approach may help explain the apparent lack of confidence in the nuclear regulatory structure that has been so prevalent in some sections of the public.

Scientists engaged in rDNA research and technology have a high degree of confidence that their activities do not involve any extraordinary hazards. They firmly believe that to the extent that hazards are present, they are no greater than those found in nature or in other more conventional laboratories, and that they can be minimized by sound research practices and procedures. In other words, they seem to be following the pattern described by Rickover of characterizing the "warnings of scientists as 'unproven' and 'exaggerated'." There are, however, three interrelated social factors that make it difficult for industry and academia alike to argue that regulation is unnecessary.

First, the technology cannot escape the heritage of its past—the moratorium, the Asilomar Conference, and the early NIH guidelines. All of these publicly proclaimed the assumption that rDNA activities involved possible hazards of sufficient dimension to require dramatic forms of intervention. It is hardly surprising, now that rDNA technology—much of it profit-oriented—has emerged, that some segments of the public will have reservations about the revised estimates of risk. Indeed, some scientists who were proponents of the moratorium now seem to believe, in retrospect, that their action served no useful purpose and merely led to undue public concern.

Second, public perceptions may be more important than reality in the political process. These perceptions often are ignited and fueled by politicians in search of issues and by outsiders who wrap themselves in a public-interest mantle. Scientists and technologists have a great tendency to advocate public education programs to rectify inaccurate public perceptions. While no-one can be critical of genuine educational efforts, too often they backfire because they are perceived by the public at whom they are directed as self-serving propaganda. For example, the atomic energy establishment has been notably unsuccessful in its efforts to educate the public as to the benign effects of nuclear power plants.

Third, the industry is inevitably linked by the phrase "genetic engineering" to fundamental and legitimate moral and policy concerns relating to the use of reproductive biology technology and to the potential use of gene splicing techniques to "improve" human beings. These concerns arise out of the changed social function of biology—from understanding and coping with biological life, to the capacity to remake and improve the forms of life. There has been a persistent interest in establishing some kind of permanent oversight commission to monitor developments in these areas of real moral and ethical concern. Although the biotechnology industry is not a direct target of these efforts, its work may increase public apprehension with respect to industrial applications of genetic engineering.

THE ALTERNATIVES FOR REGULATION

At the present time, the biotechnology industry is essentially unregulated and lives very comfortably under voluntary compliance with the NIH guidelines and the essentially benevolent oversight of the Recombinant DNA Advisory Committee (RAC). RAC is constituted with significant representation of lay members of the public, as well as scientists from areas other than gene splicing. Indeed, RAC may be regarded as still another mechanism for fostering public participation.

As noted above, the industry's products may be subject to regulatory review by FDA, EPA, or USDA, but such review impacts only tangen-

tially, if at all, on how the industry conducts its scientific and technological activities. Nevertheless, it seems inevitable that the industry itself, as well as its products, will become subject to positive regulation
of some kind, and it is important to consider four alternative modes
of regulation that might be adopted. In the discussion that follows, it
is assumed that existing agencies such as FDA and USDA will continue
to regulate to the extent that they presently have clear regulatory authority. The question considered here is the optimum locus of regulatory authority over aspects of gene splicing that are unique and therefore presently not subject to regulation.

First, NIH might attempt to stretch the laws under which it presently
operates so as to bring all rDNA activities, academic and industrial
alike, under real, mandatory regulation. This approach seems unlikely
and undesirable for the reasons discussed above, relating to NIH's lack
of regulatory experience and its conflicting responsibilities for regulation and promotion. Granting regulatory responsibility to NIH would
also invoke great uncertainty as to the character of the regulation to
which biotechnology would be subject. Academia would probably find
this new brand of regulation stifling, while industry would be faced with
perplexing questions arising out of a novel regulatory scheme. There
may, therefore, be compelling reasons for leaving academic research under the NIH guidelines and looking elsewhere for regulation of industrial activities. It may, however, be illogical or impractical, to have a
dual set of rules with different requirements applicable depending upon
whether an activity is academic or industrial.

On the other hand, NIH has created a superb technical resource—
RAC—which should not be discarded lightly. It is, I believe, safe to assume that, in one form or another, perhaps even expanded and strength-
ened, RAC will survive to provide the scientific expertise so essential
to sound health and safety decisions, applicable to both academia and
industry, in this area.

A second alternative for regulation of the industry would be to rely
upon some other existing agency with present statutory authority that
could be extended to cover industrial gene splicing technology. The obvious candidate for this regulatory role is the Environmental Protection
Agency (EPA), which believes, although the matter is not free of legal
doubt, that the array of statutes it presently administers, particularly
the Toxic Substances Control Act and the Federal Insecticide, Fungi-
cide, and Rodenticide Act, gives it authority to regulate rDNA activities. Any doubt that does exist about EPA's authority could be neatly

resolved by a simple amendment to EPA's organic legislation. Of course, EPA regulation would not exclude regulation by other agencies such as FDA and USDA with respect to matters within their jurisdiction. From industry's standpoint, one advantage of EPA regulation is that the agency has a track record and established procedures that would provide some degree of certainty as to how the regulatory system would work.

A third alternative would be enactment by Congress of new legislation, analogous to the statutes now being administered by EPA, that would establish criteria and procedures specifically applicable to the industry's activities. Such a statute could be administered by EPA or some other agency. If this route were to be followed, the resulting legislation would be shaped by unpredictable political currents and would have an unpredictable content, with attendant uncertainties as to its implementation. Moreover, the very existence of a new law, specially targeted at the biotechnology industry, would suggest, probably incorrectly, that the industry involves unique hazards.

The fourth alternative is suggested by a not implausible future scenario. There has been legislative concern about scientific gene splicing research directed towards interventions in the treatment of human beings or, more broadly, in evolutionary processes. It has been suggested that a new federal "watchdog" commission be established to monitor developments in this area. Such a commission was contemplated in legislation enacted by the 98th Congress, but the legislation was vetoed by President Reagan for budgetary reasons unrelated to the creation of such a commission.[8] These proposals have usually explicitly or implicitly recognized that perhaps such a commission should also keep its eye on what the biotechnology industry is doing.[9] It is not difficult to visualize scenarios in which such a commission would evolve into a regulatory agency. Such an evolution would inevitably confuse innocuous activities of the industry with issues of human, evolutionary, and ecological impacts which do involve genuine moral, ethical, and policy concerns.

The framework for regulation now emerging was revealed by the Reagan administration in its December 21, 1985, publication for public comment of its proposal for a "coordinated framework for regulation of biotechnology." The proposal, which is essentially consistent with the considerations discussed above, envisions coordinated regulation by FDA, EPA, and the USDA. In general, FDA would regulate food additives, drugs, and other products within its jurisdiction; USDA would

173

regulate plant pests, animal biologicals, and other agricultural products within its jurisdiction; and EPA would regulate pesticides and industrial products. Regulatory review would be conducted in similar ways on a case-by-case basis by all three agencies and each would have its own scientific advisory group. A Biotechnology Science Board would be established by the Department of Health and Human Services to oversee and coordinate the biotechnology activities of the three regulatory agencies, as well as NIH and the National Science Foundation.

APPLICABILITY OF NEPA

The question of federal regulation of the biotechnology industry should be considered in the context of the applicability of the National Environmental Policy Act (NEPA) to NIH decisions under its guidelines. It is clear that NIH actions, particularly relating to release of genetically engineered microorganisms into the environment, may be "major federal actions significantly affecting the quality of the human environment." As a consequence, before such actions may be taken it would be necessary for NIH to comply with NEPA.[10]

NEPA, enacted in 1969, requires that any federal agency, before taking major action that would "significantly affect the quality of human environment," must prepare an environmental impact statement. The environmental impact statement must first be circulated in draft form to elicit the comments of other federal agencies and the interested public, on the basis of which comments the final environmental impact statement is prepared. The environmental impact statement is required to include, among other things, a "detailed statement" of the environmental impact of the proposed action, adverse environmental impacts that cannot be avoided, alternatives to the proposed action, and the relationship between short-term uses of the environment and the maintenance and enhancement of longterm productivity.

When NIH initially promulgated the guidelines, it did so after preparing an environmental impact statement in compliance with NEPA. It is plausible, therefore, that any major changes in the guidelines also require an environmental impact statement, or at least a formal environmental assessment resulting in a so-called "negative declaration" that the proposed action is not a major action that will significantly affect environmental quality. Moreover, it is well established that a federal agency's grant of a license or permit to a private applicant may trigger the applicability of NEPA. Indeed, a significant modification of a preexisting license or permit may require an environmental impact statement.

The requirements of NEPA are sweeping and amorphous. It has spawned literally hundreds of lawsuits brought by members of the general public seeking to block or reverse federal actions on the ground of noncompliance with NEPA. The judicial decisions have generally given an expansive interpretation to the statute.

NEPA is, of course, an important tool for public involvement in federal decision making affecting the environment. Nevertheless, of all the regulatory formats that the genetic engineering industry has to fear, the most fearsome is probably the one in which regulatory actions affecting the industry would be subject to review under NEPA. Such review would not only involve long delays inherent in the time-consuming agency compliance with the procedural hurdles imposed by NEPA, but each of those hurdles would also provide an opportunity for ideologically-motivated members of the public to litigate regulatory decisions that facilitate advance of the technology. The litigation would be based on allegations that the agency had not undertaken the kind of environmental review mandated by NEPA and/or that the product of such a review — the environmental impact statement — was deficient in content and/or candor. The litigation could be endless and enormously expensive. These are precisely the tactics that the opponents of nuclear power have used so effectively and that have contributed so substantially to the present plight of the nuclear industry.

One conspicuous advantage of regulation by EPA is that, since that agency is presumably single-mindedly dedicated to promotion of environmental quality, its own regulatory actions are exempt from the requirements of NEPA.[11] This in itself would warrant industry's embracing the concept of EPA regulation as the optimum alternative.

In discussing the question of regulation of biotechnololgy, it is necessary to keep in mind the two separate communities that are involved, and also the fact that the two communities have become significantly intertwined. The community of academic science can probably live quite comfortably under the NIH guidelines, and there is no reason to assume that the interests of the public would be adversely affected by academic science done in accordance with the guidelines and with customary scientific prudence. However, where science and its resultant technology are directed towards economic profit, experience teaches us that a firmer and more positive regulatory structure is probably needed. Whatever questions may exist in the academic context about the im-

175

pact of regulation on scientific freedom, they surely are not present, or at least not to the same degree, in the context of industrial science and technology.

CONCLUSION

Gene-splicing technology was destined almost from its inception to spawn controversy and debate. When scientists who pioneered in the early research "went public" with their concerns, they set the course for decades to come. Whether or not the technology involves hazards that warrant or necessitate regulation has become almost irrelevant. Because leading scientists called for a moratorium on research and the NIH guidelines imposed restrictions, public perceptions and political forces were created that cannot be undone by development of new scientific knowledge. It is too early to predict how many of the regulatory issues will be resolved. At the moment, the exercise of regulatory authority by the federal government does not seem to threaten the policy power of the states and their subsidiaries. And the ultimate form and substance of federal regulation is more likely to be shaped by unforeseeable occurrences that feed public concerns, and by the perceived needs of politicians, than by scientific objectivity.

NOTES

1. Paul Berg et al., "Potential Hazards of Recombinant DNA Modules," *Science* 185 (26 July 1974): 303.

2. U.S., Department of Health, Education and Welfare, *Provisional Statement of the Conference Proceedings*, DHEW Pub. No. (NIH) 76-1138, p. 59; Paul Berg et al., "Summary Statement of the Asilomar Conference of Recombinant DNA Molecules," Proceedings of the National Academy of Sciences 72 (1976): 1981-84.

3. *Federal Register*, 1976, 41:27911-43.

4. U.S., Department of Health, Education and Welfare, Environmental Impact Statement on *NIH Guidelines for Research Involving Recombinant DNA Molecules*, DHEW Pub. No. (NIH) 1489.

5. Testimony of Thomas I. Emerson, U.S., Congress, House, Committee on Science and Technology, Subcommittee on Science, Research, and Technology, *Hearings*, 95th Cong., 1st sess. (1977), 875-85; John A. Robertson, "The Scientist's Right to Research," 1203f.; Richard Delgado and David Millen, "God, Galileo, and Government,"; DeWitt Stetten, Jr., "Freedom of Inquiry," 416 ff.

6. *United States v. Butler*, 297 U.S. 1 (1936); *Steward Machine Co. v. Davis*, 301 U.S. 619 (1937).

176

7. Unpublished but distributed in typewritten form by the U.S. Atomic Energy Commission.

8. U.S. Cong., S. 240, 98th Cong., 2d sess. (1984); vetoed 30 Oct. 1984.

9. U.S., President's Commission for the Study of Ethical Problems in Medicine and Biomedical and Behavioral Research, *Splicing Life* (1982), 81 ff.

10. *Foundation on Economic Trends, Inc. v. Heckler,* 756 F. 2d 143 (D.C. Cir. 1985).

11. *Federal Register* (1974)39:16186 and 39:37119.

8. State Governance through Conflict of Interest: The California Experience

HELEN LESKOVAC

State governments seldom undertake comprehensive programs to foster or regulate the growth of science and technology. More frequently they encourage industrial growth through assorted measures in areas of public education, taxation, zoning, etc. Following the 1981–82 recession, however, and the permanent layoffs of thousands of workers in traditional industries such as steel and automaking, many state governors began to view high-technology industries as the best solution to their states' economic woes. Governors in several states proposed and put through their legislatures complex legislation to attract high technology companies and foster university-research connections.

Little legislative attention has yet been given to actual and potential problems created by such links, however. One such problem is that of unreasonably high expectations—it seems unlikely that high technology in the short term can create enough jobs to compensate for more than a fraction of the jobs lost to automation and foreign competition. In addition, high technology is losing its image as a "clean" industry, as instances of toxic waste pollution and industrial injury begin to surface in areas of the country where high technology has enjoyed its greatest success, such as California's Silicon Valley. Perhaps most significantly, government sponsorship of university-industry links gives official approval to changes in the conduct of basic research that may have long-term consequences for the research enterprise.

The increasing commercialization of basic research, and along with it the substitution of the process of technology for the traditional ethos of academic science, may be the most disturbing result of the partnership of university and industry favored by many state governments today. Critics of industry-university alliances fear that the traditional mission of the university is undermined when applied research is given priority at the expense of the pursuit of knowledge for its own sake. Already it is reported that behavioral characteristics of commercial enterprise are being internalized within the scientific community, including norms of secrecy, profit making, and short-term goals.[1]

The clash between commercial and academic norms is sometimes viewed as an aspect of "conflict of interest"—a legal term roughly corresponding to the idea that an individual has no business accepting mutually inconsistent obligations and loyalties. Often these conflicts are identified and measured in terms of pecuniary gain. Hence conflict of interest codes frequently mandate disclosure of income and financial interests. Often they require individuals to disgorge their pecuniary gain or abstain from acting in situations where their conflicting interests are involved.

When conflict of interest issues are raised in connection with university-industry research ties, they generally raise questions about less tangible conflicts: Are universities and individual researchers using publicly-funded facilities and personnel for their own institutional and personal gain? Are students receiving proper instruction and training? Are the traditional goals of the university hindered? Can the public rely on university faculty as objective sources of information and advice for formulating a broad range of public policy in areas of medicine, energy, environment, agriculture, and industry?

Because the ties of universities and researchers to commercial entities are seldom disclosed, the issue of potential conflicts of interest may have bearing upon the resolution of these questions. University faculty, however, assert that existing mechanisms are sufficient to handle any conflict of interest problems that arise. Indeed, the resolution of faculty conflicts of interest has traditionally been within the province of self-regulation. One state, however, has taken the unprecedented step of requiring some university researchers to report and to disclose publicly their ties to commercial entities.

In 1982, in response to a petition from public interest groups, California amended its state conflict of interest regulations to include certain university faculty. Researchers at the University of California now must disclose publicly their significant financial interests in the private sponsors of their research at the time they apply for university approval

179

or renewal of research projects. Similar disclosure could be achieved in other states if courts construe university records of faculty financial holdings to be, public records as has been done in Wisconsin.[2]

This chapter reviews the roles played by state governments, universities, citizen groups, and existing legal doctrines in attempting to regulate potential conflicts of interest engendered by state-supported university-industry connections. It focuses on California, whose highly publicized success in attracting and strengthening high technology provides a paradigm of the issues and problems associated with that approach to economic growth. The first section highlights the problems that may accompany state encouragement of high-technology industry. The second section surveys the effects of commercialization of scientific research in academia. The third section describes the experience of California in regulating conflicts of interest in university research. The fourth section analyzes the applicability of rights of privacy and academic freedom to university conflicts of interest. The fifth section briefly analyzes some models available for regulation of faculty conflicts of interest, concluding that existing mechanisms do not adequately apprehend and address the problem.

STATE ENCOURAGEMENT OF HIGH TECHNOLOGY

As an industry, high technology includes computer electronics and software, communications equipment, computer-aided design and manufacturing robotics, fiber optics, optical instruments, vapor phase technology, medical instruments, and biotechnology.[3] The greatest concentration of this industry has been in areas of the country that feature a combination of university research centers and industrial parks. The prototype is California's "Silicon Valley" in the Santa Clara Valley south of San Francisco. Two other widely publicized centers are Route 128 outside Boston, Massachusetts, and North Carolina's Research Triangle Park.[4] Each center has benefited from the close association of university researchers and industry scientists, with incidental benefits to area economy.

State governments across the nation have sought to emulate the economic success of these centers. Many states, including Michigan, Oregon, Virginia, New Jersey, New York, Indiana, and New Mexico, have passed legislation to attract high-technology companies and to create university-industry centers that will foster technological innovation.[5] The steps taken by these states are similar to those taken in Michigan in 1982 by

Gov. William Milliken, who established a program of regulatory reform, business tax relief, reduction of workers' compensation and unemployment insurance, and financial assistance plans for new and existing industries.[6]

Michigan's efforts to revive its failing industries with investments in high technology and related research are typical of regional promotions across the nation. But forecasts of economic analysts do not necessarily support these optimistic ventures into state industrial planning. High technology, while the fastest-growing industry in terms of job creation, nonetheless represents a very small sector of the economy. The high-technology industry employs only 2.5 to 6 million people, compared to the 19 million in manufacturing, of a total workforce of 102.7 million.[7] *Business Week* in 1983 estimated that "the number of hi-tech jobs created over the next decade will be less than half of the two million jobs lost in manufacturing" in the preceding three years.[8] And Labor Department figures indicate that "high tech will provide less than 10 percent of the 25 million new jobs needed by 1995 to reduce unemployment to 6 percent."[9]

Even in California the golden future predicted for hi-tech industry does not always pan out. In the personal computer and software industry, sales in 1985 slowed from a predicted 50 percent annual growth rate to 28 percent,[10] and many companies were struggling to keep afloat; several filed for bankruptcy. Others laid off workers and moved operations to the Far East and Latin America to reduce costs.[11]

Biotech companies experienced similar reverses. In late 1984, Biogen, a multinational front-runner in the gene splicing industry, announced that it had cut 13 percent of its staff, evenly distributed between its United States operations in Cambridge, Massachusetts, and its European ones in Geneva, Switzerland. This action followed a reported loss of about $11 million in a nine-month period, about 16 percent of the company's total assests.[12] Other smaller biotech ventures have gone out of business or experienced slower growth than expected.

While high-technology industries are experiencing unanticipated reverses, hidden costs have surfaced in occupational injury and toxic pollution. For example, Dr. Joseph LaDou of the University of California, San Francisco, reports that the semi-conductor industry "provides a complete spectrum of occupational hazards . . .including exposures to chemicals, gases (and) metals."[13] Additionally, serious toxic-waste-disposal problems have been detected in Silicon Valley, and state cleanup costs are yet to be calculated.[14]

181

The aftermath of the technological revolution is already beginning to reveal a high toll in human and economic costs. Moreover, state and federal encouragement of industry-oriented education and research programs at universities may have pervasive effects on the research enterprise itself for years to come. While university and industry links are proliferating, many critics in both academia and the public have warned that commercialization is turning science into the servant of the industry. They fear this inexorably may alter universities' commitment to basic research and academic freedom and point to the example of biology, an academic field that has been transformed in just a few years by entrepreneurial alliances. Academic research biologists, who once disdained commercial involvement, now implicitly accept it. And most top-flight biologists today are in some way affiliated with one or more commercial entities in an area related to their university research.[15]

COMMERCIALIZATION OF SCIENTIFIC RESEARCH

Despite serious concerns about the impact of university-industry links of academic values, many of the nation's most prestigious universities have not hesitated to join in a variety of research affiliations with industry.[16] At the same time, individual university professors have been making private arrangements with companies interested in their research, resulting in a new role: the professor-entrepreneur.[17] Some professors have formed their own companies; a number have achieved spectacular success. The University of California, San Francisco's Professor Herbert Boyer, for example, founded Genentech, a bioengineering company whose stock, when first offered in 1980, soared from $35 to $84 in one day.[18] Nobel Prize winner Walter Gilbert, formerly professor of microbiology at Harvard, became chief executive officer of the international biotechnology firm, Biogen S.A. When Biogen went public in 1983, the entire $57.5 million offering was sold out within hours.[19]

Many universities admit that, as a result of commercial pressures, they are deviating from their own rules that promote free dissemination of knowledge, arguing that otherwise they cannot keep up with state of the art technology.[20] It is difficult to gauge the degree of secrecy involved, since many university-industry research agreements themselves are kept secret. The Hoechst agreement with Massachusetts General Hospital to fund an entire microbiology department, for example, was not disclosed until Albert Gore threatened to subpoena it during congressional investigations in 1981.[21] IBM's contract with Carnegie-Mellon University for computer software and communications networks research, estimated at $20 million, is secret, as is a similar $15 million agreement with Brown University. At Carnegie-Mellon, Douglas E. Van Nouweling, vice provost, acknowledged, "We have made a basic compromise. In return for being able to use advanced technology, we have created barriers on the interchange of information. I would not deny for a minute that this is a very uncomfortable place for a university to be."[22]

Trade Secrets. In order to accept the tens of millions of dollars companies are spending on campus research, universities like Carnegie-Mellon and Brown are agreeing to protect corporations' trade secrets and product plans.[23] Trade secrets are of potentially unlimited duration and are generally protected by state law. Thus a court can enjoin disclosure of the information (that is, order no disclosure on penalty of contempt of court), effectively preventing open dissemination of information. Trade secrets appear to be preferred to patents in some fields (biotechnology, for example), because patentable work may become outdated before the patent is issued, a process that may take up to two years.[24] Universities have in the past relied heavily on patent agreements to protect their investment in various inventions, while permitting publication of results and, after seventeen years, public use of the invention.[25]

Secrecy Among Colleagues. As a result of commercial pressures, many researchers no longer freely exchange materials and ideas.[26] Eric Holtzman, chair of the department of biological sciences at Columbia University, warns, "Unless we find ways of tempering the hectic, get-for-yourself-what-you-can atmosphere that is now flourishing, it will prove difficult to preserve the broadly cooperative structures that have sustained our individual efforts and to protect fragile practices such as open communication and peer review."[27]

An example is the dispute between Russell Doolittle of the University of California, San Diego, and Richard Lerner of the nearby Scripps Clinic and Research Foundation regarding a new method for making synthetic vaccines. According to Doolittle, he had mentioned the method to Lerner, who had come to seek advice on an unrelated problem. Subsequently Lerner published an article about the method but failed to acknowledge the conversation with Doolittle. Although Doolittle was outraged at this breach of academic courtesy, he did nothing until he learned that Scripps was seeking to patent the method and join in a

183

venture with Johnson & Johnson to produce synthetic vaccines. Doolittle decided that under the circumstances, the University of California should also seek a patent, although he believed the method should ideally not be patented at all. He wrote to the university board of patents, "Now we are locking our doors. The threat to scholarship is serious indeed."[28] Similarly, in 1981, after University of California, San Francisco's Herbert Boyer formed Genentech, a UCSF committee investigated the effects on university researchers. It found that "people were loathe to ask questions and give suggestions in seminars or across the bench, for there was a feeling that someone might take an idea and patent it, or that an individual's idea might be taken to make money for someone else."[29]

Secrecy in Publication.   Researchers interested in profiting from their university-based research may also withhold details in the publication of experiments, making their work essentially irreplicable.[30] Others may withhold publication in order to establish products in the market ahead of potential competitors. Commercial ties were decried as a source of bias by the editors of the *New England Journal of Medicine*, who reported that the problem was "rampant." In the May 1984 issue, they requested prospective authors to disclose all relevant ties with businesses related to their research. In explaining this step, the journal invoked classic conflict-of-interest principles:

> One does not have to assume that researchers are venal to appreciate that they may be affected (consciously or unconsciously) by economic incentives, which can influence the way they design or conduct their studies, how they interpret the results, or how and when they choose to report them.[31]

Conflict of Interest.   Conflict of interest, including problems generated by the mere appearance of conflict of interest, is a critical problem in university-industry relations today. First, it tends to decrease public confidence in the integrity of university research and researchers. Second, it undermines the academic principle of pursuit of knowledge for the common good. Third, it is difficult to identify and remedy. Society values academic freedom highly, and governments are reluctant to intervene too openly or harshly. Thus when California's Fair Political Practices Commission (FPPC) amended state conflict-of-interest disclosure regulations to include public university researchers, it very restrainedly targeted less than 10 percent of the research conducted at the University of California (UC).

CALIFORNIA'S REGULATION OF CONFLICTS OF INTEREST

The California Political Reform Act of 1974 established the FPPC to monitor the implementation of conflict-of-interest regulations applicable to public officials.[32] According to the act, a conflict of interest exists when (1) a public official makes, participates in making, or uses his or her official position to influence a governmental decision that (2) will foreseeably affect his or her financial interest, (3) resulting in a material effect on the official's financial interest, (4) distinguishable from its effect on the public generally.[33] The act requires every state agency, including UC, to formulate a conflict-of-interest code that directs "designated employees" to disclose relevant income and assets.[34] The university implemented a code that designated faculty members with administrative positions as public officials subject to the act. Most professors and researchers were exempted from these requirements because research decisions were not at first viewed as "governmental decisions."[35] Concerned citizens and faculty criticized the omission, pointing out that research decisions affect large sums of public money, public facilities, public employees, and students.

Conflicts of Interest at the University of California. In California, external support of research at UC historically has stirred considerable internal debate and public criticism. In the 1960s, students and public interest groups protested the conduct of defense and war research on campus, the dominance of business leaders on the boards of trustees and regents, and the education of students to meet the needs of the corporate system.[36] In the 1970s, the public interest groups invoked the university's land-grant heritage to challenge agricultural research carried out at a number of campuses. In a suit against the university and its regents, California Agrarian Action Project (CAAP) asserted that commercial mechanization research benefits agribusiness at the expense of small farmers and farm laborers, in contravention of university land-grant obligations to improve the quality of rural life.[37]

In the late 1970s, UC faculty confronted the potential problem of faculty conflicts of interest. In 1977, UC, Berkeley's Academic Senate appointed a committee to investigate the effects of faculty consulting activities on faculty members' duties and the potential conflicts of interest arising from those activities. The committee concluded that there was no need for reform of the university's consulting policies. A strongly-worded minority report protested, however, that existing regulations

185

did not adequately address the serious potential for conflicts of interest. It proposed mandatory public disclosure of faculty consulting as the surest preventive measure. The proposal was defeated, however, on the grounds that disclosure would violate researchers' financial privacy and academic freedom.[38]

Commercialization of university-based research in the biosciences revived internal debate a few years later. In 1980, under President David Saxon, the systemwide UC administration convened two committees to investigate aspects of university-industry relations and intellectual property. The report from the University-Industry Relations Project described existing university collaboration with industry. It recommended university facilitation of such links as well as of state and federal support. The report concluded that current policies dealing with consulting and conflict of interest adequately safeguarded against untoward effects of university-industry affiliations.[39]

Those policies were tested soon in a number of well-publicized incidents. In 1981, for example, the UC, Davis administration discovered and dealt with a potential conflict of interest when Professor Ray Valentine secured a $2.5 million multi-project research grant from Allied Chemical Co. to investigate nitrogen fixation in plants. Two days after the grant was awarded, Allied Chemical purchased 20 percent of the stock in Valentine's off-campus firm, Calgene. The ensuing furor led the dean of the College of Agricultural and Environmental Sciences to offer Valentine a choice of three courses of action: end his affiliation with Calgene, resign his position, or remove himself from the Allied Chemical–sponsored project. Valentine chose to withdraw from the project, with the result that the university lost $1 million in grant funds because there was no-one else in the department to undertake the research.[40]

In the meantime, both faculty and public interest groups continued to criticize UC's regulation of industry ties as inadequate to detect all but the most egregious examples of conflict of interest. On some campuses, concerned faculty sponsored public lectures. Leon Wofsy, professor of immunology (see Chapter 5), spoke on the topic, "Biology and the University on the Marketplace: What's for Sale?", at UC, Berkeley, on March 16, 1982. At UC, Davis, Paul Baumann, professor of bacteriology, organized a series of eight lectures in spring 1982, with speakers from academia, industry, and public interest groups.

Meanwhile, in their investigations for CAAP's agricultural mechanization suit, attorneys discovered what they believed to be actual and potential conflicts of interest in the relationships of UC researchers and the private sponsors of their research.[41] The state auditor general reported additional cases of conflicts of interest in relationships to UC researchers and industry.[42] As a result, California Rural Legal Assistance (CRLA) and CAAP petitioned the FPPC to apply state conflict of interest regulations to UC researchers.[43]

1982 Amendment of California's Conflict of Interest Regulations. After public hearings in 1982, the FPPC amended Section 18705 of the California Administrative Code to require faculty at state-supported colleges and universities to disclose their financial interests in the private sponsors of their research at the time they apply for project approval or renewal.[44] As amended, the state disclosure requirements affect less than 10 percent of the funds supporting scientific research at UC.[45] Researchers with financial interests in government-supported research, for example, are not affected. The regulations require disclosure only when a researcher has an "investment interest in, holds a position with, or has received income from" a private source that supports her or his university-based research. When such an interest is disclosed, the administrative code directs a university committee to undertake a substantive review.[46]

Under the new regulations, each campus forms its own review committee to evaluate research applications for potential conflicts. When the committee completes its review, it then submits a recommendation to the campus chancellor, who may accept the project as proposed, reject it, or modify it. Reports of the committee's deliberations and the chancellor's decisions are then filed with the university administration and the FPPC. The FPPC scrutinizes the disclosure and review reports to insure that all campuses are uniformly administering the law.[47]

Faculty Response to Regulation. Disclosure requirements have met with a mixed response from the faculty. At UCLA the conflict of interest committee was at first reluctant to comply with the state regulations, asserting that disclosure of their deliberations would violate the privacy and academic freedom of faculty. After consultation with the systemwide administration and the FPPC, however, the committee agreed to document their decision making and file the required reports.[48] Following this skirmish, all campuses are currently in compliance with state regulations.

The incidence of potential conflicts of interest tallied by the FPPC

187

is about 5 percent and rising slowly.[49] Many of these potential conflicts are relatively minor, involving only a researcher's expenditure of relatively small sums of her or his own money on a research project or situations in which a researcher holds a position on the board of a not-for-profit foundation such as the American Cancer Society. Others are more serious, stemming from substantial consulting income, board directorships in for-profit organizations, stock, stock options, and other equities. In these situations, the California regulation empowers the reviewing committee to balance the potential contribution of the research project to university goals against the detriment to the university posed by the conflict of interest. Thus the committee may choose to allow a researcher to continue as principal investigator despite a conflict of interest.[50]

MODELS FOR REGULATION OF CONFLICTS OF INTEREST

Internal regulation remains the primary model for regulating conflicts of interest in university-industry connections. However, this model may not be sufficient to cope with the pressures of commercialization and public demands for accountability. Because of changing conditions, ethical values and norms are not necessarily shared or adhered to within the present-day scientific community. Even when the universities prepare conflict-of-interest guidelines and set up faculty review committees, there may be little effective deterrence of conflicts of interest. Universities have limited powers to impose and enforce ethical constraints. They cannot, for example, without significant extensions of their authority, bar faculty members from taking corporate positions or making investments on their own time. Additionally, since most faculty members in certain fields are affiliated in varying degrees with private enterprise, committees they sit on may lose their claim to objectivity and freedom from bias.

The California Model. Independent regulatory agencies such as California's FPPC are presumably more disinterested than faculty committees and more likely to assure uniform implementation of conflict-of-interest regulations in university settings. In the few states that have ethics-in-government acts, such agencies have legislative authority to extend conflict-of-interest regulations to include university researchers. Such regulation serves to restate ethical norms and social values that may be lost sight of in times of flux. Additionally, by exposing to public scrutiny the financial ties of researchers to business entities, state regulation may tend to discourage actual conflicts of interest. It undoubtedly provides a means of assessing the incidence of certain categories of conflicts of interests. However, the expansion of existing legal concepts to apply state conflict-of-interest regulation to faculty-industry ties does not fully resolve the problem.

Conflict-of-interest regulation is appropriate whenever a public official's private interests appear to clash with the proper administration of her or his public responsibilities. Private interest is commonly interpreted as economic gain, hence the requirement of financial disclosure. Many of the harms associated with conflicts of interest in university-industry links, however, are not necessarily measurable in economic terms. For example, faculty with ties in industry risk damaging the credibility of university-based researchers as a source of objective information and counsel. The public may conclude that a professor's ties to a private corporation could slant the direction of the research toward the needs of the outside company. Students may be concerned that the professor is not available for counseling and assistance; graduate students may consider that the emphasis on projects benefiting private interests hampers their opportunity to attain knowledge and expertise in their chosen field. And certainly colleagues may question whether the professor's loyalty to outside interests is conducive to the collegial atmosphere of the university that fosters the advancement and dissemination of knowledge.

It is unlikely that these concerns can be addressed by state conflict-of-interest regulation. In addition, it is clearly university faculty and students who can best identify and gauge the effects of conflicts of interest within academia. From this vantage point, the historic model of internal faculty regulation is most appealing. Not all university faculty will necessarily adopt internal regulation, however. The UC, Berkeley faculty, for example, dismissed the potential for conflicts of interest in university-industry ties and did not undertake to broaden existing university regulations. Imposition of external regulation by the FPPC, negligible as it may be, followed.

The University of Wisconsin Model.   The University of Wisconsin took the problem of conflicts of interest more seriously. The university itself proposed modifications of state rules relating to the code of ethics for unclassified staff (faculty, graduate academic staff, and limited ap-

189

pointees) in the UW system.[51] The proposed order pending before the state legislature recommends filing of yearly reports of time spent on projects with the potential for conflict of interest. It also provides protection for students performing research at the university: principal investigators of research projects must reveal their financial interests in the research to their students. And any person may file a written complaint about suspected conflicts of interest with the president of the UW system or with campus chancellors. Furthermore, since the proposed order must be approved by the state legislature, there is opportunity for public comment as well.

This combination of internal and external regulation appears to include the best features of both internal regulation and state regulation. Universities and the public will be following the progress of UW's proposed order through the political process. Whether or not such a model is acceptable in other states, however, will depend upon the individual state constitutional status of their public universities and the provisions for their governance.

A Federal Model.   A possible third and distinct alternative is that of indirect federal regulation. The federal government provides the bulk of research support at all universities, public and private, channeling funds through NIH and NSF primarily.[52] Universities that receive federal grants already follow government-mandated administrative and accounting procedures, which include filing detailed reports from research investigators on a regular basis. It would add little to the administrative burden if the federal government were to require the attachment of a financial disclosure report, similar to that used by the FPPC in California, to applications for funding and renewal of research projects. This broadened application of California's transactional procedure would result in financial disclosure by most university researchers. Yet it would intrude minimally into the personal finances of faculty if it were limited to disclosure of equity interests in, and financial income from, entities that benefit from the faculty member's research.

A nonprofit public interest group, the Natural Resources Defense Council, Inc., has recommended federal legislation requiring universities to adopt codes of ethics that include financial disclosure as a condition of receiving federal funds.[53] Such legislation would leave university faculties free to regulate themselves as to the nonpecuniary but nonetheless critical aspects of conflict of interest. This approach would give universities some leeway in accommodating to local conditions and at the same time assure fairly uniform regulation of conflicts of interest in both public and private universities. It could safeguard the public's interest in the funding of university research without unduly infringing on either the financial privacy or the academic freedom of university faculty.

State regulation of potential conflicts of interest in the relations of university researchers and industry appears to run counter to the trend of state and federal legislation that fosters rapid transfer of scientific knowledge to the commercial sphere. In a time of heightened concern for economic growth, regulation of conflicts of interest in university research may be viewed as somewhat aberrant. On the other hand, regulation may encourage a thoughtful analysis in the public interest of the social and environmental consequences of the technical application of knowledge. And regulation may act as a conservative influence to preserve the notion that pursuit of knowledge is an intrinsically valuable human endeavor. In this sense, conflict of interest legislation supports the proposition that research universities are institutions entrusted with the confidence and support of the public for the primary purpose of advancing and disseminating new knowledge for the benefit of all.

NOTES

1. Nicholas Wade, "Background Paper," in *The Science Business: Report of the Twentieth Century Fund Task Force on the Commercialization of Scientific Research* (New York: Priority Press, 1984), 27.

2. *Capital Times v. Bock* (1983).

3. Monroe W. Karmin with Linda K. Lanier, Ron Scherer, Jack A. Seamonds, and Michael Bosc, "High Tech: Blessing or Curse?," *U.S. News & World Report*, 16 Jan. 1984, pp. 38–44.

4. Anne Bagamery, "No Policy Is Good Policy," *Forbes*, 18 June 1984, pp. 140–45.

5. Katherine Bouton, "Academic Research and Big Business: A Delicate Balance," *New York Times Magazine*, 11 Sept. 1983, p. 63.

6. Roger Kerson, "Will Pac-Man Eat Your Job?," *Michigan Voice*, July 1983, p. 22.

7. Karmin et al., "High Tech," 38.

8. "America Rushes to Hi Tech for Growth . . . But Not Enough Jobs Are There," *Business Week*, 28 Mar. 1983, p. 84.

9. Karmin et al., "High Tech," 38.

10. Kerson, "Pac-Man," 22.

11. Joanne Davidson, "Gloom in the Valley . . . But a Silver Lining Too," *U.S. News & World Report*, 20 Aug. 1984, p. 38.

12. Jeffrey L. Fox, "Biogen Cuts 13 Percent Including Scientists," *Science*, 7 Dec. 1984, 1175.

13. Joseph LaDou, "The Not-So-Clean Business of Making Chips," *Technology Review* 87 (May/June 1984): 9.

14. Ibid.

15. Bouton, "Academic Research and Big Business," 63.

16. David E. Sanger, "Business Rents a Lab Coat and Academia Hopes for the Best," *Time*, 28 Sept., 1981, p. 63.

17. Barbara J. Culliton, "Biomedical Research Enters the Marketplace," 1195.

18. Bouton, "Academic Research and Big Business," 63.

19. Ibid.

20. David E. Sanger, "Computer Work Bends College Secrecy Rules," *New York Times*, 16 Oct. 1984.

21. U.S., Congress, House, Committee on Science and Technology, Subcommittee on Investigations and Oversight and Subcommittee on Science, Research, and Technology, *Hearings on the Commercialization of Academic Research,* 90.

22. Sanger, "Computer Work."

23. Ibid.

24. Reid G. Adler, "Biotechnology as an Intellectual Property," *Science* 224 (27 Apr. 1984): 357.

25. Jeffrey L. Fox, "Patents Encroaching on Research Freedom," *Science* 224 (8 June 1984): 1080.

26. Nicholas Wade, "Background Paper," 27.

27. Eric Holtzman, "Competition and the Marketplace: The Need for Balance," *BioScience* 34 (June 1984): 349.

28. Wade, "Background Paper," 36–37.

29. Ibid.

30. Ibid.

31. Arnold Relman, "Dealing with Conflicts of Interest," *New England Journal of Medicine* 310 (3 May 1984): 1182.

32. Cal. Gov't code Sec. 83111 (West 1976).

33. Cal. Admin. Code tit. 2, R.R. 18700–03 (1984).

34. Cal. Gov't Code Secs. 81000–91014 (West 1976).

35. Cal. Admin. Code tit. 2, R. 18705 (filed 24 Jan. 1978).

36. Verne A. Stadtman, *The University of California, 1868–1968* (New York: McGraw-Hill, 1970), 425–29.

37. California Agrarian Action Project v. Regents of U.C., No. 5,164,225 (Super Ct. Alameda County, filed 16 Jan. 1979).

38. Memorandum, UC Berkeley Senate, 1978.

39. University of California, *Report of the University-Industry Relations Project*, 1982, p. 1–5.

40. Allen G. Marr, dean of the graduate division, interview with author, Davis, Calif., 28 July 1983.

41. Albert Meyerhoff, Ralph Abascal, Timothy McCarthy, Robert Hawk, and Paul Barnett, "Potential Conflicts of Interest Among University of California Academic Personnel: A Comment to the Fair Political Practices Commission," August 1981. (Copy on file, Fair Political Practices Commission, Sacramento, Calif.)

42. California Auditor General, *Report to the California Legislature,* 715.9, 1978.

43. Cal. Gov't Code Sec. 81000 (West 1976).

44. Cal. Admin. Code tit. 2, R. 18705 (filed 4 June 1982).

45. University of California, *Report of the University-Industry Relations Project*, 1982.

46. Cal. Admin. Code tit. 2, R. 18705(b) (amendment filed 4 June 1982).

47. Robert Leidigh, staff attorney, FPPC, interview with author, Sacramento, 22 June 1983.

48. "UCLA Conflict Rules Will Be Investigated: Panel Orders Full Probe After Disclosure that Data on 23 Professors Was Withheld," *Los Angeles Times*, 3 Aug. 1983.

49. Robert Leidigh, interview with author, Sacramento, 27 June 1983.

50. Robert Leidigh, telephone conversations with author, 9 Mar. 1984 and 26 Mar. 1985.

51. Proposed Order of the Board of Regents of the University of Wisconsin System Adopting, Amending, and Repealing Rules, submitted to the Wisconsin Legislative Council, Oct. 31, 1983.

52. National Science Foundation, *University-Industry Research Relationships: Myths, Realities, and Potentials* (Washington, D.C.: Government Printing Office, 1982).

53. U.S., Congress, House, Committee on Science and Technology, Subcommittee on Investigations and Oversight, *Hearings on University/Industry Cooperation in Biotechnology.*

193

9. Local Control of Research Involving Chemical Warfare Agents

SHELDON KRIMSKY

The U.S. Department of Defense (DOD) continues to support an active chemical warfare research and development program. DOD funds research in new chemical weapons and their deployment systems,[1] methods for protecting soldiers exposed to conventional chemical warfare agents, and procedures for detoxifying stockpiles of chemical agents when they are no longer needed.[2] To accomplish its R&D objectives, DOD transports quantities of chemical nerve and blister agents to contractees at research facilities in different parts of the country.

In Cambridge, Massachusetts, a highly-regarded consulting firm, Arthur D. Little (ADL), spent over $800,000 to construct a laboratory designed to meet DOD safety requirements for handling chemical nerve and blister agents. Several months after the Cambridge City Council became aware of the type of tests taking place at the facility, the local public health commissioner ordered the firm to cease storing and testing the chemical warfare agents in the city. Subsequently, a committee of scientists and citizens was convened to assess the public health risks of research with highly toxic chemical agents and to advise the city on managing the risks. ADL contested the city's authority to interfere with its DOD contract.

This chapter examines the origins of the controversy, the risk assessment review process, and the constitutional issues underlying the litigation of this case. The central conflicts involve local accountability for potentially hazardous defense contracts, and the preemptive authority of the national government on health and safety issues pertaining to federally-sponsored research.

Like the genetics debate that erupted nine years ago in Cambridge, the controversy over research with chemical warfare agents raises questions about the role of cities and towns in regulating, restricting, or proscribing scientific research and technological development. Comparisons and contrasts between the genetics and chemical weapons debates are also discussed in the chapter.

THE GENESIS OF CONCERN

In 1982, ADL began planning for the renovation of an existing laboratory to conform to DOD specifications for work with "chemical surety materials," a euphemism for chemical warfare agents. ADL invested over three-quarters of a million dollars in establishing the Philip L. Levins Laboratory to meet state-of-the-art requirements for handling supertoxins. In January 1983, the firm notified Cambridge city officials of the plans for a new laboratory designed for research on highly toxic materials. The city manager, police chief, and fire chief were given a briefing about the new testing facility when ADL applied for a building permit. It is unclear how much these individuals knew, at that time, about what was going to be tested in the laboratory. Beyond the minimal disclosure ADL made to selected municipal officials, the full nature and purpose of the facility were not communicated to members of the Cambridge City Council or the public prior to or during the construction of the laboratory.

Between late September and early October 1983, ADL notified selected officials in the neighboring towns of Arlington and Belmont that its new chemical testing facility was completed. A few town officials toured the laboratory and were asked to keep its use confidential. After the tour, Arlington's town manager informed ADL that he could not in good conscience withhold information about the lab's new capabilities from town residents. He planned to raise the issue of the laboratory at the next meeting of his town's selectmen. On that same day, ADL issued a news release announcing the opening of a high-security laboratory for the testing and analysis of toxic materials. The news release was skillfully written and avoided any mention that the facility would be handling chemical warfare agents or that the research undertaken there would be defense-related.

A few days later, on October 17, ADL officials met with the Arlington Board of Selectmen at a public hearing, "but revealed only limited information about the lab and its operations."[3] According to a story in the *Arlington Advocate*, "Their [ADL's] answers did not seem to fully satisfy board members who voted unanimously to contact the state Commissioner of Public Health and the city council of Cambridge. . . ."[4]

On October 20, the *Arlington Advocate* carried a front-page banner headline: "A.D. Little Toxic Chemical Testing Surprises Town." On that same day a story also appeared in the *Boston Globe*. At first, citing the classified nature of its research, ADL declined to discuss specific activities carried out at the facility. The *Boston Globe* report speculated that "it might involve research on means to detoxify old stocks of nerve gas for the army."[5]

Concerned about what they had read in the newspapers, neighborhood residents aroused members of the Cambridge City Council, who called a public hearing on October 24 to air the issues. ADL's DOD-funded research on chemical warfare agents was already under way in early October.

Spokespersons for ADL who attended the public meeting tried to assure the council that its facility had been designed with the most advanced safeguards for handling chemical toxins. But the council wanted more assurance than the company could offer. It passed an order creating a scientific advisory committee, the purpose of which was to advise the city council and the commissioner of health and hospitals on issues of public health and safety related to the environmental hazards of ADL's research with chemical warfare agents. The Scientific Advisory Committee (SAC), formally established in fall 1983, was not in operation until the following spring. The city fathers fashioned SAC after the Cambridge Experimentation Review Board (CERB), a committee of local citizenry that had helped resolve the controversy over genetics research that had erupted in 1976.[6]

At this stage, community involvement was minimal, limited to a few articulate and persistent spokespersons who followed the issue from its inception through the deliberation process. Mass community organizing did not come until months later.

Between fall 1983 and winter 1984, individual city councillors introduced orders requesting a moratorium on testing of nerve and blister agents until SAC was appointed and completed its evaluation of the risks. Orders voted on by the city council are effective only if acted upon by the city manager. In February 1984, Councillor Alfred Vellucci, who had spearheaded the city's oversight of gene-splicing research and transformed the recombinant DNA controversy into a populist issue, called for a ninety-day moratorium on the testing of chemical warfare

196

agents. The purpose of the moratorium was to give the city time to study the issue. A month later, on March 13, the city's chief public health official, Commissioner of Health and Hospitals Dr. Melvin Chalfen, issued an emergency regulation that prohibited "testing, storage, transportation and disposal of five specified nerve and blister agents within Cambridge, until the SAC and an independent hazard assessment has been completed and these recommendations have been reviewed by the Health Commissioner's office."[7]

On March 16, ADL filed suit against the City of Cambridge, requesting that the commissioner's order be enjoined. The court offered relief to the plaintiff by issuing a temporary restraining order that remained in effect through summer 1984, enabling ADL to continue its testing of the chemical warfare agents.

Meanwhile, the city developed a two-part strategy in response to the litigation. It decided to convene SAC and await the committee's evaluation of the research before pressing on with the legal case. The city solicitor needed that independent evaluation to demonstrate to the court that the emergency order was not arbitrary and capricious. Second, the commissioner of health contracted with an independent scientist to undertake a risk assessment. The scientist, representing the firm TRC Environmental Consultants, Inc., of Hartford, Connecticut, was asked to evaluate the public health risks of five chemical warfare agents being tested at ADL. On recommendations from the city council, in March the city manager appointed members to SAC, with the commissioned risk assessment study already underway. SAC held its first meeting on April 12, 1984. Frequent exchanges took place between the outside consultant and SAC up until the commissioned risk assessment was completed.

In late April, the city petitioned the court to remove the temporary restraining order, introducing the preliminary results of the TRC report as new evidence. However, the TRC risk assessment did not provide sufficient grounds for the court to overturn the order. The concluding paragraph in the affidavit filed by the risk assessment consultant on behalf of the city illustrates the consultant's lack of conviction concerning a research ban.

> In summary, accidental or intentional release of nerve gas to the environment is very unlikely but not impossible. If the amount of concentrated nerve gas maintained at Arthur D. Little is less than 100 milliliters, and the experiments do not change to involve intentional aerosol generation or large quantities of explosives, there is little chance of fatalities at a dis-

197

tance of the nearest residences even in the event of a release. There is a chance of fatalities, but not a large number, at a distance of Route 2 if more than 10 milliliters of nerve agent is released. Fatalities might involve the curious drawn to the accident. The absence of an emergency plan for the community in terms of cordoning off areas, halting traffic, or obtaining decontamination aid increases community risk. An emergency plan would need to be kept up to date particularly if experiments at Arthur D. Little changed to involve greater quantities of more toxic materials.[8]

On May 2, the court again ruled in favor of ADL and extended the temporary restraining order. Ironically, ADL's early legal defense was built on the summary of the TRC report. In its brief, ADL argued that the independent risk assessment supported the firm's contention that prohibition of its research was unwarranted. A trial date, initially set for early June, was postponed to the fall. The postponement gave the city time to hear from the Scientific Advisory Committee before continuing its litigation.

A CITIZEN-SCIENCE COMMISSION

The troubled city council, having reacted on the basis of intuitive and popular concerns over the hazards of chemical nerve and blister agents, failed to stop the research by order of the chief health officer. Since the consultant's affidavit did not overturn the restraining order, considerable attention was directed to the work of SAC.

While the order for establishing SAC came from the city council, its size and membership were determined by the city manager. Initially, the committee contained seventeen members. After several meetings one member, unable to meet the time commitments of the committee's schedule, resigned. Table 9.1 shows the membership of the committee by occupation, institutional affiliation, and residence when it was stabilized at sixteen.

Upon receiving its charge from the city manager, the committee assigned itself three distinct functions: (1) assessing the risks of the current or planned research at the ADL facility, (2) deciding whether or not the risks were acceptable, and (3) recommending a risk management plan to the city for all forms of research involving highly toxic agents.

The composition of SAC reflects an interest of city officials in combining, within a single process, the technical and policy dimensions of

TABLE 9.1. Composition of the Cambridge Scientific Advisory Committee by Occupation, Institutional Affiliation, and Residence

Occupation	Institutional Affiliation	Cambridge Residence
Physicist/ Risk Assessment	Harvard University	No
Biochemistry/ Pharmacology	Tufts University	No
Community Organizer/ National Toxics Program	Nat'l Project on Neighborhood Health & Safety	Yes
Biology/Oceanography	New England Fishery Management Council	Yes
Chemical Engineering/ Industrial Hygiene	Harvard University	No
Physical Chemist/ Environmental Measurements	Consulting Firm	No; adjacent town of Arlington
Philosopher/ Social Scientist	Tufts University	Yes
M.D./Public Health/ Epidemiology	Boston University	Yes
Architect	Architectural Firm	Yes
Ph.D. Chemist	Private Sector	Yes
Public Health	Town of Belmont	No; adjacent town of Belmont
Molecular Biologist	Harvard Med. School	Yes
Restauranteur	Cambridge Restaurant	Yes
Electrical Engineer	Private Sector	Yes
Social Service Administrator	Cambridge Committee of Elders	Yes
Occupational Health	Harvard University	Yes

this issue. Science/technology policy debates have addressed the advantages and disadvantages of establishing separate decision-making processes for the technical and value components of an issue.[9] Within the science policy field one may find positivists who believe that normative/ value issues may be isolated from technical questions and non-positivists

199

who contend that the separation is not possible. The widely debated "science court" proposal for resolving disputes among experts is a reflection of the former view, while the "citizen court" proposal is a reflection of the latter.[10]

Risk assessment is primarily a technical matter, although there are a number of windows through which values may enter into the scientific analysis. (See Chapter 2 of this volume.) In contrast, the determination of acceptable risks is largely value-laden. There are norms one can use in such cases, but they are not based on scientific fact or theory. Considerations may be given to psychological factors, benefits versus costs, the historical circumstances, and where one is situated with respect to the risks and benefits.[11].

Finally, decisions on risk management involve science and technology, the allocation of resources, and sociopolitical institutions. In some cases where public consensus exists that certain risks are unacceptable, there may be a lack of expertise as to how to manage those risks.

THE PROCESS OF INQUIRY

The early meetings of SAC were devoted to unstructured interrogation. Representatives of ADL responded to a series of disjointed free-form questions raised by SAC members. The committee's appetite for information, in both breadth and detail, seemed insatiable. To help structure its inquiry and set priorities on the use of its technical and intellectual resources, SAC developed a framework for classifying its information needs (see Table 9.2).

For each category in the classification, committee members were asked to provide a fine structure of questions they considered relevant to the decision-making process. To answer all the suggested questions would have been a sizable task. Aware of its limited resources, SAC set priorities for the principal categories in the Classification of Information Needs and formed subcommittees to report on each area. While this was taking place, TRC's consultant to the city, Dr. Brian Murphy, met with SAC on several occasions to discuss his risk analysis.

Murphy's task was limited to assessing the potential public health hazards involved in ADL's storage and use of chemical warfare agents. For his basic methodology, he chose the analysis of worst-case scenarios. In this context, a "worst case" was interpreted to mean a release into public spaces of the most hazardous agents handled by ADL. The

TABLE 9.2. Classification of Information Needs as Determined by the Cambridge Scientific Advisory Committee

A.	Physical, Chemical, & Toxicological Characteristics of Chemical Warfare Agents
B.	Internal Emergency Procedures and Planning
C.	Laboratory Facilities
D.	Risk Scenarios
E.	Comparative Risks
F.	Physical Surroundings
G.	Scope of Present ADL Activities and Constraints
H.	Operational Procedures of Inspections
I.	Life Cycle of Materials
J.	Regulations in Effect at All Political Jurisdictions
K.	Future Activities of the ADL Laboratory

consultant's job was aided by the availability of published information on the physical and chemical properties of the chemicals.[12]

In his analysis, Murphy applied standardized dispersal models that describe how gases or volatile liquids are carried through the air. Four types of releases were addressed in his study: (1) evaporation from a spill, (2) sudden release by evaporation or impact, (3) release in a fire, and (4) intentional release.

In his report, the consultant discussed the limitations and boundaries of his study. First, only hazards to the general public and not hazards to ADL employees were addressed. Second, only work currently under contract at ADL, and not anticipated work that might involve different experiments, was considered. Third, no probability values were assigned to any of the hypothetical worst-case situations cited in the study. Fourth, the consultant made no judgments about whether the risks were acceptable or unacceptable.[13]

But the TRC consultant did not explain a critical trans-scientific judgment in the study: to use worst-case scenarios as the preferred method of risk analysis. There is no single approach to risk assessment. An alternative to the analysis of worst cases is to examine the most probable scenarios for accidental release. Worst cases and most probable cases are rarely ever the same. Safety requirements for the former can be significantly greater than what would be considered reasonable safeguards for the latter. Still another approach involves examining the conditions of a facility, both physical containment and laboratory practices, and comparing those to the state of the art for handling equivalent substances.

SAC followed the same basic methodology chosen by the TRC consultant. The committee analyzed the public health effects of several worst-case scenarios. If such cases revealed insignificant public health risks, SAC was prepared to examine potential impacts of lesser consequence. By choosing this methodology, SAC was looking for limits of the possible. If one hundred milliliters of nerve agent were released into the environment, lethal doses would be carried over certain distances and some number of people would be exposed to these. The committee wished to know the details of these scenarios. Once the worst cases were modeled, there were several options available to SAC. It could proceed to estimate the probability that one of the scenarios would take place. Or, it could examine ways to reduce the probability of such an occurrence. To build a risk management policy on the basis of worst-case scenarios, without an analysis of the probability of occurrence, is predicted on the idea of minimizing regret. In other words, if there is an outcome that is possible and deemed unacceptable under any foreseeable circumstances, minimizing regret means eliminating the conditions that make the outcome a possibility, regardless of the value of the occurrence probability. This approach is consistent with public attitudes toward low-probability catastrophic events.[14]

SAC developed its information base around the issue of worst-case analysis. The committee reviewed and commented on early drafts of the TRC report. The physical models incorporated into the TRC report were acceptable to SAC. Building on the consultant's report, SAC pursued additional queries. Other than ADL employees, how many people might be exposed to lethal doses of chemical warfare agents in the event of a major accident involving a release of those agents into the environment? How does the risk of such accidents compare with other hazards facing city residents? In terms of toxicity, how do other chemical agents that are used for research in the city compare to the nerve and blister agents handled at the ADL testing facility? These questions brought the committee into an extended debate over the manner and means of regulating "supertoxins," the term given to chemicals of toxicity comparable to some of the most dangerous of the chemical warfare agents.

REGULATING SUPERTOXINS: TWO APPROACHES

According to a U.S. Army contract made available to SAC,[15] the chemical warfare agents tested at the ADL facility included: Sarin (GB), Soman (GD), VX, Mustard (HD), and Lewisite (L). In presentations before the committee, ADL representatives contended that these chemicals or close derivatives are available from chemical houses without special licenses or restrictive uses. They also claimed that chemicals of equal or greater toxicity and with similar effects on humans are used in commercial and household products such as pesticides.

Of the five chemical warfare agents used by ADL in its R&D work, the three nerve agents Sarin, Soman and VX are the most toxic and were of greatest concern to the committee.[16] The extremely high toxicity of these chemicals confounds our intuitive ideas about small quantities. On first learning about the volumes of chemical warfare agents stored at ADL, most people are not apt to be concerned. To the layperson, a pint or a quart of a toxic chemical is not likely to be viewed as a public health hazard. Nevertheless, the toxicological properties of these agents are so much greater than any we might experience in ordinary life that a reorientation to a world of minute numbers is required fully to appreciate the hazards. For example, the agent VX is most toxic through inhalation as an aerosol. The lethal dose of this agent sufficient to kill 50 percent of the adults who inhale it (LD50) is a mere .3 milligrams, or one-hundredth of a drop. The other agents GB and GD are about one-third to one-half as toxic as VX by inhalation. When we consider that a liter (approximately a quart) contains about 30,000 drops, that seemingly small amount of chemical agent begins to take on a new meeting with respect to public health and safety.

A subcommittee of SAC was formed to examine comparable risks between the chemical warfare agents and other toxic chemicals used in the city. Since large amounts of chlorine are stored to purify the city's drinking water, the Comparative Risks Subcommittee drew comparisons between the two toxic compounds.[17]

VX has an LD50 of about 30 mg-min/m3, whereas chlorine has an LD50 of about 30,000 mg-min/m3 (possibly lower). To get the same ratio of M/D [Mass to Dose ratio], when D is the LD50, we see that the mass of chlorine has to be 1000 times larger than the mass of VX. Thus, 1000kg of chlorine (1 ton) is approximately equivalent to 1kg of VX, in that these quantities of the different agents will result in the same size and shape of the area in which the total dose exceeds the LD50.

As a first approximation, 1000kg (about a ton) of chlorine released into the environment would have the same lethal effects as 1kg (about a quart) of VX.

This type of information stimulated two kinds of discussions within the committee. First, there was a lengthy debate over the role of comparative risk analysis. Second, there was a protracted discussion over whether it was reasonable to classify a special group of chemicals as supertoxins for the purpose of regulation.

The logic underlying comparative risk analysis can be very compelling. Its basic idea may be summarized as follows: activities involving risks no greater than those with which we ordinarily live are rationally acceptable. There is, however, a glaring problem with this approach. Gertrude Stein might have said, "A risk is a risk is a risk." But decisions on acceptable risk inevitably involve a consideration of benefits. As a result, the tolerance for situations of comparable risk may vary considerably.

Building on the distinction between risk and risk-benefit, some members of SAC considered it fallacious to compare the risks of research involving VX with those of chlorine storage tanks in the city. The tanks are considered an essential asset to community health since the chlorine is used to purify the Cambridge water supply. SAC did not view the research with chemical warfare agents as providing any benefits to the city. A few members of the committee had serious reservations about the benefits of the research to the country as a whole.

Comparative risk analysis was also criticized for failing to take account of the critical distinction between voluntary and involuntary risks. In cases where two activities involve about the same actuarial risk, there may be vastly different public perceptions of acceptable risk, for example, if one of the activities is freely chosen and the other is externally imposed.

SAC also struggled with the issue of defining a class of chemicals called "supertoxins." Once the committee recognized that chemicals of toxicity comparable to the nerve agents were not regulated by federal and state health and safety laws, it investigated the number of such chemicals in common use. If Cambridge were to establish regulations for highly toxic chemicals, SAC wished to know how many compounds the health commissioner would have to oversee. Would it be a dozen, hundreds, thousands, or tens of thousands? A Data Search Committee was formed to answer these questions. The committee undertook a computer search of two registries of chemical compounds: the Registry of Toxic Effects of Chemical Substances (RTECS) and data base of the National Institutes of Environmental Health and Safety (NIEHS).

In the RTECS registry there were 66,954 substances listed, and 50,811 (76 percent) reported at least one LD50 (lethal dose to 50 percent of an exposed population) in any model. Using a threshold LD50 of 2 mg/kg, the estimated LD50 of ethyl parathion, a highly regulated anticholinesterase organophosphate widely used as a pesticide, the search identified 295 substances with an LD50 less than or equal to the threshold. In the LD50 range of 2–10 mg/kg the search revealed 1,354 substances. Ironically, the nerve agents used by ADL under its DOD contract were not listed in the chemical registries.

The NIEHS data base is similar to RTECS, but smaller. The search located about 300 substances with an LD50 of 1 and 2mg/kg. This search was more restricted since it only yielded LD50 values that were integral numbers and ignored intermediate values.

This data base search of very low LD50s (high toxicity) proved useful in that it gave SAC an estimate of how many chemicals of toxicity comparable to the chemical nerve agents would be covered by a municipal ordinance regulating supertoxins. The implementation of a city ordinance might be impractical if more than a few hundred compounds were targeted by the regulation. Several other considerations were raised in discussions about a municipal ordinance.

1. Currently, whether used in industry, R&D firms, or university research, the class of supertoxins is regulated neither by public nor occupational health legislation at the state or federal level. From a health and safety standpoint, DOD is the primary overseer of ADL's handling of chemical warfare agents. The same agency is, therefore, responsible for both promoting and regulating research with very hazardous materials.

2. If SAC were to come up with a regulation that covers the use of the supertoxins in R&D activities, members of the committee posed the following questions. Should it be targeted exclusively to firms like ADL, in other words, the for-profit sector, or should it also cover university research? For the purpose of regulation, should all supertoxins be treated equally? Or should the intent of the research and the uses of its results be considered in an ordinance? Some members of SAC argued persuasively for equal treatment. The local control of supertoxins, they held, should not depend on whether the sub-

205

stances are used for cancer treatment in a university medical complex or by a for-profit firm under contract with DOD in the form of chemical warfare agents.

Considerable opposition came from some SAC members to the suggestion that all supertoxins be treated the same from a regulatory standpoint (supertoxin equity rule). Since "acceptable risk" considers the benefits as well as risks, they argued that an ordinance designed to manage the risks should distinguish supertoxins by type of use. Some members of SAC believed that the DOD work with chemical warfare agents was of dubious value to society and may be even part of a new escalation in chemical weapons development. Others believed that the appropriate way to regulate these substances was by toxicity and volume, without reference to the intentionality of the work on the source of funding. They supported the supertoxin equity rule and argued that the work at ADL should be restricted because the volumes of supertoxins used pose a hazard to the community. The same substances used in micrograms (millionths of a gram) would pose no hazards beyond those to the investigators.

After weeks of debate, two distinct positions emerged. The first held that if supertoxins were to be regulated, then the rules should cover all such chemicals, regardless of (1) the nature of the application, i.e., whether it is pure research or development; (2) the institutions involved, i.e., whether profit, nonprofit, public or private; or (3) the source of funding for the research, i.e., public or private. This "supertoxin equity rule" requires that all supertoxins be treated on an equal basis for purposes of regulation.

The second position called for rigorous regulation of chemical warfare agents as a distinct class of chemicals. These agents would be defined by the purpose of the research. Since the military publishes a list of chemical warfare agents, any institution working under DOD contract and using one of the designated agents would fall under the city ordinance. The same substances used for biomedical research under contract from the National Institutes of Health (NIH) might not be covered by such a regulation. This second position is referred to as the "supertoxin intentionality rule."

A consensus was finally reached by SAC on one of the two approaches to regulating research with supertoxins. The final outcome was not a compromise of the two positions. Advocates for the "supertoxin intentionality rule" won the debate by sheer persistence. Others, somewhat reluctantly but in a spirit of cooperation, joined to make the final decision of SAC unanimous. (At the meeting where the final vote was taken, thirteen members present voted in favor of the final recommendations.)

THE DECISION

The final report of SAC contained discussions for each of the three areas pertaining to risk: risk assessment; acceptable risk; and risk management. Building its analysis of risk on the consultant's worst-case model, SAC concluded that releases of 100ml of VX into the air could expose people to substantial lethal doses of the nerve agent approximately 300 feet away at a bowling alley and a major highway. For a release of 500ml of the same compound, substantial lethal doses could reach a 500-foot radius, within which is located a motel and a large athletic field where tournament games are played. Much smaller lethal doses of the nerve agent could enter residential neighborhoods. The report stated that "an accident in which chemical warfare agents are released from the ADL facility is unlikely but not impossible."[18] SAC did not attempt to quantify the probability of a worst-case accident. Such calculations are very complex, involve many assumptions, and result in a considerable margin of error.

On the issue of acceptable risks, SAC concluded that:

> the benefits of research with these chemicals do not justify lethal risks to the general public. For this reason, the SAC believes that storage and testing of these chemical warfare agents within the densely populated city of Cambridge in the quantities and concentrations used by ADL is inappropriate. Furthermore, the majority of the SAC members judge the risks associated with any such work to be unacceptable.

Although the committee was divided on the question of acceptable risks, the split had little effect on its recommendation to the city. There was a consensus that the quantities of nerve agents stored at the ADL facilities were unacceptable. However, a few SAC members seemed willing to accept a testing program involving very small quantities of those agents. Nevertheless, a substantial majority of the committee did not feel there was justification for a single lethal exposure of the public to these chemicals in the name of chemical weapons research.

Finally, the committee developed a plan for the city to regulate research with supertoxins. The risk management plan introduced by SAC contained the following provisions.

207

1. Certain designated hazardous materials proposed for testing, use, storage, or disposal within the city must be reported to the commissioner of health and hospitals at least three months prior to the date of planned entry into the city.
2. The substances designated for reporting include: chemical warfare agents (as provided in a list); other nerve agents of chemical structures different from those listed, when used in chemical weapons R&D; biological warfare agents; and other highly toxic agents as may be designated by the commissioner.
3. Each proposed use of regulated agents must be reviewed by the commissioner and given a site evaluation in writing after appropriate information is provided. Any citizen of the city may petition for a public hearing.
4. If the commissioner finds that the use of the regulated chemical agents presents an unacceptable hazard to public health or safety, then a site assignment shall not be given and the use of such materials by the petitioner shall be prohibited.
5. In addition to chemical warfare agents, the City of Cambridge shall develop policies to regulate other supertoxins.

The final recommendations of SAC were predicated on the "supertoxin intentionality rule" discussed in the previous section. At this stage in the committee's deliberations, the primary distinction for the regulation of supertoxins was not based on toxicity or volume but on the use for which the chemicals of the research were designated. The final report stated:

> Chemical warfare agents are of a particular concern as a separate class of hazards because of their nature and purpose. They are highly toxic, designed for ready dispersal, and are intended to kill great numbers of people. Currently, these agents are largely unregulated by local, state or federal statues.[19]

SAC did not introduce small-volume exclusions into its recommendations. It left that to the discretion of the commissioner. However, it did exempt from the reporting requirement any retail products, pharmaceuticals available at drug stores, and materials used in a therapeutic setting by a physician.

UNCERTAINTIES IN THE REGULATORY AGENDA

Despite the long deliberations that went into the final report, there were a number of unresolved questions. SAC did not provide a carefully worded definition of a chemical warfare agent. For purposes of regulation, it is unclear whether a substance has to appear on a designated list or simply be an essential ingredient in chemical weapons research. Also, the committee did not address the question of concentrated versus dilute agents. In assessing the risks of toxic chemicals, there is a tradeoff between volume and concentration. A small volume of highly concentrated nerve agent may be as hazardous as a large volume of dilute material. However, highly dilute solutions of nerve agents are used in a variety of circumstances that may already be regulated.

To turn SAC's recommendations into a municipal ordinance, several problems must be resolved. For example, suppose an academic scientist is planning to study the properties of a highly toxic compound that does not appear on the city's list of regulated substances but is used in research funded under DOD contract. SAC's recommendations do not make it clear whether this situation would fall under "chemical weapons research."

In another hypothetical case, a university scientist is using extremely small quantities (micrograms) of a nerve agent that is on the DOD's inventory of chemical warfare agents. It is not clear whether the committee intended such uses to fall under the reporting requirement. It would seem so, although the intention of the committee is not to obstruct such research, only to have the city make note of it.

The SAC report has important implications for Harvard and MIT scientists who work with supertoxic agents. First, it requires the universities to take account of the chemicals in use. Second, DOD-funded research involving supertoxins must be reported to the commissioner of health and hospitals. At a time when Massachusetts universities are seeking exemptions from a state "right to know" law requiring disclosure to workers about chemical exposures, researchers and administrators are not eager to face another layer of local regulations of toxic substances.

JUDICIAL PROCESS

With the completion of SAC's report in September 1984, the city had two risk assesssment documents to present to the court. The judge's order, enjoining the city from enforcing its prohibition against research with the nerve and blister agents, was still in effect. The case was heard by a circuit judge in Superior Court of Massachusetts. After an initial hearing, the judge divided up the legal issues into two parts. First, he

209

wanted to hear briefs on the question of supremacy. ADL claimed the city had no legal right to prohibit its experiments since they were funded by DOD and the chemical agents were owned by the federal government. The city's regulation prohibiting ADL from conducting defense-related testing of chemical warfare agents, the argument continued, imposes a clear conflict with the federal interest. In such conflicts, the federal role takes supremacy over local interests. Second, if it were found that supremacy does not stand, the judge agreed to hear arguments on the reasonableness of the city's order to proscribe the testing of the five chemical warfare agents in question.

Arguments on the supremacy issue were presented to the court in mid-November 1984. Counsel for the City of Cambridge (defendent in the case) argued that, for federal supremacy to hold, one of two conditions must be satisfied. Either the federal government has preempted the field of toxic substances regulation, or a fundamental conflict exists between the federal and local governments on the regulation of these substances. The defense counsel maintained that neither condition is satisfied. Congress has never stipulated that testing of toxic substances would be exclusively occupied by the federal government. Under the Federal Hazardous Substances Act, as a general rule, defense contended, local governments may regulate non-manufacturing activities. On the issue of conflict between federal and local laws, defense counsel cited the following points:

1. Language in the DOD contract states that the contractee must follow all local and state laws in addition to DOD regulations. This implies that no fundamental conflict exists among political jurisdictions.
2. The government could always do the testing on federal property; the facts do not show that there is an actual conflict.
3. Under the municipality's police powers it may alter a previously established contract.

Counsel for ADL raised the following points in building an argument for federal preemption over the city's action:

1. Congress has authorized DOD to establish a chemical warfare program, and this includes regulations for handling, use, and disposal of the agents.
2. The framers of the U.S. Constitution as well as Congress intended the federal government to have exclusive responsibility for national defense. The city's regulation prohibiting ADL from conducting defense-related testing of chemical warfare agents is tantamount to

interference with governmental functions and represents a clear conflict with the federal interest.

3. If Cambridge is free to prohibit such work, then so too is any other community. If all jurisdictions followed Cambridge's lead, federal programs in chemical warfare research would be frustrated.

4. Since ADL is a contractor of the government, the firm is invested with "derivative sovereign immunity" which allows the supremacy clause of the Constitution to apply to it with equal force as to the federal government. Council for ADL contended that reasonable additions to the safety regulations of DOD do not represent a fundamental conflict between the city and the federal government. The conflict arises when the city's regulation effectively prohibits ADL from performing its contracted work for DOD.

The decision on the supremacy question was entered by the court in a twenty-one-page brief on December 14, 1984. The ruling stated, "The Cambridge ordinance does not run afoul of the Supremacy Clause nor is it preempted by federal law."[20] The judge reasoned that this was not a case in which Congress left no room for state and local governments to supplement federal regulations. Furthermore, the local regulation is not an obstacle "to the accomplishment of the full purpose of Congress."

Two months later, on February 26, the Superior Court ruled on the second part of the issue declaring that there was no procedural defect in the city's order prohibiting use of the chemical agents. The following day, the judge declared the September 1985 order "valid and enforceable." However, the judge filed an unusual addendum to his decision which stated his personal belief that ADL was not treated fairly in this process. He expressed his hope that the appellate courts or the state legislature will change the current law that guided his decision.

ADL appealed the case to the Massachusetts Appeals court on March 12, 1984. The court gave the company immediate relief by reinstating the injunction against the order pending the outcome of the appeal. In response, the city petitioned the Supreme Judicial Court (SJC) and asked that it take the case over from the Appeals Court. The SJC agreed with the city's petition, heard the case on April 4, 1985 and issued its ruling four months later on August 1.

The SJC found that the commissioner's order was a permissible attempt by the city to protect its inhabitants under the local police powers. It rejected arguments by ADL that the order violated the firm's right to due process or constituted an unjustified interference in its contract

211

with DOD. The SJC also failed to find within federal statutes congressional intent to preempt local communities from passing health and safety regulations for chemical warfare agents. The court affirmed the right of local health authorities to prohibit activities so long as the regulations are not "unreasonable, whimsical, or capricious." ADL chose not to appeal the SJC decision to the U.S. Supreme Court. The experiments on the chemical warfare were halted and, subsequently, the agents were transported out of the city.

GENETIC RESEARCH AND CHEMICAL
WARFARE AGENTS: CONTRASTING ISSUES

To many observers, the ADL affair conjures up memories of the recombinant DNA (rDNA) controversy that took place in Cambridge in 1976. There are similarities, but equally important are the differences between the two episodes. Nine years ago, the Cambridge City Council was confronted by a scientific community polarized over the issue of the safety of gene-splicing research. To resolve the local controversy, the council created a committee called the Cambridge Experimentation Review Board (CERB). As in the conflict over chemical weapons research, the event that precipitated local concern in the rDNA episode was the construction of a laboratory designed for hazardous experiments. Basic research in molecular genetics was at issue. In contrast, the testing done at ADL involves applied research. It is designed with a particular end-product in mind, i.e., detection kits for nerve agents, or methods of detoxifying chemical weapons. The salient comparisons between the two episodes are outlined in Table 9.3.

The grassroots public reaction to the testing of chemical warfare agents was considerably more intense than the response of the Cambridge non-academic citizenry to the genetic debate. However, the response by public officials to both controversies was about the same. In the genetics controversy, scientists brought the issue to the attention of the city council. Their concern about the postulated risks of gene-splicing research was a critical factor in convincing the council to take action. The issues rDNA research were obscure and esoteric to members of the council, whereas experiments with chemical warfare agents are much more comprehensible to the ordinary citizen. Since such agents are designed as instruments of death, the hazards of these agents are not hypothetical or mysterious. During the rDNA debate much was un-

TABLE 9.3. Comparisons and Contrasts in Debates Over Genetics Research and Testing of Chemical Warfare Agents in Cambridge, Massachusetts.

Category of Issue	Genetics Research (1976)	Chemical Weapons Research (1984)
Type of Research	New technique in molecular genetics; basic science	Applied chemical-engineering research
Origins of Controversy	Initially national in scope and centered within the scientific community	Local in nature and centered on a city and two towns
Origins of Local Involvement	Newspaper story about plans for renovation of a Harvard lab for high containment genetic experiments	Newspaper story on newly renovated lab for testing chemical warfare agents
Nature of Risks	Hypothetical; possibility of creating a pathogen from mixing genetic information	Proven hazards of chemical warfare agents; main problem is containment
City Response	Public hearing; Call for a good-faith 3-month moratorium on certain types of gene-splicing experiments; Established citizens panel— 8 members chosen with ethnic, m/f, racial mix	Public hearings; Call for a moratorium on testing nerve & blister agents; Convened science-citizens— 15m/1f, no members panel of 16 ethnic, racial mix Emergency ban issued by health commissioner
Response to City Council Action	Universities accept moratorium on research	ADL seeks court order restraining city ban on testing chemical warfare agents
Outcome of Review Process	Research can continue with some additional safeguards; ordinance recommended to cover all rDNA research	Testing of chemical warfare agents deemed inappropriate; it should not continue; ordinance recommended covering use of supertoxins for chemical warfare agents
Legal Process	No legal test of rDNA ordinance or city moratorium on research	Legal test of city directive banning use of chemical warfare agents
Community Involvement	Primarily from academic sectors; no grassroots organizing; some organized opposition from young scientists, Ph.D. candidates, and post-docs	No community groups organized at the early stages; some community activism begins after SAC report is released; intense organizing in Oct-Dec. 1984

known; for example, few of the postulated risk scenarios had been tested, and none had been confirmed. With respect to chemical warfare agents, however, not only is there an informative literature about their toxicological properties, but there are reliable models that describe how those agents would behave when released into the environment. Moreover, past accidents involving nerve agents provide useful information about risks.[21]

Another striking difference in the two controversies is in the response to the city's action by the research institutions involved. During the gene-splicing debate, both Harvard and MIT accepted a good-faith moratorium on certain types of experiments until the city could complete its assessment of the risks. In contrast, when ADL was asked to accept a moratorium on its research with chemical warfare agents, it refused. The company initiated litigation as soon as the commissioner of health issued a cease-and-desist order.

The gene-splicing moratorium applied only to a restricted class of experiments, and the impediment to research in Cambridge was minimal. The research affected by the moratorium was of a basic nature, funded primarily by NIH. The research ban affecting ADL was restricted to a group of experiments, namely, those involving the use of five chemical warfare agents. But unlike the genetic experiments, ADL's research on chemical warfare agents is more typical of engineering work than applied science. As a consequence, scientists did not view the city's research ban as a threat to scientific inquiry. No scientists or R&D companies came to the side of ADL in a public forum.

CONCLUSION

This case illustrates the exercise of power by a local government to restrain federally-funded research in a private facility. The salient focus here is the shared powers of federal and local jurisdiction to protect public health and safety. The right of a local jurisdiction to impose limits on R&D activities involving highly toxic substances is protected when the following conditions are met: (1) Congress has not explicitly preempted such activities, (2) the actions taken do not thwart the federal government from exercising its functions, and (3) there is reason to suspect that the research may have an adverse impact on public health or safety. The response to potential or actual risks must not be arbitrary and capricious.

Following Loren Graham's taxonomy of public concerns over science and technology,[22] testing of chemical warfare agents fits most appropriately in the category "accidents in science." Certainly that was the basis upon which the city acted. But just as in the rDNA controversy, where there were underlying issues such as ethical problems with genetic engineering, the testing of chemical warfare agents also carries with it concerns other than public health hazards.

During their deliberation, members of the Cambridge Scientific Advisory Committee discussed the ethics of research with chemical warfare agents. Some individuals were suspicious of the putative values behind the research. ADL described the research as fundamentally humanitarian and strictly a defensive nature. But taken in the context of other national trends, such as increased spending for chemical warfare programs and military plans to restockpile the U.S. chemical weapons' arsenal, some SAC members were skeptical about the role ADL's research played in the military total picture. It is quite likely that if the research had been considered unambiguously humanitarian, both the city council and the citizen-science advisory committee would have approached the issue differently. But this research is viewed as neither basic nor neutral in the current political landscape. Furthermore, it is shrouded in secrecy and cloaked in military euphemisms that offend people's sensibilities. The planning and construction of the ADL laboratory for this research was also kept secret for at least a year after it was conceptualized. The type of research planned for the facility became public when it was no longer possible for ADL to obtain promises of confidentiality from local officials. Finally, some SAC members did not look favorably upon the idea that DOD both funds the research and also regulates the use of the chemical warfare agents. Cambridge passed its own recombinant DNA ordinance when it considered the dual roles of the NIH as both promoter and regulator of genetics research to be in conflict. The combined effect of these factors made the type of research undertaken at ADL particularly vulnerable to regulation by the City of Cambridge.

While local control of DOD-sponsored chemical weapons research at a private firm seems far removed from academic science, there are some potential points of intersection. First, universities may accept classified research involving chemical warfare agents. Second, there are chemicals found in university warfare agents. Second, there are chemicals found in university laboratories with toxicities equal to or greater than the chemical warfare agents. When concentrations and volumes of these chemicals are factored into a risk assessment, a local community may find a compelling case to regulate their use in research.

The control of scientific research, whether publicly or privately funded, whether in academia or private industry, is still under negotiation.[23] The regulation of supertoxic chemicals is the latest in a series of federal and local interventions into science, joining human and animal experiments, fetal research, gene splicing, and control of radioactive materials. Each of these cases establishes a delicate balance point between the autonomy of the research community and the social accountability of science and technology. The negotiated balance for research with supertoxins, called into question by the City of Cambridge, is very much in flux.

NOTES

1. Stephen Hilgartner, "The Binary Weapons Controversy," in *Controversy: The Politics of Technical Decisions*, ed. Dorothy Nelkin, 143–58.

2. U.S. Army, Contract to Arthur D. Little, Inc., No. DAAK11–82–C–0065 (22 Aug. 1983). The contract objectives include developing methods for increasing the sensitivity of detection tests for chemical warfare agent testing kits.

3. A.M. Reidy, "A. D. Little Toxic Chemical Testing Surprises Town," *Arlington Advocate* 111 (20 Oct. 1983): 1, 26.

4. Ibid.

5. Paul Hirshon, "Arthur D. Little Opens High Security Lab in Cambridge to Test Hazardous Chemicals," *Boston Globe*, 20 Oct. 1983.

6. Sheldon Krimsky, "Local Initiatives for Regulation," in Krimsky, *Genetic Alchemy* (Cambridge: MIT Press, 1982), 295–311.

7. Melvin Chalfen, commissioner of health and hospitals, City of Cambridge, "Order on the testing, storage and transportation of chemical nerve and blister agents" (13 Mar. 1984).

8. TRC Environmental Consultants, Inc., *Community Risks from Experiments with Chemical Warfare Agents at Arthur D. Little*, Project No. 2631–N81, Hartford, Conn. (5 June 1984).

9. See, for example, Sheldon Krimsky, "Social Risk Assessment and Group Process," in *Group Decision Making*, ed. Walter C. Swap, 151–80 (Beverly Hills: Sage, 1984); and Harvey Brooks, "The Resolution of Technically Intensive Public Policy Disputes," 39–50.

10. Sheldon Krimsky, "A Citizen Court in the Recombinant DNA Debate," *Bulletin of the Atomic Scientists* 34 (Oct. 1978):37–43.

11. Social and cultural aspects of risk assessment are discussed in Mary Douglas and Aaron Wildavsky, *Risk and Culture* (Berkeley: Univ. of California Press, 1982); and William Lowrance, *Of Acceptable Risk* (Los Altos, Calif.: William Kaufmann, 1976).

12. Matthew Meselson and J. P. Robinson, "Chemical Warfare and Chemical Disarmament," *Scientific American* 242 (Apr. 1980):38–47.

216

13. TRC Environmental Consultants, *Community Risks*, 1.

14. Baruch Fischhoff, Paul Slovic, and Sara Lichtenstein, "Lay Foibles and Expert Fables in Judgment about Risk," *American Statistician* 36 (Aug. 1982): 240–55.

15. U.S. Army, contract to Arthur D. Little.

16. For a discussion of the toxicological properties of chemical warfare agents, see John Cookson and Judith Nottingham, *A Survey of Chemical and Biological Warfare* (New York: Monthly Review Press, 1969).

17. The measurements of LD50 toxicity are in units of either mg-min/m³ (vapor inhalation) or mg/kg (intake in liquid or solid state). Cambridge Scientific Advisory Committee, "Comparative Risks Subcommittee report," *Report to the City Manager* [on testing of chemical warfare agents at Arthur D. Little, Inc.], Sept. 1984.

18. Ibid.

19. Ibid.

20. Robert J. Hallisey [Superior Court Judge of Massachusetts], *Memorandum of Decision on Severed Issue*, Arthur D. Little, Inc. v. Melvin H. Chalfen, Civil Action, 84–1529, 13 Dec. 1984.

21. In March 1968, VX leaked from a F4 Phantom jet at the Dugway Proving Ground in Utah. The cloud of VX was carried twenty miles and killed an estimated six thousand sheep. See S. Murphy, A. Hay, and S. Rose, *No Fire, No Thunder* (New York: Monthly Review Press, 1984), 17.

22. Loren R. Graham, "Concerns About Science and Attempts to Regulate Inquiry," *Daedalus* 107 (Spring 1978): 1–21.

23. Dorothy Nelkin, "Threats and Promises: Negotiating the Control of Research," 191–209.

PART III

RECONCILING SCIENCE AND TECHNOLOGY WITH DEMOCRACY

Having examined changes, challenges, and institutional responses, the three chapters in Part III confront the larger and perhaps more difficult question of how science and technology can be governed more democratically. The approach in this section is first to determine the adequacy of current institutional mechanisms and then to examine a number of alternative arrangements for meeting the challenges that confront the many institutions that govern science and technology.

Bruce Jennings' Chapter 10 sets the tone for this concluding, prescriptive section of the book. Jennings searches the various conceptions of democracy for a set of criteria to use in evaluating the appropriateness of proposed institutional arrangements for governing science and technology in a working democracy. He settles on two measures of system performance: participation and representation.

Like other contributors to this volume, Jennings notes that, at the height of the social and antiwar movements of the 1960s, the post–World War II optimism concerning the promise of science and technology began to wane; and by the 1970s, the existing oversight mechanisms of democratic representation—congressional committees, advisory commissions, and interest groups—seemed woefully inadequate to protect the public interest. In the late 1960s and early 1970s, many turned to the procedural ideal of democratic self-government—"power to the people." But in the aftermath of some of the disappointments of participatory democracy, many reflected that rule by the people is not always rule for the people. As Jennings puts it, "Procedural democracy does not always produce substantive democracy." To achieve the substantive ideal, the revisionists argued, requires a "two-tiered conception" of de-

219

mocracy, with the few deciding what is in the best interest of the many, and the many choosing who among the few are best able to make wise decisions.

Jennings rejects the "two-tiered" system, flatly stating that democracy and expertise are not antithetical, that democratic governance of science and technology is not only logically possible but in the public interest. Instead of the two-tiered system, Jennings looks to a "symbiosis" of what he labels "revisionist" and "participatory" theories of democracy as the solution to past failures of representational democracy. Taking the example of the Cambridge Experimention Review Board both as proof that lay members of the public are educable, interested, and capable, and as an example of the possibilities of popular control of science and technology, Jennings concludes his chapter by making the case for more informed publics and increased citizen participation in the governance of science and technolgy.

In Chapter 11, Leonard Cole examines three specific proposals that have been made to improve the institutional processes by which decision makers make public choices among alternative solutions to controversial scientific and technological issues. He recommends a science hearings panel as the one reform that balances the scientist's need for autonomy with the citizen's desire for accountability. In advocating a science hearings panel Cole stresses the linkages between scientific and technological literacy and the democratic governance of science and technology. In this sense, his chapter foreshadows the section on institutional reforms that follows.

Cole reviews the histories of nuclear power and gene-splicing research, the potential hazards of which stimulated the search for a governing scheme that went beyond the traditional institutions of representative government. He reviews two proposals that emerged from disputes over nuclear energy and genetic engineering — a science court and a citizen court — and finds both wanting. In advocating a science hearings panel instead, Cole uses the emerging disputes over secrecy, patent protection, and controls over experiments in the private sector — disputes connected with the still-controversial rDNA research — to illustrate the panel's advantages over other alternatives. What makes the science hearings panel so attractive to Cole is that, because it relies on existing institutions of governance, it requires little innovation. Furthermore, it enhances the scientific and technological literacy that is a necessary condition of democracy; it meets the democratic requirements of open discussion, informed decision making, and accountability that are suggested in the concluding chapter.

Chapter 12 takes up the question of how science and technology should be governed in a democracy. The premise is that there is an underlying tension between the norms of science and technology and the democratic imperative. That is because those who do science and technology seek to maintain their professional autonomy, while democrats (including some scientists and engineers as well as others) demand greater accountability, even at the expense of some of that autonomy. The chapter summarizes the book's thesis: governing science and technology more democratically will reconcile science and technology with democracy. Both science and society would be better off if the United States were to move in the direction of more, rather than less, public governance of science and technology.

I argue that there is a crisis of governance in science and technology, and that one way to solve the crisis is to encourage more public participation in all phases of the science policy making process — from setting the agenda to formulating alternatives to adopting laws and regulations to implementing them. To succeed, however, it is necessary first to lower some of the barriers to broad-based participation — by solving the problem of widespread scientific and technological illiteracy in the country, by making the institutions of governance more accessible, and by encouraging public discourse. This, of course, is no easy task.

The book ends on a prescriptive note: reform and modernize governing institutions so that they can deal more effectively with the challenges that have been presented to them by recent changes in science and technology and in society, with one precondition for reform being the removal of some of the impediments to public participation in science and technology policy making. While the proposed reforms are merely suggestions, they include prescriptions as to who should make policy, at what point in the process, where, and to what effect.

10. Representation and Participation in the Democratic Governance of Science and Technology

BRUCE JENNINGS

Despite important philosophical and methodological differences separating them, policy analysis and political theory are fields of inquiry that have much to contribute to one another. Nowhere is their conversation more needed, or more conspicuous by its absence, than in the area of science and technology policy. The current debate over the proper governance of science and technology in the United States is studded with assertions about the nature and purpose of democratic representation, accountability, and participation. Proponents of scientific autonomy and professional self-regulation often equate democratic governance with some kind of populist anti-intellectualism or bureaucratic Lysenkoism.[1] Proponents of greater political accountability or of increased citizen participation in the policy-making process often assume that formal or procedural mechanisms alone are sufficient to attain democratic objectives.

Arguments of this kind do little to advance our understanding of the values at stake in the governance of science. Although I won't attempt to make it here, there is an affirmative case to be made for what Robert Dahl has aptly called scientific guardianship—professional autonomy and the delegation of authority to scientific elites in public policy decisions concerning basic research and technology development.[2] Too often, however, the case for autonomy is made, not by defending the distinctive values—wisdom, the unfettered pursuit of truth, efficiency—intrinsic to it, but by defending autonomy *faute de mieux*, as an antidote to the disturbing excesses and distortions supposedly inherent in a democratic mode of governance.

Similarly, the case for a more democratic governance of science and

223

technology must be made on its own terms; it cannot finally stand or fall solely on the basis of our assessment of the merits of the case for guardianship. Moreover, the case for democracy requires more than a pragmatic defense of democratic *means* or procedures, important as these are. In considering the prospects for democracy in the governance of science and technology, as in political life and public policy-making generally, it is essential to mount a principled defense of democratic *ends*, to distinguish among the various moral values democracy may serve, and to explore the possible institutional arrangements that are likely to further the substantive democratic objectives we have defined.

In this chapter I will attempt to make, or at least to examine carefully, the affirmative case for the democratic governance of science and technology. Science policy debates are a microcosm in which much broader and more abstract controversies of twentieth-century democratic theory are replayed. By bringing this broader theoretical context to bear on the question of science and technology governance, I hope to underscore the importance of democratic ends as well as means and to offer a framework within which the institutional reforms discussed elsewhere in this volume may be assessed.

RECONCILING SCIENCE AND DEMOCRACY

What is distinctive about American society in the late twentieth century? What forces shape our way of life, define our deepest ideals and aspirations, and propel us toward a future containing both greater possibilities and greater dangers than humankind has ever known before? Among the many characteristics that could be mentioned in response to these questions, surely two stand out as essential: our reliance on science and technology, and our recourse to democratic principles and procedures in evaluating and justifying the exercise of public authority and power. Without the former most of our major social and economic institutions could not function; without the latter those institutions would be left without an overriding sense of public purpose. Throughout our history America has been seen as the exemplar of some new kind of social experiment, as a place where special human goals, untried or unrealized elsewhere, could be fulfilled. Over time the content of the mission defining America has changed, but the quest to fulfill some kind of higher human *telos* has remained a constant feature of

American cultural self-identity. Today, at least in part, that quest is to reconcile the energies of science and technology with basic democratic values. Foremost among these values are individual autonomy and self-development, political equality, and the right of those significantly affected by public decisions to participate meaningfully in the decision-making process. Such notions still give us our moral bearings in the political world, yet a suspicion is growing that these traditional democratic values are becoming obsolete in an era of increasingly specialized knowledge and technological complexity.

Although it has always been a prominent theme in American social thought, the reconciliation of science and democracy did not emerge clearly as an aspect of the distinctive mission of America until the late 1940s.[3] Despite the long shadows cast by the atomic bomb, the prognosis for reconciliation in the postwar years was generally optimistic. Scientific discovery and its technological applications seemed to offer the promise of virtually open-ended control over natural limits to the fulfilment of human and social goals. Science itself was widely taken to be a symbol of the power of human intelligence, reason, and freedom of thought in an open society. For social theorists like John Dewey, the ethos of science was a fertile breeding ground for the pragmatic, experimental temperament essential to a viable democratic culture. Finally, science and technology seemed to hold the key to a new era of economic growth, thereby eliminating the kind of class conflicts that had proved fatal to liberal democratic values and social stability in Europe in the 1930s.

The apparently benign *modus vivendi* between science and democracy was badly shaken in the 1960s and 1970s. During the Vietnam War the New Left began a critique of the social consequences of technology and the political influence of scientific elites. This critique was subsequently extended and given wider currency by the environmental movement.[4] In the process the image of science and the optimistic promise of technology have been transformed in the public mind. Questions largely glossed over in the postwar years now have become salient. Are the forces driving basic scientific research and the incentives operating within the professional scientific community necessarily responsive to public needs and interests? Are these forces adequately sensitive to ethical considerations and social values? Does social and economic dependence on science and technology in turn create a political dependence on scientific and technological expertise that undermines effective demo-

225

cratic accountability and decison making? Has the influence of science in the culture produced an active democratic ethos, as Dewey expected, or has it inclined instead toward a technocratic elitism?

However one answers these and similar questions, it is clear that the reconciliation of science and democracy can no longer be considered a simple problem, much less an accomplished fact. The practice of contemporary science — organized, expensive, bureaucratic science — is deeply entwined in the political, economic, and moral fabric of our culture, shaping that fabric and in turn being shaped by it. Increasingly, the conduct of scientific research and the technological applications of basic scientific knowledge raise social, political and ethical questions that cannot — and should not — be resolved by the professional scientific community alone. Just as external political decisions, economic forces, and social values shape the basic direction of scientific and technological development, that development also profoundly affects society as a whole. Long gone is the era in which the practice of science was the "private" activity of scientists and was solely their concern. Today, both basic research and technological development are "public" activities and are increasingly being held accountable as such. Tax dollars subsidize the education and capital investment that make modern science possible. All citizens have a shared interest in the activities and decisions of professional researchers, technologists, and scientifically knowledgeable elites.

In saying this I do not mean only that citizens as private individuals have interests — economic interests and interests in personal health and safety, for example — that are affected by science and technology, although such interests are certainly important and deserve due consideration and protection in any scheme of science governance. I also mean that citizens as members of an integrated political community have an interest, a stake, in being meaningfully involved in determining the ends served by science and technology and in fashioning the policies which will guide science and technology toward those ends. The distinction between these two types of interests, which we might call the citizen's *private interests* and her or his *democratic interests*, is conceptually useful because these two types of interest place different sorts of demands on governance and science policy. Private interests call for governance by accountable and responsible elites; fulfilling these interests primarily requires protection from the destructive or disruptive consequences of science. Democratic interests, on the other hand, call for active citizen participation; they require not so much protection from, as shared involvement in, science and technology. For democratic interests to be served, elite accountability and responsiveness are necessary but not sufficient; democratic interests require the further conditions of representative and perhaps participatory governance as well.

The regulatory and budgetary oversight exercised by representational institutions — Congress and executive agencies — has traditionally been considered sufficient to protect the public interest (understood as an aggregation of private interests) against the abuse of science and the misuse of technology. This traditional arrangement has usually, and perhaps necessarily, involved governmental overseers' granting a large measure of autonomy and discretion to individual scientists or to professional associations. In recent years, however, the perceived shortcomings of these oversight mechanisms have led to a search for new ways to institutionalize more direct citizen involvement in shaping public policies concerning scientific research and technological development. It is important to note that this search, and its underlying quest for reconciliation of science and democracy, can be inspired by a concern for either the protection of private interests or the promotion of democratic interests. In order to protect the former, many critics now assert, we must move beyond the current mechanisms of democratic representation, for they alone are insufficient to assure adequate accountability and responsiveness, and develop stronger mechanisms of democratic participation. Alternatively, as we shall see, arguments based on an appeal to positive democratic interests are also available which lead even more directly — and, I think, more persuasively — to the same conclusion.

This particapatory impulse — also evident today in many other social and policy areas — has reopened important questions, not only about the relationship between science and democracy but also about the meaning and limits of democracy itself in the face of public policy issues that are exceedingly complex and technical in nature.[5] The demand for greater citizen participation in science and technology policy began by challenging the optimistic assumptions about the automatic social benefits of science. As it has developed, however, it has been met by countervailing response which challenges some equally optimistic assumptions about the viability and justification of enhanced participatory democracy. Interesting variations on this latter challenge have been developed by two critics of greater governmental regulation of scientific research, George Ball and David Baltimore.

In an address on "Biology and Politics" delivered to the American Political Science Association in 1977, Ball took a strong position in favor of professional self-regulation of scientific research:

> Scientifically trained men and women are far better equipped to decide whether and how certain types of research should be conducted so as to safeguard [the] public interest than legislatures or administrative tribunals or courts . . .
> [They] should be permitted maximum freedom to decide what research to undertake and how to undertake it, subject only to such safeguards as they might individually or collectively impose to prevent experiments being conducted in such a manner as to threaten the public health or welfare.[6]

At the same time David Baltimore advanced a similar, albeit more nuanced and qualified, case for scientific autonomy:

> The traditional pact between society and its scientists in which the scientists is given the responsibility for determining the direction of his work is a necessary relationship if basic science is to be an effective endeavor. This does not mean that society is at the mercy of science, but rather that society, while it must determine the pace of basic scientific innovation, should not attempt to prescribe its directions.
> . . . As I see it, we are being faced today with the following question: Should limits be placed on biological research because of the danger that new knowledge can present to the established or desired order of our society? . . . I believe that there are two simple, and almost universally applicable, answers. First, the criteria determining what areas to restrain inevitably express certain sociopolitical attitudes that reflect a dominant ideology. Such criteria cannot be allowed to guide scientific choices. Second, attempts to restrain directions of scientific inquiry are more likely to be generally disruptive of science than to provide the desired specific restraints . . . [These] arguments pertain to basic scientific research, not to the technological applications of science. As we go from the fundamental to the applied, my arguments fall away. There is every reason why technology should and must serve specific needs. Conversely, there are many technological possibilities that ought to be restrained.[7]

The nature and significance of these arguments are worth pursuing in some detail. Ball's position rests on what he sees as the superior competence of scientists to understand the real — as opposed to the popularly imagined — hazards of research and the superior effectiveness of professional self-regulation over political regulation in protecting the public interest. Baltimore's position rests on a firm demarcation between basic and applied research, and on a concomitant distinction between regulating the pace and regulating the direction of research. Finally, and most importantly for our purposes here, Baltimore suggests that democratic attempts to regulate the direction of basic research are counterproductive on their own terms as well as antithetical to the flourishing of the scientific enterprise itself.

These claims have a wide bearing on the challenge that contemporary scientific research and technology development poses for the continuing viability of democratic institutions. At bottom these arguments reveal an underlying skepticism about the capacity of democratic procedures to cope with a wide range of technological, environmental, and economic problems. The line of reasoning behind this skepticism runs something like this. A fully democratic polity, the skeptics assert, cannot devise rational public policies when science is the *object* of policy; neither can it inject sufficient expertise and technical knowledge into decision making in order to utilize science rationally as an *instrument* of public policy.[8] In other words, democratic citizens and their political representatives cannot rationally manage the development of science and technology, nor can they understand modern science and technology sufficiently to use science effectively in other policy areas. Direct citizen participation should be mainly limited to electoral participation, and political representatives (both elected and appointed public officials and interest-group activists) should largely defer to scientific and technological experts and ratify the substantive policies those experts recommend. Those who would move governance in the United States closer to the theoretical democratic ideal — by demanding a more assertive role in decision making by elected representatives and new institutional mechanisms for direct citizen participation in policymaking — are out of step with the realities of a technological society. Their reforms would create a "democratic overload" or a "democratic distemper" that would cripple or even paralyze rational, efficient governance in the public interest.[9]

This, then, is the new elitism that has developed on one side of the guardianship/democracy debate in science policy. Its roots run deep in the tradition of Western political thought (in many respects it echoes Plato's critique of classical Athenian democracy). More importantly, however, in the contemporary American context it does not appear to be an explicit antidemocratic argument at all. Rather, it parallels and draws upon one important theoretical current in twentieth-century democratic theory and mainstream political science, a current of thought that has been called "democratic revisionism" or "democratic elitism." To grasp the force and bearing of this elitism in science policy, we would do well to consider its place in democratic political theory more broadly.

229

What classical theoretical problems give rise to it? And what arguments for a more full-bodied conception of representation and participation can be made in response to it?

THE CONTESTED TERRAIN OF DEMOCRACY

Generally speaking, three distinct streams of democratic thought now vie with one another in contemporary political theory. I shall refer to them as liberal democracy, democratic revisionism, and participatory democracy. Liberal democracy is the oldest and most inclusive of the three; it is the core theory from which the revisionist and participatory perspectives have departed in the twentieth century, while nonetheless remaining linked to it in important ways. Before turning to these more recent perspectives, therefore, it will be useful to review the basic tenets of problems of liberal democracy.

Liberal Democracy. Liberal democratic theory in general holds that the legitimate authority of the government rests on the consent of the governed, and that individuals have a right to take part in decision making that significantly affects their own interests or affects the interests of the entire society.[10] The government is not the privileged domain of a particular individual or class (Louis XIV's "L'état c'est moi"); it is the instrument of the political community as a whole. The actions of the government are the actions of the people (or at least of the majority); when this is the case, the democratic *procedural* ideal of popular sovereignty or popular self-rule is achieved. Democracy, the rule of the people, is rule by the people.

There are two principal procedural mechanisms through which this fusion of the government and its citizens, rulers and ruled, can be accomplished. Democratic participation achieves this fusion directly and literally—the assembled citizenry forms a legislature of the whole which becomes the government and acts through collective deliberation and decision making. Democratic representation achieves this fusion indirectly and figuratively—a subset of the citizenry, elected by and accountable to the entire citizenry, forms the government and makes decisions. But it is not they who rule; rather those they represent rule through them.

Democratic theory has always had to face the following dilemma in its choice between participation and representation as procedural arrangements. Democratic participation fulfills the procedural ideal best, but it seems practical only in a very small setting such as the classical Greek *polis*, the traditional Swiss canton, or the small New England town. On the other hand, democratic representation is practical in larger settings, but it opens up the risk of significant deviation from the procedural ideal. Representatives may easily fail to be the instruments of the represented, and thus subvert democracy by transforming it into an oligarchy (rule of the people by the few). To guard against this danger, some mechanism must be found to keep the representatives accountable and responsive to those they are supposed to represent. This requires an open flow of information between representatives and constituents, a capacity on the part of the citizens to understand and evaluate what the representatives are doing, and periodic renewal of democratic consent via free and competitive elections.

Moreover, in addition to its procedural ideal, liberal democratic theory contains a *substantive* ideal which demands that the actions of the government must in fact protect the rights of individuals and promote the public good. That is to say, the rule of the people must be both rule by the people and rule for the people—rule in their interest, rule in the service of their human flourishing and individual self-development. Here democratic theory confronts a second dilemma. There is no a priori reason to assume, and most democratic theorists have not in fact assumed, that rule by the people (either directly or indirectly) will automatically be rule for the people. Procedural democracy does not always produce substantive democracy. The resolution of this dilemma requires that some means be found to assure that democratic citizens have adequate intelligence, judgment, and the quality of civic virtue, a moral commitment to justice and the good of the community as a whole.

In regard to the substantive ideal, one might argue that the relative advantages and disadvantages of participatory and representative forms of democracy are reversed. Representative democracy seems less likely to deviate from the substantive ideal because it demands less cognitively and morally from the bulk of the citizenry. The few who are chosen as representatives must be capable of deciding what the public interest requires, but ordinary citizens need only be able to recognize those who have this capability; they need not have it fully themselves. On this view, then, representative democracy introduces a more realistic division of moral labor, so to speak, and a two-tier conception of the distribution of political knowledge and wisdom.

On closer inspection, however, this two-tier solution to the substantive dilemma of democracy breaks down. There has never been a democratic political community or state, not even Athenian democracy at its height, that did not combine representational and participatory institutions and practices in some fashion.[11] Similarly, balancing substantive and procedural values is a problem that both representational and participatory institutions must face. Rather than pitting representation and participation or substantive and procedural values against each other and forcing some artificial tradeoff between them, a more promising theoretical approach is to explore the complementarity and symbiosis that could be achieved under various institutional arrangements.[12]

Consider, for example, the ways in which the character of political representation is affected by the kinds of participatory opportunities available to citizens at the community level. The democratic obligation of representatives (members of Congress, say) is to give voice to and promote the interests of the represented in the policy-making process. But it is not clear what to make of this obligation until we know more about the nature of those interests, how they are formed and evolve, and the dynamics of reciprocal communication between representatives and constituents. Whether or not a process of representation serves the substantive ideal of democracy depends not only on the character and activities of representatives but also on the character and activities of the represented. It is one thing to attempt to represent a passive, alienated constituency and quite another to represent a constituency whose own community life is richly textured with a variety of participatory deliberations and activities. It is at least arguable that representation in the latter context will more readily serve substantive democratic goals because democracy from above will be supplemented and reinforced by democracy from below.

In principle, theories of representative democracy should be able to distinguish conceptually between a responsive, accountable body of representatives and a benevolent, paternalistic political oligarchy, even though empirically the representatives and the oligarchs may legislate exactly the same policies. Democratic theories that set up a rigid antithesis between representation and participation are unable to capture this distinction.

From Rousseau through Madison and John Stuart Mill, the most significant debates among modern democratic theorists have centered on the relationship between representation and participation and on various strategies for resolving the procedural and substantive dilemmas I have mentioned. More recently these debates have been carried on in the rivalry between a perspective commonly known as democratic revisionism and a growing body of work that emphasizes the positive value and practicality of participatory democracy.[13] The revisionist position grew out of several sources, including empirical studies of public opinion and the pessimism about the future prospects for liberal democracy that many political theorists and social scientists began to feel when faced with the growth of totalitarian mass movements in the twentieth century. Participatory theory, by contrast, has been impressed by the significant rise of grassroots political activity in the United States and Western Europe beginning in the 1960s, activity generated by the New Left, the Civil Rights Movement, feminism, environmentalism, worker self-management, and a host of similar developments. These movements have called for, and to some extent have created, greater civic inclusion in powerful social institutions and important decision-making processes.

Democratic Revisionism.   The basic goal of revisionist democratic theory has been to replace the aspirations of traditional democratic thought with a putatively more realistic and much more modest set of expectations about the necessary limits of democratic governance.[14] The revisionists have, in effect, redefined the notion of democracy to make it compatible with a much larger substantive and procedural role for professional experts and other elites than most earlier democratic theorists would have found acceptable. For the revisionists, the difference between oligarchy and democracy is not the difference between the rule of an elite versus the rule of the people; it is the difference between the rule of a single elite versus the rule of competing elites.

Democratic revisionism dismisses direct or participatory modes of democratic governance as both unworkable and undesirable in the context of the modern nation-state and in the face of what it calls "mass society."[15] Participatory democracy requires small, decentralized political units and a fairly high degree of cultural homogeneity. Public policy making in the modern state, by contrast, requires systemic coordination and cannot presuppose cultural consensus, but must artificially construct it by reconciling pluralistic interests and values. Also, participatory institutions are sociologically and psychologically unable to realize their own ideal of democratic self-rule. They inevitably produce their own dominant elites who informally impose their own priorities and interests onto collective deliberations and decisions in accordance with what Robert Michels called the "iron law of oligarchy."[16] Finally, participatory politics has a dangerously antidemocratic and illiberal potentiality in modern societies marked by a high degree of alienation and the breakdown of secondary associations. Under these conditions charismatic leaders and antidemocratic elites can mobilize mass movements which, under the misleading banner of democratic and populist values, overthrow liberal constitutional government and establish totalitarian control.

Thus, according to the democratic revisionists, participatory democracy fails both procedurally and substantively; it achieves neither rule by the people nor rule for the people. It must be discarded as an outmoded model of governance.

The revisionist critique of representative democracy also mounts both a procedural and a substantive attack. Procedurally, representative institutions are unable to maintain their theoretically prescribed fusion between the representatives and those whom they represent. At best, electoral competition can ensure only that competing elites will be somewhat restrained in their use of political power by their temporary tenure in office and by the need to avoid doing anything that would arouse widespread public opinion against them.

This argument casts representative democracy in a new light and gives it a considerably more negative substantive purpose. Representative institutions are not to be seen as the vehicles for the expression of some positive public mission. Modern publics have no coherent or concrete purposes or programs to express; they live in a condition of general political apathy punctuated only be discrete interests, preferences, and fears.[17] Therefore, the realistic and appropriate function of representative bodies is to protect particular interests from undue domination by other interests and to protect their constituents from the power wielded by private, unrepresentative, and unaccountable elites. The goal of those elites who compete for positions of democratic political authority is to prevent public harm rather than to promote public good.

For revisionist democratic theory, then, democratic institutions have only a negative instrumental value. They are a means to achieve the values of political order and liberty by protecting against the permanent monopolization of political power by any single elite, and by protecting citizens against the unjust or exploitative exercise of private power in society. Representative institutions do not actually represent the citizenry in the process of governance, but they do provide the arena where elites seeking political power to realize their own interests are forced to compete for public favor in order to achieve their ends, and hence are effectively restrained in their tendency to promote their own interests at the expense of the public interest. With arguments of this kind, democratic revisionists have constructed a new account of how the interests of the rulers can be made to coincide with the interests of the ruled. And this, for them, is the only necessary defining characteristic of a "democratic" political system; under contemporary social conditions no more idealistic aspiration for democracy is realistic.

Participatory Democracy.   It is not surprising that such a sharp critique of traditional democratic hopes has occasioned an equally sharp response. Participatory democratic theorists share many of the revisionists' reservations concerning liberal representative democracy as it has historically functioned in the United States and Western Europe. But they draw diametrically opposed conclusions from their reading of democratic political history.[18] The failure of representation to realize its normative goals in a democratic polity, for them, can be traced to the gradual withering of participatory activity at the community level and to the privatization of self-identity in a bureaucratic capitalist (or state socialist) system. Under these conditions ordinary individuals feel powerless and alienated from political life, not because they are inherently private egoists rather than civic beings by nature, but because they in fact are relatively powerless. The solution to the past failures of representative democracy is not *less* democracy and greater reliance on authority entrusted to elite experts, professionals, and managers; but *more* democracy and more empowerment growing out of a combination of widespread participatory opportunities throughout society (in the neighborhoods, the workplace, and the various levels of government) and governmental representation based on increased accountability and better mutual communication between representatives and constituents.

A central thesis of participatory theory is that the experience of democratic participation itself enhances the political reasonableness, judgment, and civic sensibilities of the participants. Only by being directly and meaningfully involved in the process of dialogue, deliberation, and decision making about matters of public concern can an individual develop a motivating sense of citizenship and civic commitment. For this reason, participatory theorists maintain that there is a crucial linkage between fulfilling the procedural and the substantive requirements of traditional democracy. Achieving government for the people (the substantive condition) requires the creation of a certain kind of "people," a political community composed of genuine citizens. Concomitantly, achieving government by the people (the procedural condition) is the

235

principal means to that end, forging the political being of citizens through the self-transforming activity of their political doing.

The revisionists are surely correct in holding that substantive democracy cannot be achieved merely by empowering mass publics or lonely crowds composed of defensive, fearful, self-interested individuals. But, the participatory theorists counter, the way to achieve the civic sensibility substantive democracy requires is by gradually introducing more public, participatory opportunities into people's lives. The mistake the revisionists make is in assuming that a political system must be made up of ideal democratic citizens before they can be trusted to exercise democratic power responsibly. For the participatory theorists the issue is at once more complex and open to greater possibilities. On this view, the intriguing thing about democracy as a form of governance is that it must continuously create and recreate the preconditions of its own existence as it operates. Democracy is a ship of state that not only must be repaired but also must be built and rebuilt while at sea.

Finally, participatory theorists differ from democratic revisionists in that they view the democratic process as an intrinsic and not merely an instrumental good. This is an important theme in their work because they realize that making a case for citizen participation in a decision-making process solely on the grounds that participation gives individuals a way to protect their own private interests is vulnerable on two counts. First, if it can be shown that these interests are adequately protected in some other way, for instance through representational oversight or through professional self-regulation (George Ball's point), then the case for participation fades away. Second, the educational, self-developmental possibilities of the experience of participation are likely to be short-circuited if participation is seen merely as a protective device. In order to realize these possibilities, participation must be seen as a more positive phenomenon, as an occasion for the sharing of pertinent information, for the deliberative refinement of political and moral judgment, and for the exercise of civic responsibility. It is when the impulse toward participation is not informed by the promotion of democratic interests, in the sense I defined earlier, but only by the protection of private interests, that the self-defeating nature of participatory governance (Baltimore's point) looms as a serious problem.

How the basic purpose of participation is seen will also affect the institutional arrangements we devise to facilitate participatory activity. And it will further affect the likely relationships between citizen participants and the professionals or experts concerned with particular policies or issues under discussion. When participation is viewed as a protective device these relationships are likely to be highly adversarial, with each side attempting to defend itself against or co-opt the other. If participation were seen in a broader, more positive way, as a process which has both instrumental and intrinsic value for those taking part and for society as a whole, then there is no reason, in principle, why the exercise of participatory (or representative) democratic governance need undermine the legitimate and valuable role played by experts or professionals in the policy-making process. Democracy and elitism may be antithetical, but democracy and expertise are not. It may be worth stating this obvious point because it so often seems to get lost in discussions of the democratic governance of science.

DEMOCRATIC LESSONS FOR
INSTITUTIONAL REFORM IN SCIENCE POLICY

What bearing do the points raised in this review of contemporary democratic theory have on the governance of science and technology? As the debate over the governance of science and technology develops in the years ahead, both proponents and opponents of greater democratization in science policy making must more clearly identify the values that democratic governance is supposed to serve or threaten. And they must more clearly distinguish between the relative strengths of representational and participatory institutions in realizing these values. The broader but parallel debate between democratic revisionists and participatory theorists indicates some of the directions this discussion could take. Other chapters in this volume explore some of these directions in detail. Here I shall conclude simply by outlining a few points that, in my estimation, merit special emphasis.

As a starting point let us return to the arguments of George Ball and David Baltimore. Earlier I noted that their arguments, which I take to be fairly typical of mainstream science policy analysis, echo many of the central tenets of democratic revisionism. These arguments were made in the context of the controversy over the regulation of recombinant DNA (rDNA) research. In the late 1970s this controversy was – and it has remained – paradigmatic in shaping the terms of the debate over the governance of science and technology in the United States. It has been a useful prism through which to view this topic because it brings together several important facets of the complex relationship between one segment of the research community and governmental institutions at both federal and local levels. The dynamics at work here indeed may illustrate a pattern of events that could become increasingly common in similar controversies in the future.[19]

The story of this dispute is well known, so I shall only reiterate a few salient points here.[20] In 1974, in advance of any widespread public awareness or concern about the possible environmental or health hazards of DNA research, a group of concerned researchers took it upon themselves to press for self-regulation and restraint within the scientific community. In so doing, however, these researchers set in motion a sequence of broader political responses that they probably did not anticipate and certainly could not control. These responses led to the promulgation of NIH guidelines in 1976 and to the creation of the NIH Recombinant DNA Advisory Committee (RAC) and Institutional Biosafety Committees (IBCs) at individual research institutions. In an attempt to include a carefully circumscribed form of citizen participation in the regulatory process, each of these committees included lay members or "public representatives." During the same period an initially tumultuous political controversy in Cambridge, Massachusetts, activated direct citizen involvement of a much more challenging kind.

The DNA debate shocked the scientific community for at least two reasons. First, it brought substantive governmental regulation into the domain of bench science and basic research, a domain previously affected by budgetary policies at the federal level, but traditionally subject to regulation only by peer review.

Second, it raised the specter of a highly diverse and inconsistent regulatory environment controlled by the vagaries of local politics. This prospect troubled federal policy makers as well as researchers because it would make the goal of creating a consistent and predictable national science policy very difficult, if not impossible, to achieve. In the years following World War II, the scientific community had successfully established a cooperative working relationship with key policy makers and legislators at the federal level. This relationship virtually assured that professional attitudes and priorities would play a dominant role in the formation of science policy — both regulatory and budgetary policy — in Washington. At the local level, however, no such *modus vivendi* between scientific elites and politicians had been established or was likely to be. Local politicians were much less insulated from volatile public pressures and fears than federal officials. They appeared less likely therefore to give overriding priority to the value of scientific advance in their decision making.

Scientific lobbying groups, joined by private industries which had an interest in the commercial development of genetic engineering techniques, fought strenuously in 1978 against a bill introduced in Congress by Rep. Paul Rogers that endorsed the legitimacy of local community control of laboratory research. Faced with a choice between federal and local regulation, professional organizations such as the American Society of Microbiologists were willing to opt for the former as the lesser of the two evils, but only if the principle of federal preemption over local laws was firmly established. The success of this lobbying effort forestalled radical change in the structure of the science policy-making process. But the traditional pact or "social contract" between science and society, to which Baltimore refers, was beginning to show signs of strain. A hitherto "private" domain of science, basic research, was being transformed into a "public" domain legitimately subject, as things public generally are and things private generally are not in our society, to democratic controls. Democratic authority and power were gradually being shifted downward and outward.

In his provocative analysis of the rDNA controversy, David Dickson argues that "technocratic" science policy ultimately triumphed over "democratic" policy.[21] The efforts that were made to institutionalize citizen participation in the policy-making process were counterproductive, he says, because they merely created a facade of democratic accountability which masked the deeper consolidation of effective control in the hands of scientific and corporate elites. Dickson's analysis is less incisive, however, concerning an alternative to incremental attempts to institutionalize enhanced citizen participation in science and technology policy. Earlier I argued that meaningful participation and effective representation are vitally linked in a democratic political system. If we conclude that participatory reforms are inevitably prone to co-optation and degeneration into a legitimating facade for elite power, then we can hardly afford to be sanguine about the capacity of representative institutions, be they Congress, state governments, or city councils, to achieve better scientific accountability.

Despite the limited participatory goals that were achieved, the rDNA case does contain, in my estimation, some constructive lessons for the institutional reform of science and technology governance. First, it illustrates the fact that even when policy disagreements initially arise within the professional scientific community, they can quickly spill over into the public domain if those knowledgeable about the technical aspects of the controversy are willing and able to grasp the ethical and social dimensions of the problems and make them explicit. For, at bottom, it is the ethical issues that transcend specialized professional and bureaucratic expertise. These normative issues become the focal point for public interest and concern, and provide the basis upon which compelling claims for civic inclusion and democratic decision making can be made.

In addition, the rDNA case provides one of the most interesting and promising examples of productive citizen participation in recent years. In Cambridge, after the initial period of sensationalism and political posturing had passed, the deliberations of the citizen's advisory group demonstrated that when a participatory body is given sufficient time, information, and opportunity to make decisions that will have a real impact on issues that truly matter to the participants, it can achieve a high level of sophistication and understanding. And it can produce decisions and recommendations on complex technological problems that are as well informed and reasonable as those made by expert, professional elites.[22]

Generalizing from these observations brings us back to the symbiotic relationship between representational and participatory institutions. Democratic representatives can be co-opted by self-interested experts as readily as ordinary citizens, or perhaps even more readily. If public officials at the federal, state, or local level are to cope in democratically responsible ways with the issues raised by science and technology, they must be supported by informed publics.[23] And it is surely through more widespread participatory activities—both formal ones, like the Cambridge citizen's advisory group, and informal ones, like the workshops, debates, and town hall meetings once sponsored by the NSF Science for Citizens program—that the kind of informed citizenry that makes democratic representation possible will be fashioned.

Moreover, building a richer social infrastructure of participatory activity cannot be limited to the domain of science and technology decisions alone. My own view is that achieving greater civic inclusiveness and democratic accountability in the process of science policy making will be possible only if it proceeds in tandem with a parallel democratization of decision making in other areas. Conversely, since the growth of science and technology has such a significant ripple effect throughout our society, and since it plays such an important role in determining which groups control the direction of social change, an effective democratization of decision making in other policy areas will hardly be possible unless we somehow ensure that the uses of science and technology reinforce rather than impede that democratization. This is not to say that what I referred to earlier as the "participatory impulse" currently abroad in our society should be directed at science and technology policy only after it has triumphed in other areas. But it is to say that the effective democratization of science governance will not be achieved except as a part of a broader movement toward greater participation at all levels of our society. Indeed, the fact that science and technology issues permeate many other important areas of public policy — for example, the emerging domain of "industrial policy"[24] — may provide the most compelling argument for greater citizen participation in science policy making. For if citizens lack, or are precluded from developing, an informed, engaged understanding of scientific and technological issues and options, citizens will find themselves less and less able to comprehend and take part in all other policy debates. Scientific and technical illiteracy is fast becoming tantamount to civic illiteracy as such; it poses one of the gravest threats to meaningful citizenship in contemporary democratic societies.

With or without greater participatory governance, social and economic forces are transforming science, and nostalgia for a pristine state of professional autonomy can only distort our capacity to grapple with these changes. While no one can confidently predict the precise direction in which science and technology policy will move, two things do seem reasonably certain. First, policy and investment decisions made either in the public or in the corporate sector will produce new institutional pressures on scientists and will curtail the autonomy that the scientific profession had enjoyed in the past. The question is not whether that autonomy will be curtailed, but how much, by whom, and how democratically accountable those who curtail it will be. Second, science policy decision making will become increasingly politicized, both by lay groups and organizations demanding a greater role and a greater voice in the policy-making process and by corporate decision makers who seek to invest in basic research and to exploit technological applications commercially.

Given that the politicization of science is inevitable in any case, one democratic challenge facing future science policy making will be to integrate increased citizen participation into the policy-making process by devising creative new institutional mechanisms and procedures. A

241

second democratic challenge will be to channel the politicization of science toward a constructive and reasonable social consensus about the ends and priorities of technology development and the growth of potentially applicable scientific knowledge. How well we meet these challenges will be determined — not wholly, but in part — by the clarity, rigor, and imaginativeness of the democratic arguments we make, and by the democratic vision we embrace.

NOTES

1. Leonard A. Cole, *Politics and the Restraint of Science*, 3–13.

2. Robert A. Dahl, *Controlling Nuclear Weapons: Democracy Versus Guardianship* (Syracuse, N.Y.: Syracuse Univ. Press, 1985).

3. Leo Marx, *The Machine in the Garden* (New York: Oxford Univ. Press, 1964); and John Kasson, *Civilizing the Machine: Technology and Republican Values in America, 1776-1900* (New York: Grossman, 1976).

4. For careful and suggestive discussions of this new technology critique, see Langdon Winner, *Autonomous Technology* (Cambridge: MIT Press, 1977), and William Ophuls, *Ecology and the Politics of Scarcity* (San Francisco: Freeman, 1977).

5. For a general overview of this participatory impulse in science governance and in public policy generally, see Stuart Langton, ed., *Citizen Participation in America* (Lexington, Mass.: Lexington Books, 1978); James C. Petersen, ed., *Citizen Participation in Science Policy*; U.S., Congress, Senate, Subcommittee on Health and Scientific Research, *Biomedical Research and the Public*, 95th Cong., 1st sess., (Washington, D.C.: Government Printing Office, 1977); and Dorothy Nelkin, "Technology and Public Policy," in *Science, Technology, and Society*, ed. Spiegel-Rösing and Price, 393–442.

6. Quoted in Sissela Bok, "Freedom and Risk," *Daedalus* 107 (Spring 1978): 118.

7. David Baltimore, "Limiting Science: A Biologist's Perspective," 37, 41–42.

8. See Jean-Jacques Salomon, "Science Policy Studies and the Development of Science Policy," in *Science, Technology, and Society*, ed. Spiegel-Rösing and Price, 46ff.

9. These terms are borrowed from Samuel P. Huntington, "The Democratic Distemper," in *The American Commonwealth—1976*, ed. Nathan Glazer and Irving Kristol, 9–38. I have discussed this skepticism about the prospects of liberal democracy in the face of environmental problems more fully in Bruce Jennings, "Liberal Democracy and the Problem of Scarcity," *International Political Science Review* 4 (1983): 375–83.

10. The best general survey of democratic theory is J. Roland Pennock, *Democratic Political Theory* (Princeton: Princeton Univ. Press, 1979).

11. See M.I. Finley, *Politics in the Ancient World* (Cambridge: Cambridge Univ. Press, 1983), 70–96.

12. See Hanna F. Pitkin and Sara M. Shumer, "On Participation," *democracy*, 2 (Fall 1982):43–54; and Dennis F. Thompson, *John Stuart Mill and Representative Government* (Princeton: Princeton Univ. Press, 1976).

13. For a critical but thorough review of democratic revisionism, see Peter Bachrach, *The Theory of Democratic Elitism*. On participatory theory see Carole Pateman, *Par-*

ticipation and Democratic Theory; and J. Roland Pennock and John W. Chapman, eds., *Participation in Politics* (New York: Lieber-Atherton, 1975).

14. The *locus classicus* of democratic revisionism is Joseph A. Schumpeter, *Capitalism, Socialism, and Democracy*, 3rd ed. (New York: Harper & Row, 1950), 232–302. Other influential works in the revisionist tradition include: Gabriel Almond, *The American People and Foreign Policy*; Robert A. Dahl, *A Preface to Democratic Theory*; Robert A. Dahl and Charles Lindblom, *Politics, Economics and Welfare* (New York: Harper & Row, 1953); Earl Latham, *The Group Basis of Politics: A Study in Basing Point Legislation* (Ithaca: Cornell Univ. Press, 1952); William Kornhauser, *The Politics of Mass Society*; Seymour M. Lipset, *Political Man* (New York: Doubleday, 1960); Nelson Polsby, *Community Power and Political Theory* (New Haven: Yale Univ. Press, 1965); and Aaron Wildavsky, *Dixon-Yates: A Study in Power Politics* (New Haven: Yale Univ. Press, 1962).

15. See Kornhauser, *The Politics of Mass Society*; and Bachrach, *The Theory of Democratic Elitism*, 26–46.

16. Robert Michels, *Political Parties* (Glencoe, Ill.: Free Press, 1949), esp. 365–408.

17. See Paul F. Lazarsfeld et al., *The People's Choice: How the Voter Makes Up His Mind in a Presidential Campaign* (New York: Columbia Univ. Press, 1944): Bernard Berelson et al., *Voting: A Study of Opinion Formation in a Presidential Campaign* (Chicago: Univ. of Chicago Press, 1952); Angus E. Campbell et al., *The American Voter* (New York: Wiley, 1960); and Philip E. Converse, "The Nature of Belief Systems in Mass Publics," in *Ideology and Discontent*, ed. David E. Apter (New York: Free Press, 1964), 202–61.

18. Representative selections of the work of participatory theorists are contained in Terrence E. Cook and Patrick M. Morgan, eds., *Participatory Democracy* (San Francisco: Canfield Press, 1971). In my view the best and most significant work in this area is Benjamin Barber, *Strong Democracy* (Berkeley: Univ. of California Press, 1984).

19. See Allan Mazur, *The Dynamics of Technological Controversy*.

20. For a detailed account see Sheldon Krimsky, *Genetic Alchemy*.

21. David Dickson, *The New Politics of Science*, esp. 217–60. See also David Dickson, "Limiting Democracy: Technocrats and the Liberal State," *democracy* 1 (Jan. 1981): 61–79.

22. For suggestive evidence on this point consult Public Agenda Foundation, *Science Priorities and the Public* (New York: Public Agenda Foundation, n.d.).

23. See Kenneth Prewitt, "Scientific Illiteracy and Democratic Theory," 49–64.

24. It is instructive to consider science policy in the context of the industrial policy questions raised in Robert B. Reich, *The Next American Frontier* (New York: Times Books, 1983).

11. Resolving Science Controversies: From Science Court to Science Hearings Panel

LEONARD A. COLE

In the wake of the accomplishments of the atomic physicists during World War II, scientists enjoyed a period of extraordinary esteem throughout American society. Their position was enhanced by a rush of scientific and technological innovations in a variety of areas. The discovery of antibiotics, pesticides, food preservatives, plastics, and novel uses of materials like asbestos, lead, and freon seemed to offer the citizenry a future of splendid comfort. Scientists largely governed their own activities, constrained only by their wits and funding resources. As Blanpied and Hollander point out in Chapter 3 of this volume, the relationship between scientists and society was codified into law and policy. Since the scientists understood their work, and presumably its dangers, best, they were assumed to understand any risks to the public that might be associated with their activities.

But by the 1970s, as one after another of the earlier innovations proved unexpectedly hazardous, the vision of the new scientific age lost its glitter. A majority of the public still believed that the benefits of science outweighed its harmful effects, but many wondered what had gone wrong with the earlier promise.[1] Some began to consider how society might better confront scientific problems and avoid such miscalculations.

In recent years several proposals have been made to improve the institutional processes by which decisions about controversial scientific and technological issues are made. This chapter will compare three such proposals: the science court, the citizen court, and the science hearings panel. While not the only suggestions for reforming the decision-making process, these represent distinctive approaches that encompass features of other proposals as well. Moreover, they have the potential to address a wide spectrum of science and technology controversies.

A review of these proposals provides a perspective on the changing emphases of the debate about public welfare and the regulation of science. Although the proposed institutions would deal with various science and technology controversies, discussions have often focused on their relevance to nuclear or recombinant DNA issues. Before examining these issues and their relationships to the proposed institutions, a comment about science policy in a democratic society is appropriate.

SCIENCE IN A DEMOCRACY

Elsewhere in this book Bruce Jennings distinguishes between representative and participatory democracy. He cautions that in contemporary society, problems that hamper democratic governance are intrinsic to both approaches. Purely representative government may generate into competition among elites, while participatory democracy, in which citizens directly determine policies, is too cumbersome to be effective.

To the extent that a science court is elitist, and a citizen court populist or participatory, Jennings's discussion anticipates some of the criticisms that will be offered about these institutions in this chapter. Beyond questions about the shortcomings of particular institutions, however, one proposition is incontestible. Any activity that affects the wellbeing of the public should be of public concern. Whatever the nature of the activity — whether related to business, agriculture, education, or science — the ultimate guardians of the public interest should be the public and its political representatives, not the experts and specialists concerned with the activity. Does a scientist have more or less right to grow bacteria than a farmer to grow potatoes? This must depend on whether the consequences would be detrimental to the public good. If a scientist's or farmer's activities endanger the public welfare, then restraining those activities by political authority is legitimate. If the public interest would be advanced or unaffected, restraint is plainly inappropriate.

Are scientists justified in wanting to retain exclusive control of their own work? Are they better suited to regulate science than are businesspersons exclusively to regulate their activities, or lawyers to regulate theirs, or farmers to regulate theirs? Some argue that this is the case,[2] but there is ample reason for doubt. Whether in the commitment of fraud,[3] or miscalculation of the consequences of their activities,[4] scientists reveal weaknesses common to the rest of humanity. Scientists themselves are ambivalent about the legitimacy of governmental interference in their work, but survey results indicate that they recognize the responsibility of government to protect the citizenry from harmful scientific activities.[5]

THE RIGHT OF THE PUBLIC TO PROTECTION

Another aspect of the question of governance is more problematic: the extent to which external authority might inhibit or pervert scientific activities. The ethical dimensions of the problem were demonstrated during the 1970s when the public learned that government agencies had been conducting secret experiments on unwitting human subjects. The first such revelation involved a study in Tuskegee, Alabama. For four decades hundreds of syphilitic black men were observed but untreated by U.S. Public Health Service doctors who wanted to assess the course of the disease. Even if the health of the subjects had not been at risk, the experiment would have been inappropriate. Perhaps the ethical issues involved in such research were ambiguous in the 1930s when the project was begun, but well before 1972, when the experiment was stopped, the Tuskegee researchers should have recognized that their work involved a breach of ethics. Details of the Nazi medical experiments on concentration camp inmates were revealed during the Nuremberg trials in 1948. After the trials, the notion of informed consent by experimental subjects became part of the norms of research.[6]

Besides the Tuskegee case, two other federally-sponsored experiments that disregarded the rights of human subjects were revealed in the 1970s. They purportedly were conducted in the interest of national security and thus added another complication to the question of governing science. The Central Intelligence Agency tested mind-altering drugs on unsuspecting subjects to observe the effects on their behavior. Several experienced psychotic episodes, and on two occasions subjects committed suicide after they unknowingly consumed drinks containing the drugs.

The other unethical experimental project was even more shocking. For twenty years the U.S. Army secretly exposed millions of citizens to bacteria and chemical particles in simulated germ warfare attacks. Hundreds of tests were conducted during the 1950s and 1960s over populated areas to determine the dissemination patterns of the bacteria and particles in preparation for an attack by an enemy. The bacteria and particles were supposedly harmless, although questions should have been raised about health problems that arose after the population had been exposed. In any case, millions of people served as experimental subjects without their knowledge or consent.

These cases highlight the conflict of interests that has taken place in recent decades — between a scientist's right to inquire and a subject's right to protection; between the intentions of scientists who perform experiments in secret in the name of national security or for commercial gain, and the welfare of citizens endangered by these experiments; between the needs of scientists conducting research intended to better the human condition and the protection of a larger society that faces unexpected hazards. Recognizing these conflicts helps us move past the questions of whether science should be governed by external authority. We should ask, as several contributors to this book have, How should the authorities who represent the public govern scientific activities that threaten the health and welfare of the citizenry?

NUCLEAR AND RECOMBINANT DNA POLICIES

In the 1970s concern about potentially dangerous activities prompted several suggestions for institutional changes in the governance of science. No issues received wider attention in this regard than nuclear and recombinant DNA (rDNA) policies. A review of the two issues will clarify their relationships to the proposed science court, citizen court, and science hearings panel.

For thirty years after World War II, the United States' commitment to a nuclear future was reflected in political institutions that, to encourage development of nuclear power, had been distorted in form. The Atomic Energy Commission (AEC) was established in 1946, but unlike any other regulatory agency, it was charged with the contradictory responsibility of promoting the enterprise it was supposed to regulate.[7]

At the same time, contrary to the traditions of the Congress, a single permanent committee composed of members of both houses was empowered to oversee all atomic affairs. No other committee in either house had authority to consider nuclear issues. Thus, the usual regulatory and oversight arrangements that are supposed to promote public education and discourse were suspended. Members who served on the Joint Committee on Atomic Energy, like the regulators on the AEC, were almost all unstinting enthusiasts about nuclear development. The notion of protecting against the dangers of nuclear development was far less their concern than encouraging its growth. Legislation provided incentives for private industry to invest in the development of nuclear power, while the occasional scientist who raised questions about safety was stifled.[8]

By the mid-1970s, members of the public had become aware of the nuclear establishment's miscalculations and misrepresentations concerning the safety of the nuclear enterprise. Information about the danger of meltdowns at nuclear power plants, the consequent release of radioactive material into surrounding areas, inadequate evacuation plans, the inability to provide for safe permanent storage of nuclear wastes—all these stimulated questions about the wisdom of proceeding with nuclear power, and about the political institutions that had been created to accommodate its development. Recognition that the protective responsibilities of government had been sacrificed to the demand for development helped prompt institutional changes. The 1974 Energy Reorganizing Act abolished the AEC and provided for the establishment of the Nuclear Regulatory Commission (NRC) the following year. Congress's joint committee was later dissolved and congressional oversight of nuclear affairs was taken over by separate Senate and House committees.

The newly created NRC was charged with regulation, while promotion became the responsibility of a separate agency later incorporated into the Department of Energy. Some observers believe that nuclear affairs need still more rigorous control, but the institutional changes implemented in the mid-1970s at the regulatory and congressional levels mollified most critics.

At the time that inadequate governance of nuclear matters was prompting concern, the issue of rDNA research began to receive national attention. In the early 1970s, conditions seemed ripe for a biological rerun of the atomic experience. A technology was discovered in which genes could be transferred from one organism to another. The ability to recombine DNA, the chemical basis of genes, was hailed as the key to curing cancer, heart disease, and other illnesses. But a current of skepticism has arisen among several molecular biologists about the safety of rDNA research. Some felt that genetic tampering might produce dangerous organisms or otherwise harm future generations. A series of scientific conferences during the mid-1970s led to a moratorium on rDNA research.

The issues were reported by the news media and debated in city councils and before congressional committees. Ultimately the National Institutes of Health issued guidelines that were restrictive in proportion to the perceived danger of the experiment. Some types of experiments were prohibited entirely.

The manner of developing rDNA policies stood in contrast to that used in nuclear power policy development. Nowhere is this better demonstrated than by the effort to disseminate broadly the points at issue. The proceedings of a conference on rDNA sponsored by the National Academy of Sciences, for example, were published as "an attempt to help the layman and the scientist understand those facts that are already established, those facts that are in dispute, and the practical and moral considerations that must be part of any attempt to make final policy." Readers and observers were urged to examine the arguments of the DNA protagonists "at leisure," and "hopefully, this will allow a wider constituency to inform themselves and clarify the issues in this vital area of scientific development."[9] The spirit of this approach could hardly have been more at odds with the one that prevailed during the development of nuclear policies.

The media gave broad coverage to the debate, and the spectacle of scientific experts, challenging each other's interpretations of scientific facts, heightened popular discomfort about the issue. Yet by the end of the decade the controversy had largely subsided. Abetted by experimental evidence, a consensus had developed among scientists that earlier concerns about the dangers of rDNA research had been exaggerated. The NIH guidelines were relaxed, and the public seemed less apprehensive. The sequence of events, like that in the debate concerning nuclear oversight, had important implications for proposals then circulating about new institutions to improve the governance of science.

THE SCIENCE COURT

In response to the controversy about the safety and ethics of various scientific and technological activities, the idea of a science court attracted considerable attention in the mid-1970s. Articles in support of the proposal appeared in the professional journals, the issue was discussed in the popular press, and government spokesmen endorsed a trial effort. A two-day conference on the subject was held in September 1976 under the sponsorship of the Department of Commerce, the National Science Foundation, and the American Association for the Advancement of Science. More than 250 scientists, government officials, lawyers, and businessmen attended. While some expressed skepticism about the contribution that a science court might make, almost everyone agreed that the idea was worth trying.

Secretary of Commerce Elliot L. Richardson summarized the concern that prompted the conference: "We are made uncomfortable—indeed, made anxious—by the awareness that the processes by which we now arrive at important decisions are to such a degree nonrational." He expressed hope that a science court could help resolve controversies by separating scientific facts from political and value judgments.[10] In this he was joined by many others, including President Ford's science adviser, H. Guyford Stever. By the end of the conference a consensus had emerged that the idea should be implemented on an experimental basis.[11]

The model under consideration at the conference had been outlined a month earlier by the Task Force of the Presidential Advisory Group on Anticipated Advances in Science and Technology.[12] Articles in support of the court were published by members of the task force, including its chairman, Arthur Kantrowitz. Kantrowitz presented a detailed set of specifications for a court experiment that would involve three broad stages: initiation, organization, and procedure. Each stage was further divided into steps to facilitate its implementation.[13]

The initiation stage included establishment of a science court administration to make funding and hosting arrangements, to consult with regulatory agencies to find a suitable issue, and to obtain the cooperation of these agencies in procuring information. The second stage, organization, would entail soliciting personnel for a trial, including case managers to represent each side of an issue, and referees or judges.

The third stage, procedure, was the most elaborate. It included twelve steps, from formulation of factual statements by the case managers, through cross-examination and challenges by the adversaries, to the judges' opinions on contested statements of facts.[14]

The idea of an experimental court seemed to gain momentum after the conference. No other proposed institution concerning the governance of science received as much attention, before or since. Several scientific associations expressed interest, and Supreme Court Justice Warren Burger appointed a judicial task force to examine its feasibility.[15]

Yet no experimental court was ever convened. Enthusiasm for the idea soon waned, and by the end of the decade had virtually disappeared. There are two reasons for this: external events and weaknesses in the proposed model. Although the court would supposedly deal with a variety of issues, concerns about two of the most pressing, nuclear and rDNA policies, were being addressed in other ways. As discussed, institutional changes involving policy decisions in each of these areas were implemented in the mid-1970s. Yet another body to deal with them seemed superfluous.

Additionally, as the court idea came under more scrutiny, concerns mounted about several of its features. Most troublesome was the assumption that facts could be separated from values in assessing the wisdom of science policies. Proponents of the court suggested, for example, that the court could decide whether a particular nuclear power plant should be licensed or not, based on facts alone.[16] But which facts? Would they include the attitudes and values of nearby residents? Should they be based on the chances of an accident, which vary from one study to another?

Critics also doubted that truly disinterested judges could be found. Every human being unavoidably brings his own values to an interpretation of "facts." The frequency of divided decisions by the Supreme Court, and the predictability of how certain members will vote on particular issues are continuous reminders of this fact. Kantrowitz's response to the fact-value dilemma was uninspiring: "While it can be argued that the separation can never be complete, it must be admitted that we can do a better job of separating facts from values if we address ourselves to that goal."[17]

Another criticism lay with the aura of authority that would attach to the judges' verdicts. Even if venality and self-interest were not in question, the judges' decisions could never be value-free (for a discussion of this point, see Longino's chapter in this volume). Yet the decisions would appear as conclusive judgments made by supposedly disinterested scientists. Such verdicts would not likely be overriden by political officials who could make no equivalent claims of understanding the issues.

A final problem involved the court's addressing only issues that were already publicly controversial. The court's design made no provision for bringing anticipated problems to the public's attention, or for uncovering existing ones not yet widely familiar. During the early decades of nuclear development, when a few scientists sought to express concerns, they were stifled by the regulatory, congressional, and business establishments. There were no institutional provisions for dissent. The public remained oblivious to the problem until years later, when the nuclear issue evolved into one of public controversy.[18] The science court would do little to ameliorate such situations.

THE CITIZEN COURT

As the science court ideal lost momentum, a court with a sharply different format was suggested. Sheldon Krimsky proposed that a panel of lay citizens might be best suited to render decisions about science policies in their local communities. Elsewhere in this volume he reviews such an effort regarding chemical warfare research in Cambridge, Massachusetts. Most of his ideas about a citizen court, however, are based on his experience in the same community with an earlier group that had considered rDNA research policies.[19]

After learning early in 1976 that scientists at Harvard were planning to perform rDNA experiments, the mayor and city council of Cambridge, Massachusetts, held public hearings on the issue. Large crowds attended, as eminent scientists took contradictory positions. Some argued that the research would be safe and should not be restricted; others testified that it was dangerous and should be prohibited.

The council appointed a panel of eight citizens to offer advice on whether the federal guidelines for rDNA research offered sufficient protection to the community. The panel, which Krimsky used as his model for the court idea, was composed of local residents with varied backgrounds, though none had expertise about the rDNA issue. The citizen court functioned from August 1976 until January 1977, when it issued its final report.

Initially the members divided over which of the two sides in the issue had the greater responsibility to justify its positions. Some felt that safety and need had to be proved by the scientists who wanted to do the research; others believed that the case for restrictions had to be made by the critics. The court then heard testimony over a period of three months.

The procedural format was established by the members of the court. Scientific experts did not cross-examine each other, but the members questioned witnesses from both sides. Unlike a civil court proceeding, in which the judge, advocate, and jury are usually different people, the citizen court as a body assumed all three roles.

Krimsky acknowledges other shortcomings with the citizen court procedure. A few members had difficulty grasping some of the scientific arguments, though this was partly overcome when they sought comprehensible explanations from witnesses. Additionally, the members could meet for several hours a week, only as their personal and business schedules permitted. Between meetings they were expected to read reports, articles, and background material. Some worked harder than others and were better prepared to assess the issues.

Another problem involved the balance of time given to witnesses for either side of the issue. More supporters than opponents of the newest NIH guidelines were invited to testify. While this imbalance did not necessarily affect the court's ultimate judgment, the question of apparent partiality could be raised. Krimsky felt the problem was more a matter of flawed procedure than bias on the part of the members. Witnesses were often invited based on recommendations of others rather than according to any organized plan to seek balance. In the end the court's suggestions involved a compromise solution including careful monitoring, public disclosure of activities, and broad participation by the public in risk assessment. The city council voted unanimously to accept the court's recommendations.

Krimsky mentions the possibility of a citizen court working as an adjunct to a science court. The science court, he suggests, might help people understand the norms of science in a particular situation. But he envisions the citizen court as a superior forum to "assess the locus of controversy when scientific experts disagree."[20] In this regard he cites the Cambridge court as a credible group without special interests, whose proceedings were perceived as dignified and rational.

Despite Krimsky's report of success, in a broader perspective three characteristics of the citizen court idea raise questions about its value. The first involves an issue that Krimsky alluded to — the inability or unwillingness of many lay people to understand scientific issues that must enter into rational conclusions. Understanding such issues is not necessarily beyond the grasp of nonscientists, as some of the Cambridge court proved. But the manner of choosing capable people and establishing fair procedures remains undefined and problematic.

A second issue involves interpersonal dynamics — the potential for articulate people to be disproportionately influential in a group of nonexperts. There may be little connection between understanding an issue and ability to persuade others to take a position. People who are uninformed but articulate might be unduly convincing, leading to inappropriate court decisions.

Finally, allowing citizen courts to decide about major issues like DNA research or nuclear power could lead to dangerous inconsistencies. If the identical issues were to be heard by courts in hundreds or thousands of communities, this would mean not only wasteful repetition but also contradictory verdicts. Research deemed safe by one court might be ruled

253

unsafe by another, and something in between by a third. Rather than clarifying scientific and technological issues, a profusion of citizen courts would likely cause more confusion.

THE SCIENCE HEARINGS PANEL

As Table 11.1 suggests, many observers are uncomfortable with the notion of empowering a court of scientists or laymen to render verdicts about science policies. Some critics have suggested that controversies would be better dealt with through mediation, improved review procedures, or enhancement of public understanding. Such approaches reject institutions like a court that might interfere with the traditional manner of decision making.[21]

In line with these objections, a science hearings panel was subsequently proposed to enhance the decision-making process. The panel would be instructed on the premise that American political culture and existing political institutions are suitable to address science policy questions no less than questions about other areas of public interest. The panel would act as a body to receive reports of proposed or ongoing scientific activity deemed dangerous to the public and to respond in a prescribed series of steps.[22]

The science hearings panel could be composed of three or four distinguished scientists and an equal number of nonscientists, appointed by the president for five-year terms. Petitioners would initially submit a written document stating their concerns, but they might be invited to clarify their positions in person. As incentives, recognition and awards could be bestowed on those whose petitions prove valuable. If a petitioner preferred anonymity, however, this wish should be respected.[23] The priority would be to institutionalize a means to encourage scientists and others to express suspicions of danger. Whistle-blowing in the interest of public safety should be honored, at least by protecting the whistle-blower and his job.

Second, all inquiries or expressions of concern, except obviously frivolous ones, along with responses from experts, should be published in a periodical. Appropriate oversight agencies should be invited to comment as well. In areas involving research on humans, institutional review boards where the research is taking place would be expected to make a statement. In questions about the use of certain chemicals, the Food and Drug Administration or the Environmental Protection Agency would comment. Government agencies appropriate to almost every area of scientific concern already exist. Their comments, along with the petitioners' and those of recognized experts, would receive exposure through such publication.[24]

If published responses do not resolve the questions about safety or ethics, a third step would be necessary. The science hearings panel would convene a forum consisting of experts and nonscientists acting as participants and observers. The issues would then be publicly debated and the debate reported in the media.

The forum would employ an adversarial process approximating that for the proposed science court. But the forum would differ fundamentally in purpose. Unlike the court, whose judges would ostensibly decide issues of fact separately from values, the forum would offer no verdict or decision. The court proposal was based on the implausible premise that facts and values can be separated during an adversarial proceeding. Evidence presented to support any position is likely to be value-laden insofar as one advocate chooses to enhance his argument. To presume that judges could ignore the advocates' values or their own when rendering a decision is unrealistic. Still, while the science court's narrowly designated functions and purposes are problematic, elements of its proposed structure and procedures would be valuable. An adversarial process including cross-examination by opposing advocates might best expose the issues in contention and could be employed at a forum. A forum should be an educational rather than a decision-making medium. Disposition of the issues should lie with the people's representatives, the government. Employment of a forum would create a far larger base of informed citizens and representatives to make decisions than usually has been available in the past.

The proposed model resembles the sequence of events that evolved in consideration of the recombinant DNA issue. In the early 1970s, a few scientists were worried about the newly devised capability to recombine genetic material of different organisms. Their concerns were first reported in the magazine *Science* and later in the mass media. Several publicized conferences were held during the mid-seventies, at which supporters and critics of DNA research presented their views (though not in formal adversarial proceedings). The issues were debated within local and state governmental bodies, and advocates testified before congressional committees. Public exposure to the issues was broad.

The National Institutes of Health were assigned the task of formulating policy, and NIH proposed guidelines for rDNA research were

TABLE 11.1. Comparative Characteristics of the Science Court, Citizen Court, and Science Hearings Panel

	Science Court	Citizen Court	Science Hearings Panel
Principal Authorities	Judges who are scientists but not experts in areas under consideration; no number specified.	Laymen, 8 to 15 local citizens.	Equal number of scientists and laymen; total 6 to 8.
How Chosen	Science Court Administration (tenure and method of selection unspecified) chooses judges and case managers for each case.	Appointed by local governmental officials (mayor and council); tenure lasts for period that issue is under consideration.	By presidential appointment, 5-year terms, no reappointment. Other personnel, including advocates (adversaries), chosen by panel for each issue.
Role Differentiation	Separate administrators, judges (referees), and case managers (advocates).	No differentiation; members perform all functions as unit.	Panel members act as administrators, not judges. They are responsible for all functions, including appointment of personnel to specified positions, e.g., advocates, publication staff.
Goal	Verdict or decision by court intended to steer public policy.	Verdict or decision by court intended to steer public policy.	To provide information and education for the public and traditional decision makers. Nondirective in terms of policy making.

Nature of Issues for Consideration	Scientific or technological issues that are already publicly controversial; different court apparently for each issue.	Scientific or technological issues that are already publicly controversial; different court for each issue.	Publicly controversial issues as well as potentially dangerous or unethical ones not yet familiar to the public.
Period in Session	Unspecified—apparently only while a particular issue is under consideration.	New court for each issue; exists only during period that issue is under consideration.	Continuous existence as body (though individuals may serve only single 5-year term).
Decision-Making Process	Predetermined procedures: advocacy by case managers who represent different views; cross-examination (adversarial); final verdict by judges.	Each court establishes own procedures. In Cambridge experience, all members interrogated witnesses and joined in final verdict.	Panel acts as sponsor at various stages. 1) Receives controversial issues and solicits responses. 2) Disseminates information through publication. 3) Convenes forums for debate and adversarial challenges. 4) Does not render verdict, but lays out information for consideration by public and its political representatives.
Assumptions about Facts and Values	Explicit belief that scientific facts can be separated from values and that judgments can be made on factual considerations apart from values.	Implicit belief that scientific facts can be judged apart from values.	Assumes facts and values can never be entirely separated.

widely disseminated in the scientific community and the popular press. By the end of the decade, not all questions about safety had been resolved, though a consensus on regulated research had been reached. The issues had been considered and disposed of before the public.

In the 1980s, new issues concerning rDNA research emerged. As private industry entered the biotechnology field, questions about secrecy, patents of new life-forms, and controls over privately conducted experiments unsettled many observers. If the four-step sequence had been successful in dealing with the questions of the 1970s, the new issues have yet to be resolved. As Harold Green indicates in this volume, regulation of the genetic engineering industry seems inevitable, though the form it will take is debatable. Application of the science hearings panel format to the new issues could mediate the current controversies.

The four stages in the rDNA experience in the 1970s ought to become a standard procedure for other scientifically contentious issues concerning the well-being of the public. The concern initially raised by a few scientists about DNA research was welcome but uncommon. A science hearings panel to which scientists and others could bring their concerns without fear of penalty would make the process easier.

Second, though *Science* reported the controversy and helped provide information later disseminated by the popular press, the development was fortuitous. A journal published by the science hearings panel could reduce the uncertainty about exposure for other issues. Third, a formalized means to convene a forum would avoid uncertainties about ground rules and effectiveness that troubled conferences held on rDNA policy. Finally, as with the DNA controversy, after broad public exposure the issues may be better understood and disposed of by traditional legislative, executive, and judicial processes.

The suggested steps would require little innovation in political structure. A panel — to act as a depository for scientific concerns, to publish responses, and to sponsor an occasional forum — would constitute the only substantial innovation. The intention is not to organize a new system of judgment, but to enhance the process of decison making in the existing political apparatus. Scientific issues that affect the public should be decided no differently from nonscientific issues — before the public and their representatives.

CONCLUSION

The science hearings panel would not be encumbered by liabilities inherent in the science or citizen court models. Unlike the courts, the panel format does not assume that facts can be separated from values. As a result, expectations and outcomes would be more realistically based. Since no verdict would be rendered, there is no implicit claim that science policy issues can be resolved "above" politics.

Another valuable feature of the panel is its provision for soliciting and exposing anticipated problems. The court models allow for addressing issues only if they have already become matters of public controversy. A final advantage of the panel would be its continuing procedural mechanism. The science and citizen court formats require that an organization be reestablished for each new issue under consideration. The science hearings panel, in contrast, would be a permanent body whose procedures, once established, are systematic and predictable.

The principal weakness of the science hearings panel is that it might be no more capable than other forums of resolving problems related to certain secret work. Whether for purposes of national defense or proprietary interest, some scientific activities are carried out in secret. Unless one argues that secrecy is never legitimate, a plainly untenable position, the risk remains that the public can be exposed to dangers without its knowledge or consent. Nevertheless, the existence of a science hearings panel, insofar as it promotes the ethos of openness, might help discourage unnecessary secrecy. It would stand as an important symbolic as well as practical reminder of the rights of citizens.

The success of the science hearings panel presupposes that the integrity of existing political institutions be scrupulously respected. If their functions and purposes are perverted, as was the case with nuclear affairs, the public interest may be undermined. Open debate, informed decision making, and accountable officials are all requirements in the formulation of appropriate policies.

The criteria are not guaranteed to lead to the wisest policies, but neither are courts of scientists or laypeople. The most appropriate methods, those that have best served this country throughout its history, involve public accountability. With respect to science policies, institutional arrangements should enhance exposure to key issues by the public and its political representatives, the people who should ultimately make the policy choices.

The most desirable proposals in this regard are not novel means to

259

establish policy; rather, they suggest vehicles to educate. Public understanding of science controversies requires public airing of these controversies. If this can be promoted by an institution like a science hearings panel, a more informed electorate could make better decisions through its governmental representatives. The effort should be directed at enhancing traditional democratic practices, whether in legislative or administrative decision making. In this manner should science be governed, when governance is required outside the scientific community.

NOTES

1. L. John Martin, "Science and the Successful Society," 18.
2. Keith M. Wulff, "Research Regulation, the Public, and Professional Organizations," in *Regulation of Scientific Inquiry*, ed. Keith M. Wulff, 219–20.
3. William Broad and Nicholas Wade, *Betrayers of the Truth* (New York: Simon and Schuster, 1982).
4. Rachel Carson, *Silent Spring* (Boston: Houghton Mifflin, 1962); Ralph Nader and John Abbotts, *The Menace of Atomic Energy* (New York: Norton, 1977); Adeline Gordon Levine, *Love Canal: Science, Politics and People* (Lexington, Mass.: D.C. Heath, 1982).
5. Leonard A. Cole, *Politics and the Restraint of Science*, ch. 9.
6. Jay Katz, *Experimentation with Human Beings* (New York: Russell Sage Foundation, 1972), 292–306.
7. For a more comprehensive review of the nuclear policies summarized here, see Cole, *Politics and the Restraint of Science*, 121–36.
8. Ibid., 126–28.
9. National Academy of Sciences, *Research with Recombinant DNA: An Academic Forum, March 7-9, 1977* (Washington, D.C.: National Academy of Sciences, 1977), 3.
10. *New York Times*, 22 Sept. 1976, p. 11.
11. Ibid.
12. Task Force of the Presidential Advisory Group on Anticipated Advances in Science and Technology, "The Science Court Experiment: An Interim Report," *Science* 193 (20 Aug. 1976): 653–56.
13. Arthur Kantrowitz, "The Science Court Experiment: Criticisms and Responses," *Bulletin of the Atomic Scientists* 33 (Apr. 1977), 44–50.
14. Each step is delineated, in ibid., 45.
15. Philip M. Boffey, "Science Court: High Officials Back Test of Controversial Concept," *Science* 194 (8 Oct. 1976), 167–69.
16. Task Force of the Presidential Advisory Group, "The Science Court Experiment," 654.
17. Kantrowitz, "The Science Court Experiment," 46.
18. In ch. 6 of this volume, Leon Trachtman notes the role of the press as an imperfect though important outlet in lieu of governmental provisions.
19. Discussion in this section derives largely from Sheldon Krimsky, "A Citizen Court in the Recombinant DNA Debate," 37–43.

20. Ibid., 43.

21. Barry M. Casper, "Technology Policy and Democracy," *Science* 194 (1 Oct. 1976), 29–35; Nancy Ellen Abrams and R. Stephen Barry, "Mediations: A Better Alternative to Science Courts," *Bulletin of the Atomic Scientists* 33 (Apr. 1977), 50–53; Nancy E. Abrams and Joel R. Primack, "The Public and Technological Decisions," *Bulletin of the Atomic Scientists* 36 (June 1980): 44–48; and Mark E. Rushefsky, "The Misuse of Science in Governmental Decisionmaking," *Science, Technology and Human Values* 9 (Summer 1984): 47–59.

22. The science hearings panel was first proposed in Leonard A. Cole, "Science Watch," *The Sciences* 21 (Dec. 1981): 9, and further discussed in Cole, *Politics and the Restraint of Science*, 154–57.

23. An argument in favor of anonymous whistle-blowing is made by Frederick A. Ellison, "Anonymous Whistle-Blowing: An Ethical Analysis," *Business and Professional Ethics Journal* 1 (Winter 1982), 39–58.

24. In late 1984 the National Academy of Sciences began publishing *Issues in Science and Technology*, a quarterly intended to air "all points of view," according to the academy's president, Frank Press, (No. 1 [Fall 1984], 2). There is no indication whether the journal will employ a systematic method to seek various points of view, or how it intends to achieve balance. This effort to publicize different points of view is laudable, however, and, if successful, would perform the publication function of the proposed science hearings panel.

12. Governing Science and Technology: Reconciling Science and Technology with Democracy

MALCOLM L. GOGGIN

In addressing the post-war changes in science, technology, and society and their effects, the authors who have contributed to this book have commented critically on the nature of institutional responses to some perplexing governance problems and have evaluated the extent to which these responses have been successful. If there is one message that these chapters convey, it is that there is an underlying tension between the rules by which science and technology live and the rules of democracy.

Despite its internal system of democratic self-government, Science is one of those activities that lives by elite criteria, exercising claims to autonomy that are anathema to democrats. Democracy is more egalitarian than science, and even the United States' special brand of republican democracy was designed to prevent the concentration of power in the hands of any one interest or faction. This underlying tension between democracy and expertise has created problems for society, problems which, not surprisingly, are not easily resolved. The principal aim of this chapter is to reconcile science and technology with democracy so that all will flourish.

How one proceeds from this point depends upon whether or not the argument that there is a governance problem at all is credible, and, beyond that, whether the crisis of governance is due to too much or too little democracy. On balance, the contributors to this volume tend to support the views that there *is* a crisis of governance and that it is due to *too little*, rather than too much, democracy. No single dogma is preached by all of the contributors. Yet, if I can speak for the group, I am convinced that both science and society would be better off if the

United States were to move in the direction of more, rather than less, public governance of science and technology. The question that is addressed in this chapter is, How can science and technology be governed more democratically?

One answer to this question is to remove some of the impediments to public participation in science and technology policy making. The first part of this chapter identifies four barriers to democratic governance and recommends ways of lowering them. Next, the chapter takes up a number of issues related to structural changes in the science policy making and implementing apparatus — who should make policy, at what point in the process, where, and to what effect.

BARRIERS TO DEMOCRATIC GOVERNANCE

The multi-disciplinary research that is reported in this volume identifies at least four impediments to the democratic governance of science and technology. They are: (1) the learned attitudes and behavior of the average citizen, (2) a tightly-knit community of experts who are not so willing to share power, (3) powerful profit-seeking industrialists, and (4) universities that are heavily dependent on both industry and government for their survival. Let us examine these four barriers to public participation in turn.

An Apathetic, Scientifically Illiterate Citizenry. First, lay members of the public have little influence over policy for science and technology because the vast majority are apathetic, unorganized, and scientifically and technologically illiterate.

That most Americans are not actively involved in science and technology issue resolution is well documented.[1] Yet this same evidence supports the theory that power in America is shared, not concentrated — that a minority of interests governs most public policy domains.[2] And there is no reason to believe that science and technology would be an exception to this "rule by minorities" principle of governance.[3] The "alienation breeds distrust" proposition that was explicated in Chapter 1 helps explain why there are such low levels of public participation in the making of public policy for science and technology.[4]

In blaming the victim for her or his lack of participation, however, this explanation points to *psychological* barriers as conditioning, if not determining, political behavior. For example, the "cult of expertise," so

263

goes this argument, conditions many members of the public to behave as spectators, thus allowing elected representatives to be the gladiators in the arena of Congress. This *passive* behavior on the part of the public is learned and internalized as part of the socialization process. The belief in partisan mutual adjustment among competing elites that Don Price contends is part of the "unwritten Constitution" is an *ideological* barrier to more direct social control of science and technology. Of course, Price's solution—to give more power to the President—might make it even more difficult for ordinary citizens to have access to governing institutions.

Another more sinister explanation for low levels of citizen participation is a conspiracy theory. Scientists and engineers use a variety of *structural* devices to protect their privileged positions. With their special knowledge and education, they mystify science and technology, rely heavily on technical jargon in communications, form exclusive professional associations, and use professional, specialized journals that are not widely circulated in order to communicate results. Those with expert knowledge and training are rewarded for these types of professional behaviors and discouraged from other, more public ones, via university and professional reward systems. The end result is a fairly narrow set of activities directed at a very limited audience. And this mystification process discourages public understanding of science and technology.

Experts Who Believe in the Republic of Science.   Second, there is a powerful, organized, politically active community of experts that can mobilize its members when necessary. As part of their socialization into the profession, most accept what Michael Polanyi has described as a "Republic of Science."[5] Most agree that science and technology should be left to scientists and engineers.

Although the ultimate power to determine research priorities rests with members of the public, laypersons usually either consciously or by default delegate much of this responsibility to others. Whereas the Constitution designates Congress as the law-making branch of government, on many scientific and technical matters much of the responsibility for making policy has been delegated to non-elected officials in the executive agencies. Through this two-stage process of deferral to expert opinion, those with specialized knowledge gain considerable power. When it suits them, members of this group of scientists and technologists—and their non-credentialed allies in industry and the university—

can use their power to discourage public participation, or at least to neutralize its effects.

One of the best examples of the power of the scientific lobby was cited earlier in this book, namely the concerted effort by scientists in 1977 to block legislation that would have institutionalized a public voice in making national policy for scientific research. In 1977, at the height of the rDNA debate, Sen. Edward Kennedy, in response to considerable public pressure, introduced legislation in the Senate to establish a "balanced" committee to oversee gene-splicing research. But as a result of organized lobbying on the part of scientists and technologists, his proposal was withdrawn. Writing of the "victory" in the *New Republic*, James Watson said that the bill's defeat would have occurred sooner if "all scientists had said in public what we were endlessly boring ourselves with in private." He continued,

> This proposal naturally depresses me since it opens up the prospects of people with no scientific qualifications deciding what scientific work we should not do. Naturally, we have called on everyone we know in the White House to alert them to the new folly at HEW . . . only we scientists can judge unquantifiable conceptual risks.[6]

Corporate Capital Which is Short-Sighted.   Third, corporate capital, in the form of major science-based industries that are rich in resources, seek to maintain the current "two-tiered" system for governing science and technology. This is a system that relegates the majority of citizens to the sidelines in the policy-making game. Business interests fear a "tyranny of the majority."

The story of what happened to the Kennedy proposal for a "balanced" recombinant DNA committee is typical of "interest groups liberalism," a vulgarized form of pluralist theories of power in America.[7] Interest group liberalism grants special interests the rights to make public policy, which is then ratified by the state. In this theory of the state, the government protects the right of special interest groups to make policy decisions, and the regulatory powers that are granted to the state are used primarily for maintainance of existing power arrangements rather than for protection of the public or for system reform or structural change. Another example of the influence of interest groups in the formation and implementation of technology policy is what happened in the early years of the funding and development of the totally implantable artificial heart. Mary Lasker and her associates, and Dr. Michael

DeBakey, were very influential in shaping the path of the medical device's development.

A University that is Losing its Autonomy.   Fourth, a university that is, to use Ralph Nader's words, fast becoming "a vanguard of mercantilism", is a threat to democratic governance as well. The unversity's autonomy is threatened because of its heavy reliance for its future survival not only upon the genius of its faculty, student tuition, and alumni contributions, but also upon donations from government and industrialists.

The autonomy of the university, which is so vital to the nurturing of more and better citizen participation in science, is in danger of being eroded because of the commercialization of biology. Since the discovery of the double helix, biology has undergone rapid change. Like computer science and atomic physics, molecular biology has suddenly become commercialized. In the area of biotechnology, the contract between science and society has been rewritten to include the industrialist as middleman. There is a real danger that, as happened with other new technologies, experts with commercial interests will promise more than can be delivered, or exaggerate potential benefits and minimize potential risks and harms.

The autonomy of the university is also threatened by the related problem of conflict of interest, which surfaces in several ways, for example, as a conflict between the obligations of a university researcher to the norms of science and the purposes of the university, on the one hand, and the pressures from a patron — either to come up with a marketable product or to keep secret a report of a finding that might have commercial value. If science and technology are to be governed democratically in the future, then ways must be found either to avoid or quickly to resolve conflicts of interest.

WAYS OF LOWERING BARRIERS

No solution to the crisis of governance can be found unless positive steps are taken to overcome psychological, ideological, and structural barrier to public participation in the governing of science and technology.[8] By taking several practical steps to overcome these deep-seated obstacles, it is possible to establish the preconditions for a science and technology that will be governed more democratically. These steps are predicated on the assumption that existing institutions (some more representative than others) for governing science and technology in a democracy are inadequate. Given this generally negative assessment of existing institutions, there are at least three ways in which credibility can be restored. The strategies outlined below are directed towards building a "democratic character" and towards improving the quality and quantity of public participation in making and implementing public policy for science and technology.

First, lay members of the public have to *improve their understanding* — of science and technology and of the requirements of citizenship. Aristotle, in making the distinction between the legal framework of constitutional government and actual behavior in the polity, makes the point that a crucial component of political stability is learned, supportive behavior, not merely "book-learning." In Book V, Aristotle wrote:

> The education of a citizen in the spirit of his constitution does not consist in his doing the actions in which the partisans of oligarchy or the adherents of democracy delight. It consists in his doing the actions by which oligarchy or a democracy will be enabled to survive.[9]

Second, members of various publics must recognize that in order for any political solution to work, they will have to *respect the autonomy of others* with legitimate, competing claims. Democratic politics requires mutual respect and a recognition that in order to reach a solution, bargaining will be necessary. This requires that lay members of the public have an equal right to a place — and not just token representation — in the institutions that make decisions about priorities in science and technology. One way to guarantee parity with experts is either to educate public members of decision-making bodies or to give them access to scientific and technical advice upon which to make sound judgments.

Third, steps must be taken to encourage *public discourse*, or discussion, on matters scientific and technical. To do this requires improved access to policy formulation and adoption processes. Improved access necessitates a variety of participatory mechanisms, from more town meetings and community forums to intervenor funding to the demystification of science and technology. The critical aspect of public discourse is not only what is discussed, but where and when. In this regard, the antiwar movement is an appropriate model — local discussion in small groups with the supposition that fundamental assumptions can be assessed at any point in the policy process. Broadly speaking, what is indicated is a restoration of some of the communitarian institutions of

267

earlier times, but in a form that is consistent with modern life. Invigo-rating the democratic character of citizens will require opening up many social institutions — factories, universities, and families, for example — to democratic governance. In this manner, science and technology can be reconciled with democracy.

But these are merely preconditions, and say very little about the struc-ture of the science policy-making apparatus and how it can be made to operate more democratically. There are a number of tough questions that still need to be addressed. In the remainder of this chapter, four of them will be examined:

1. Who should govern?
2. When should science and technology be governed?
3. Where should power to direct modern science be lodged?
4. What should be the ends of science and technology?

WHO SHOULD GOVERN AND WHEN?

The results of our cross-disciplinary research underscore two points about who is currently governing and how. First, science and technology, which in this volume have been examined more as objects than as in-struments of policy, operate within a "two-tiered" political system of representative democracy where elites, responding to a variety of pres-sures, including the preferences of both organized interests and the elec-torate, make all the important political judgments, and non-elites vote periodically in order to select leaders who commit the collective to a particular course of action or inaction. Second, the social activities that have been defined as science and technology are carried out within a capitalistic economic system in which a relatively small group of power-ful individuals controls the processes of production, distribution and consumption. Convinced that what is good for corporate capital is good for America, at the moment this dominant interest has decided that us-ing science and technology to restore industrial capacity and build mili-tary might are in the public interest. Is this the dominant interest that should be governing?

In an article written a quarter-century ago, Wallace Sayre observed of our democratic system for governing science policy,

> In a democratic order all policies of significance must secure a wide range of consent, not merely from the general public but also from the many organized groups and institutions that see their interests importantly

involved. Scientists do have a special involvement in science and policy, but under the rules of a democratic society they have no monopoly in its development or maintenance, nor have they inherently any greater legitimacy or relevance as participants than all the other claimants who aspire to influence the content of science policy.[10]

Like Sayre, many of the authors of the chapters in this book have also observed that no one interest either should or does govern science and technology. And the question of who governs science and technology is inextricably linked to the question of who ought to govern them. In fact, in spite of a tangled web of relations among interest groups, federal agencies, and congressional committees and subcommittees that tends to produce a convergence of interests, the unique characteristics of the U.S. system of government have encouraged a divergent, uncoordinated, directionless, and, at times, contradictory "non-policy" for science and technology.[11] Furthermore, although much U.S. science and technology policy-making is conducted within the legislative and executive branches in Washington, power is not centralized but is widely shared between national and subnational governments and between governments and subgovernments, especially corporations, professional associations, the military, public interest groups, and universities.

Since fact and value questions relating to science and technology policy are so inextricably linked, it is not feasible to think in terms of one group with one set of credentials adjudicating matters of fact, and another group with other qualifications settling value questions. Thus, in answer to the question, Who should govern?, I agree with Wallace Sayre that *all who see their interests importantly affected should be involved in deliberations* about the course and conduct of science and technology. I am also convinced that all citizens, regardless of formal education, are also capable of being educated about facts and values. Therefore, in answer to the question, At what stage of the policy process should all these interests of which Sayre speaks be represented?, I would answer, *Interested citizens should participate actively at all stages.*

WHERE SHOULD SCIENCE AND TECHNOLOGY BE GOVERNED?

Among the various authors who have contributed to this book, there is considerable disagreement over where policy for science and technology should be made. Trachtman is satisfied with existing institutions but thinks they can be made to work better. Krimsky and Florig, on the other hand, argue for more decentralized decision making, with more local control. Blanpied and Hollander would like to see the current piecemeal system of allocating resources for science and technology scrapped in favor of more central coordination. What are the advantages and disadvantages of less and more centralized decision making? To best serve science and democracy, where should be the locus of power — at the center or at the periphery?

Interestingly, advocates for both centralization and decentralization have claimed that their respective governing scheme is superior — that it can maximize equity. This is because there are two ways of approaching the problem of how to organize and manage modern science. The first is the "centralization as equalizer" approach: the more concentrated the power to make decisions, the more likely it is that the distribution of benefits and burdens will be fair. The second view — the "decentralization as maximizer" approach — holds that the more dispersed the authority to allocate scarce resources, the more responsive and accountable will be the people who make policy. And they will feel more politically efficacious as well. Decentralization improves the chances of participation, and as a civic culture develops in a region, and as channels of influence open up for plural interests to affect resources allocation decisions, opportunities for each group to get what it deserves improve.

The traditional approach to the study of organizations favors highly centralized organizational structures on the grounds of administrative efficiency. A structure where power is concentrated is one where the top or central positions in the hierarchy maintain control over the sub-units by controling all of the major resources of the organization.[12] Centralized administration consists of an elite and professional structure that can implement the ideological interests of policy makers in an efficient fashion.[13]

Efficiency in the administration of science and technology can be understood in terms of the uniformity of policy administration among all branches of science throughout the country. Uniformity in administration implies that centralized administrative structures are more impervious to the demands of competing interest groups. Moreover, the interests of wider segments of the public, especially minority interests — for example, those afflicted with "orphan" diseases — are taken into account in making public choices. Consequently, a centralized authority structure is assumed to result in greater equality.

Another advantage of centralization, so argue the proponents of concentrated power, is the capacity to set and enforce uniform national standards. If the principle is applied to the science and technology policy arena, then one can assume that the federal government is more likely to protect minority interests and guarantee even-handed treatment of all groups. Furthermore, a centralized national administration can provide incentives to the states to coerce or entice them to implement the laws of the land, especially federal health and safety regulations.

The counterargument is that the egalitarian aspects of centralization are more than offset by the disadvantages of making decisions in Washington, with a loss of responsiveness and adaptability. In this case, decentralization, rather than centralization, improves performance of the system with respect to representation. And, so goes this argument, a system which is more representative is likely to allocate rewards and burdens more equitably. Advocates of a more decentralized administrative structure question the assumption that highly integrated and bureaucratically organized forms of governance lead to more effective operations. Instead, the proponents of decentralization suggest that it is the decentralized system of administration that is both more effective and fairer.[14]

All this said, it seems to me that a "balanced" system must be devised, one that takes into account the existing federal system, yet looks for new ways of tapping one of the country's major resources — human capital. One solution would be to go ahead with plans to create a Department of Science, and to give that institution the authority to centrally coordinate national policy for science and technology.[15]

Creating a cabinet-level Department of Science responds to the criticism that is expressed in Chapters 3 and 6 that science and technology policy making is fragmented and incoherent. It also addresses the problem of administrative inefficiency by creating an institution that would, through its planning and coordinating functions, help reduce redundancy and duplication. Minimizing overlap is especially critical during periods of fiscal retrenchment. In passing a law that would specify the structure and functions of this new agency, Congress would be advised to consider the interests of the many constituencies that have a stake in science and technology policy. Therefore, the new Department of Science should be staffed with people who go well beyond the scientific and technological establishment. By recruiting managers who can speak for a broad range of interests who are importantly affected by science and technology, a Department of Science can serve both science and democracy.

But as several authors of this volume have pointed out, mechanisms of procedural democracy do not necessarily guarantee substantive democracy. One institutional arrangement for increasing the likelihood that science and technology would serve democracy is the Dutch "science shop," a loosely coupled organization of local scientists and engineers who volunteer their time to advise local residents on local problems that lend themselves to scientific or technological solutions.[16] Usually attached to a local university, this decentralized service-oriented institution is staffed by local professionals who are responding to local needs. It would be a valuable complement to the centralized Department of Science by providing an important community-based forum for local debate of local issues, the results of which could be communicated to the Department of Science in Washington. In this manner the science shops would serve as a conduit for broadly-based input from both experts and non-experts. A network of science shops would also serve as a valuable means of involving large numbers of citizens in the science policy making process, thus reducing scientific and technological illiteracy and restoring confidence in science and technology.

TO WHAT ENDS SHOULD SCIENCE AND TECHNOLOGY BE PUT?

The United States, according to Kenneth Prewitt, "has lost its number one status,"[17] and this has resulted in a number of changes in policies for science and technology, especially with respect to budget priorities. During the Reagan administration's first term, the nation's priorities for scientific research and technological development and diffusion have been reordered, and significant changes within the technoscience agencies have taken place as well.

Science, Technology, and Human Values.   Science and technology, according to the Reagan formula, should serve society by stimulating industrial growth and by improving the nation's security. Although the administration has been less vocal on this point, most people would agree that improving health status is another major objective of the nation's research and development effort. There are other ways in which science and technology can serve society, however, and this chapter addresses two of the most important ones: science and technology have a responsibility to *democracy*; and they also have an obligation to *justice*.

Science's Obligation to Democracy.   In its obligation to serve democracy, the scientific republic must, to use the phrase of Don K. Price, the former dean of the John F. Kennedy School of Government at Harvard University, "speak truth to power." One of the principles of the United States' democratic republic is that government is limited by the Constitution, and the very concept of limited government implies that the tendency towards tyranny will be checked in part by an analysis of the constraints imposed by the physical and socioeconomic worlds. Speaking truth to power in this manner forces the asking and answering of such questions as "What are the likely social dislocations, if any, that will be created by the widespread introduction of robotics in American industry?", "Does acid rain pose a serious threat to human health on the North American continent?", "Are the likely benefits of a space station greater than its projected cost?", and "Will Star Wars work?"

In reflecting on the relationship between science and democracy, we identify a number of cases of "disputed" (risky to human health or safety or damaging to the environment, coupled with a high degree of uncertainty and/or ethical controversy) scientific research and technological development. For example, scientists have argued on both sides of, and have been unable to resolve, safety issues related to nuclear power or acid rain; and controversy still rages over the ethics of conducting experiments on human reproduction, cross-species organ transplants, or gene therapy. And several new processes and products have raised a host of questions equally troubling for the federal government. Three of the most timely and controversial ones are the effects of robotics and computers on employment, the commercial use of the space shuttle, and, perhaps most controversial of all, the Strategic Defense Initiative, or Star Wars.

Science's Obligation to Justice.   In an obligation to justice, the benefits *and* burdens of scientific discoveries and technological developments should be distributed to improve individual "well-being" — so that those individuals and groups in society who are already disadvantaged are not made worse off psychologically, physiologically, economically, or socially. This particular rule of distribution does not, of course, deny the existence of a number of other values — equity, need, or equality, for example — that one might employ as a basis for distributing the costs, risks, and benefits of scientific discoveries and their applications. At the heart of this issue are technology transfer, especially in the highly-

273

charged area of biotechnology; and the distribution of products and processes of value that are or will be in high demand and scarce supply, for example, artificial organs and costly medical procedures. Particularly hazardous technologies such as chemical fertilizers, pesticides, and nuclear waste, also raise serious value questions, especially in relation to the distribution of their risks and costs. Hence, science can serve justice by projecting the most likely distributional consequences (who benefits and who loses, for example) of various policy options. Nowhere is this issue of distributive justice more obvious than in the area of life-extending medical technology.

Value Tradeoffs. There are, then, at least five "masters" that a national policy for science and technology might serve: (1) increased ability to defend the nation militarily, (2) increased ability to compete more effectively in world markets, (3) improved health status, (4) a more democratic society, and (5) a more just society. One intriguing question for future research is the extent to which these goals of a national policy for science and technology are compatible. It is possible that the best way to strengthen democracy and to make America's least advantaged class better off is to put science and technology more exclusively in the service of industry. It is also possible that the current policies that favor federal support for basic rather than applied research, for hard rather than the social and behavioral sciences, and for projects that show high potential for commercial or military application, while serving the nation's industrial policy may impede progress towards a more just and democratic society. And it may also be the case that by adopting an industrial policy fashioned after the one pursued by our commercial rivals in Japan, France, Federal Republic of Germany, or the United Kingdom, or an armament policy to match our military rivals in the Soviet Union, justice and democracy will be imperiled. Given the constraints imposed by the physical world and by growing budget and trade deficits, for example, what are the tradeoffs, if any, among improved economic vitality, a healthy people, a just society, a vigorous procedural and substantive democracy, and an impenetrable defense?

The issue of the ends to which science and technology should be put is illustrated in the case of genetic engineering. This research is not only yielding products that can be used to solve some of the world's most pressing problems, but also potent weapons in the military's arsenal for biological warfare. How new discoveries are to be used, and for whose benefit or harm, are important policy questions that arise as a result of an emerging biotechnology industry. In state legislatures and chambers of commerce, there is ample discussion of the glamorous side of high tech industry.[18] Yet there is a darker side of biotechnology — biological warfare, occupational health hazards to workers, and environmental pollution, for example — that also cries out for analysis.[19]

There are some who believe that the direction of genetic engineering should be determined entirely by the market, with scientists choosing the problem for research, the method of inquiry, and how the findings are to be used. Others believe that politics is a better allocating mechanism. Given the extent of government's and industry's involvement in funding research and development, it hardly seems possible that there is a free market operating. Since politics is already affecting the patterns of funding and the choices of goals, why not choose the goals of this important new knowledge through negotiations among a wide variety of political actors? To answer the question about ends more directly, *I would prefer that Margaret Mead called a "humane" science*,[20] one that has as its objective a better world in which to live, one that nurtures freedom and equality. And I am convinced that if goals are negotiated, they are likely to be more humane.

CONCLUSION

Having addressed issues of changes, challenges, and institutional reforms, we return to what Hunter Dupree has called the "unresolved dilemma" of all attempts at central scientific organization.[21] In this chapter, the dilemma has been posed as a question, How can science and technology be reconciled with democracy? The solution to the dilemma lies in the answers that have been offered to four questions that were asked in the Introduction to this book.

First, all people who are importantly affected should share equally in the task of governing science and technology in a democracy.

Second, these various interests should be meaningfully involved in policy making early and often. Voting in elections, and leaving these matters to specialists between elections, serves neither science nor democracy.

Third, a "balanced" system of governance — one that combines central coordination with decentralized, communitarian institutions accessible to all and designed to encourage public discourse on both national and local issues — has been recommended.

Fourth, science and technology should serve humanity, and whether

275

humanity is best served by directing science and technology to the needs of a failing economy, national security interests, or substantive democracy is something to be negotiated.

NOTES

1. See Miller, Suchner, and Voelker, *Citizenship in an Age of Science.*

2. This does not negate the finding that socioeconomic class is positively related to involvement in political life. While access to the institutions of government may be equal, those opportunities are not evenly taken advantage of across the social strata.

3. Robert A. Dahl, *A Preface of Democratic Theory,* calls this system "rule by minorities."

4. Most citizens have limited time and resources and a limited attention span. On his trip to America in the 19th century, deTocqueville noted that America is a participatory society. As Emmett Redford pointed out in a symposium on the governance of science and technology in Houston, May 21-22, 1985, today there are even more means of access to the policy process — for example, citizen lobbies, the media, litigation, advisory committees, hearings, etc. For examples of citizen participation in science, see the excellent volume, James C. Petersen, *Citizen Participation in Science Policy.*

5. Michael Polanyi, "The Republic of Science," 54-73.

6. James D. Watson, "DNA Folly Continues," *New Republic,* 13 Jan. 1979, pp. 14-15. If there is still any question as to whether scientists are above politics, see Charles E. Hess, "Freedom of Inquiry: An Endangered Species," *Science* 225 (20 July 1984): 273.

7. See Theodore Lowi, "The Public Philosophy: Interest Group Liberalism," *American Political Science Review* 61 (Mar. 1967): 5-24; and Malcolm L. Goggin, "Social Policy as Theory," in *Public Policy and Social Institutions,* ed. Harrell Rodgers, Jr. (Greenwich, Conn.: JAI Press, 1984).

8. For a while, participatory democracy was very much in disfavor. But recent developments in politics at the national level have revitalized intellectual discourse on this subject. In one of the most coherent arguments for democratic governance to date, Benjamin Barber, *Strong Democracy* argues for a democracy in which the ordinary citizen is very active in public affairs. His broad themes, which are consistent with our own recommendations, are citizenship, participation, and political activity.

9. Aristotle, *Politics,* Book V, trans. Ernest Barker (Oxford: Oxford Univ. Press, 1946), 1310a.

10. Wallace Sayre, "Scientists and American Science Policy," in *Scientists and National Policy-Making,* ed. Robert Gilpin and Christopher Wright (New York: Columbia Univ. Press, 1964), 97.

11. According to Don K. Price, this reluctance of political leaders to coordinate policy centrally constitutes America's "unwritten constitution." As a solution to the problem of what some political scientists have called "partisan mutual adjustment," Price advocates a parliamentary system in which the president, rather than congressional committees and interest groups, dictates public policy. With this proposed reform, coherent, long-range plans for the nation could be established and implemented. See Don K. Price, *America's Unwritten Constitution: Science, Religion, and Political Responsibility* (Baton Rouge: Louisiana State Univ. Press, 1983). For the contrasting view that policy can at times be centrally coordinated and at other times be the product of accommodation, see

Malcolm L. Goggin, "Health Policies, Priorities, and Politics: Two Decades of Analysis," paper presented at the Annual Meeting of the American Political Science Association, Chicago, Sept. 1983.

12. F.J. Weed, "Centralized and Pluralistic Organizational Structure and Public Welfare," *Administration and Society* 9 (1977): 111–36.

13. H.H. Gerth and C. Wright Mills, *From Max Weber: Essays in Sociology* (New York: Oxford Univ. Press, 1946):214–24; and A.L. Stinchcombe, "Social Structure and Organization," in *Handbook of Organizations*, ed. James C. March (Chicago: Rand McNally, 1965).

14. Richard Nathan, "Special Revenue Sharing," in *Restructuring the Federal System: Approaches to Accountability in Postcategorical Programs*, ed. J.D. Sneed and S.A. Waldhorn (New York: Crane, Russak, 1975).

15. The idea of a Department of Science has been discussed in several recent articles in *Science*. See U.S., Congress, House, Committee on Science and Technology, *Subjects and Policy Areas for Consideration Report* (Washington, D.C.: Government Printing Office, Apr. 1983), 5 and 54–59. One of the earliest arguments for more central direction can be found in an OECD report principally authored by Harvey Brooks, Organization for Economic Cooperation and Development, *Science, Growth, and Society: A New Perspective* (Paris: OECD, 1971). On the need for more central coordination, see National Research Council, *International Competition in Advanced Technology: Decisions for America* (Washington, D.C.: National Academy Press, 1983); and Frank Press, "Annual Report to the President," 26 Apr. 1983 (mimeographed).

16. Dorothy Nelkin and Arie Rip, "Distributing Expertise: A Dutch Experiment in Public Interest Science," *Bulletin of the Atomic Scientists* 35 (May 1979): 20–23, 54; Ad Meertensand Onno Nieman, "The Amsterdam Science Shop: Doing Science for the People," *Science for the People* (Sept./Oct. 1979):15–17, 36–37. For more on local participatory mechanisms in countries other than the U.S., see Dorothy Nelkin and Michael Pollak, "Public Participation in Technological Decisions," 55–64; Dorothy Nelkin, *Technological Decisions and Democracy*; and K. Guild Nichols, *Technology on Trial: Public Participation in Decison-Making Related to Science and Technology* (Paris: OECD, 1979).

17. Kenneth Prewitt, "Scientific Illiteracy and Democratic Theory," *Kettering Review* (Summer 1985):32. A number of other articles in the same issue of *Kettering Review* speak to the issue of the relationship of science to society in the modern world.

18. Many see a veritable "gold mine" in high-tech industry, and many see distinct advantages to encouraging joint university-industry projects in this area. For a sober view, see National Science Foundation, *University-Industry Relationships: Myths, Realities, Potentials*. As far as the government's role in encouraging cooperation goes, the NSF believes that it is inappropriate for government to "make science do something related to the marketplace" (p. 31).

19. That the "new" biology has benefited enormously from the explosive growth of NIH funding in this area is well established. One issue that has received much less attention is the suggestion that the government seek a greater return on its research investment, either in the form of lower prices or as a tax. See Philip Siekevitz, "Biomedical Research and Contracts: A Commentary on Goggin's Article," *Politics and the Life Sciences* 3 (Aug. 1984):59–61; and Malcolm L. Goggin, "Threats to Freedom from a Tyranny of the Minority," 71.

20. Margaret Mead, "Towards a Human Science," *Science* 191 (5 Mar. 1976):903–9.

21. A. Hunter Dupree, *Science in the Federal Government*, 379.

Bibliography

BOOKS

Achinstein, Peter. *Concepts of Science*. Baltimore: Johns Hopkins Univ. Press, 1968.

Almond, Gabriel A. *The American People and Foreign Policy*. New York: Praeger, 1960.

Ames, Mary E. *Outcomes Uncertain: Science and Political Process*. Washington, D.C.: Communications Press, 1978.

Averch, Harvey. *A Strategic Analysis of Science and Technology Policy*. Baltimore: Johns Hopkins Univ. Press, 1985.

Bachrach, Peter. *The Theory of Democratic Elitism: A Critique*. Boston: Little, Brown, 1967.

Barber, Benjamin. *Strong Democracy: Participatory Politics for a New Age*. Berkeley: Univ. of California Press, 1984.

Ben-David, J. *The Scientist's Role in Society: A Comparative Study*. Englewood Cliffs, N.J.: Prentice-Hall, 1971.

Benveniste, Guy. *The Politics of Expertise*. Berkeley: Glendessary Press, 1972.

Blissett, Marlan. *Politics in Science*. Boston: Little, Brown, 1972.

Blume, Stuart S. *Toward a Political Sociology of Science*. New York: Free Press, 1974.

Boffey, Philip M. *The Brain Bank of America: An Inquiry into the Politics of Science*. New York: McGraw-Hill, 1975.

Boorstin, Daniel J. *The Republic of Technology: Reflections on Our Future Community*. New York: Harper & Row, 1978.

Broad, William, and Nicholas Wade. *Betrayers of the Truth*. New York: Simon and Schuster, 1982.

Brooks, Harvey. *The Government of Science*. Cambridge: MIT Press, 1968.

———. *Technology and Society in the 1980s*. Paris: OECD, 1981.

Burger, Edward J. *Science at the White House: A Political Liability*. Baltimore: Johns Hopkins Univ. Press, 1980.

Burnham, John C., ed. *Science in America: Historical Selections*. New York: Holt, Rinehart and Winston, 1971.

Bush, Vannevar. *Science: The Endless Frontier*. Washington, D.C.: U.S. Government Printing Office, July 1945.

Caldwell, Lynton; Lynton R. Hayes; and Isabel M. Mac Whirter. *Citizens and*

279

the Environment: Case Studies in Popular Action. Bloomington: Indiana Univ. Press, 1976.

Carson, Rachel. *Silent Spring.* Boston: Houghton Mifflin, 1962.

Cole, Leonard A. *Politics and the Restraint of Science.* Totowa, N.J.: Rowman and Allanheld, 1983.

Commoner, Barry. *The Politics of Energy.* New York: Knopf, 1979.

Cook, Terrence E., and Patrick M. Morgan, eds. *Participatory Democracy.* San Francisco: Canfield Press, 1971.

Dahl, Robert A. *A Preface to Democratic Theory.* Chicago: Univ. of Chicago Press, 1956.

Dahl, Robert A., and Charles Lindlom. *Politics, Economics and Welfare.* New York: Harper & Row, 1953.

Dahl, Robert A., and Edward R. Tufte. *Size and Democracy.* Stanford, Calif.: Stanford Univ. Press, 1973.

Dickinson, John P. *Science and Scientific Researchers in Modern Society.* Paris: UNESCO, 1984.

Dickson, David. *The New Politics of Science.* New York: Pantheon, 1984.

Douglas, Mary, and Aaron Wildavsky, *Risk and Culture.* Berkeley: Univ. of California Press, 1982.

Dupree, A. Hunter. *Science in the Federal Government: A History of Policies and Activities to 1940.* Cambridge: Harvard Univ. Press, Belknap Press, 1957.

Ebbin, Steven, and Raphael Kasper. *Citizen Groups and the Nuclear Power Controversy: Use of Scientific and Technological Information.* Cambridge: MIT Press, 1974.

Ellul, Jacques. *The Technological Society.* Translated by J. Wilkinson. New York: Knopf, 1967.

Encel, Sol, and Jarlath Ronayne, eds. *Science, Technology, and Public Policy: An International Perspective.* Elmsford, N.Y.: Pergamon, 1979.

Eulau, Heinz, and Kenneth Prewitt. *The Labyrinths of Democracy: Adaptations, Linkages, Representation, and Policies in the United States.* Indianapolis: Bobbs-Merrill, 1973.

Freeman, James O. *Crisis and Legitimacy.* Cambridge: Cambridge Univ. Press, 1978.

Fudenberg, H. Hugh, and Vijaya L. Melnick, eds. *Biomedical Scientists and Public Policy.* New York: Plenum Press, 1978.

Fusfeld, Herbert I. *Science and Technology Policy: Perspective for the 1980s.* New York: N.Y. Academy of Science, 1979.

Gilpin, Robert. *American Scientists and Nuclear Policy.* Princeton: Princeton Univ. Press, 1962

Gilpin, Robert, and Christopher Wright, eds. *Scientists and National Policymaking.* New York: Columbia Univ. Press, 1964.

Gofman, John. *Radiation and Human Health.* San Francisco: Sierra Books, 1981.

Golden, William T. *Science Advice to the President.* Elmsford, N.Y.: Perga-mon, 1981.

Greenberg, Daniel S. *The Politics of Pure Science: An Inquiry into the Relationship between Science and Government in the United States.* New York: New American Library, 1967.

Grobstein, Clifford. *A Double Image of the Double Helix: The Recombinant DNA Debate.* San Francisco: W.H. Freeman, 1979.

Haberer, Joseph. *Politics and the Community of Science.* New York: Van Nostrand Reinhold, 1969.

————. *Science and Technology Policy: Perspectives and Development.* Lexington, Mass., Lexington Books, 1977.

Habermas, Jurgen. *The Legitimation Crisis.* Boston: Beacon, 1975.

Hagstrom, Warren O. *The Scientific Community.* New York: Basic, 1965.

Holton, Gerald, and Robert S. Morison, eds. *Limits of Scientific Inquiry.* New York: Norton, 1979.

Johnston, Ron, and Philip Gummett, eds. *Directing Technology.* New York: St. Martin's Press, 1979.

Kaplan, Norman, ed. *Science and Society.* Chicago: Rand McNally, 1965.

Katz, Jay. *Experimentation with Human Beings.* New York: Russell Sage Foundation, 1972.

Kenny, Martin. *Biotechnology: The University–Industrial Complex.* New Haven: Yale Univ. Press, forthcoming.

Knorr, Karin D.; Roger Krohn; and Richard Whitley, eds. *The Social Process of Scientific Investigation.* Boston: D. Reidel, 1981.

Kohlstedt, Sally G. *The Formation of the American Scientific Community.* Urbana: Univ. of Illinois Press, 1976.

Kornhauser, William. *The Politics of Mass Society.* Glencoe, Ill.: Free Press, 1959.

Krimsky, Sheldon. *Genetic Alchemy.* Cambridge: MIT Press, 1982.

————. *Public Participation in the Formation of Science and Technology Policy.* Washington, D.C.: National Science Foundation, 1979.

Krohn, Roger G. *The Social Shaping of Science.* Westport, Conn.: Greenwood, 1971.

Krohn, Wolfgang; Edwin T. Layton; and Peter Weingart, eds. *The Dynamics of Science and Technology.* Dordrecht, Holland and Boston: D. Reidel, 1978.

Kuehn, Thomas J., and Alan L. Porter, eds. *Science, Technology, and National Policy.* Ithaca: Cornell Univ. Press, 1981.

Kuhn, Thomas. *The Structure of Scientific Revolutions.* 2d ed. Chicago: Univ. of Chicago Press, 1970.

Lakoff, Sanford A. *Science and the Nation.* Englewood Cliffs, N.J.: Prentice-Hall, 1962.

Lambright, W. Henry. *Governing Science and Technology.* New York: Oxford Univ. Press, 1976.

281

Langfitt, Thomas W.; Sheldon Hackney; Alfred P. Fishman; and Albert V. Glowasky. *Partners in the Research Enterprise: University-Corporate Relations in Science and Technology.* Philadelphia: Univ. of Pennsylvania Press, 1983.

Langton, Stuart, ed. *Citizen Participation in America.* Lexington, Mass.: Lexington Books, 1978.

Lappé, Marc. *Genetic Politics: The Limits of Biological Control.* New York: Simon and Schuster, 1979.

Lawrence, William. *Of Acceptable Risk.* Los Altos, Calif.: William Kaufman, 1976.

Lear, John. *Recombinant DNA: The Untold Story.* New York: Crown, 1978.

Lester, John, and Bowman, Ann O'Malley, eds. *The Politics of Hazardous Waste Management.* Durham, N.C.: Duke Univ. Press, 1983.

Levine, Adeline Gordon. *Love Canal: Science, Politics and People.* Lexington, Mass.: D.C. Heath, 1982.

Lieberman, Jethro K. *The Tyranny of Experts: How Professionals Are Closing the Open Society.* New York: Walker, 1970.

Lindblom, Charles E. *The Intelligence of Democracy.* New York: Free Press, 1965.

———. *Politics and Markets.* New York: Basic, 1977.

Lipscombe, Joan, and Bill Williams. *Are Science and Technology Neutral?* Stoneham, Mass.: Butterworth, 1979.

Lipset, Seymour Martin. *Political Man.* New York: Doubleday, 1960.

Lipset, Seymour Martin, and William Schneider. *The Confidence Gap: Business, Labor, and Government in the Public Mind.* New York: Free Press, 1983.

Lomask, Milton. *A Minor Miracle: An Informal History of the National Science Foundation.* Washington, D.C.: National Science Foundation, 1976.

Long, T. Dixon, and Christopher Wright, eds. *Science Policies of Industrial Nations.* New York: Praeger, 1975.

Lovins, Amory. *Soft Energy Paths.* New York: Harper & Row, 1979.

Mahoney, M.J. *The Scientist: Anatomy of the Truth Merchant.* Cambridge, Mass.: Ballinger, 1976.

Markle, Gerald E., and James C. Petersen, eds. *Politics, Science, and Cancer: The Laetrile Phenomenon.* Boulder, Colo.: Westview, 1980.

Marx, Leo. *The Machine in the Garden.* New York: Oxford Univ. Press, 1964.

Mazmanian, Daniel, and Jeanne Nienaber. *Can Organizations Change?* Washington, D.C.: Brookings, 1979.

Mazur, Allan C. *Disputes Between Experts.* London: Minerva, 1973.

———. *The Dynamics of Technological Controversy.* Washington, D.C.: Communications Press, 1981.

Merton, Robert K., ed. *The Sociology of Science.* Chicago: Univ. of Chicago Press, 1973.

Miller, Howard S. *Dollars for Research: Science and Its Patrons in Nineteenth-Century America.* Seattle: Univ. of Washington Press, 1970.

Miller, Jon D.; Robert W. Suchner; and Alan M. Voelker. *Citizenship in an Age of Science: Changing Attitudes Among Young Adults.* New York: Pergamon, 1980.

Mitroff, Ian I. *The Subjective Side of Science: A Philosophical Inquiry into the Psychology of the Apollo Moon Scientists.* Amsterdam and New York: Elsevier, 1974.

Nelkin, Dorothy, ed. *Controversy: Politics of Technical Decisions.* 2d ed. Beverly Hills, Calif.: Sage, 1984.

———. *Science as Intellectual Property.* New York: Macmillan, 1984.

———. *Technological Decisions and Democracy: European Experiments in Public Participation.* Beverly Hills, Calif.: Sage, 1977.

Nelson, William R., ed. *The Politics of Science: Readings in Science, Technology and Government.* New York: Oxford Univ. Press, 1968.

Noble, David F. *America by Design: Science, Technology and the Rise of Corporate Capitalism.* New York: Knopf, 1976.

Norwood, Hanson. *Patterns of Discovery.* Cambridge: Cambridge Univ. Press, 1958.

Ophuls, William. *Ecology and the Politics of Scarcity.* San Francisco: Freeman, 1977.

Passmore, John. *Science and Its Critics.* New Brunswick, N.J.: Rutgers Univ. Press, 1978.

Pateman, Carole. *Participation and Democratic Theory.* Cambridge: Cambridge Univ. Press, 1970.

Pennock, J. Roland. *Democratic Political Theory.* Princeton: Princeton Univ. Press, 1979.

Pennock, J. Roland, and John W. Chapman, eds. *Participation in Politics.* New York: Lieber-Atherton, 1975.

Petersen, James C., ed., *Citizen Participation in Science Policy.* Amherst: Univ. of Massachusetts Press, 1984.

Price, Derek John de Solla. *Little Science, Big Science.* New York: Columbia Univ. Press, 1963.

———. *Science Since Babylon.* New Haven: Yale Univ. Press, 1961.

Price, Don K. *America's Unwritten Constitution: Science, Religion and Political Responsibility.* Baton Rouge: Louisiana State Univ. Press, 1985.

———. *Government and Science: The Dynamic Relation in American Democracy.* New York: New York Univ. Press, 1954.

———. *The Scientific Estate.* New York: Oxford Univ. Press, 1965.

Primack, Joel, and Frank von Hippel. *Advice and Dissent: Scientists in the Political Arena.* New York: Basic, 1974.

Raffaele, Joseph Antonio. *The Management of Technology: Change in a Society of Organized Advocacies.* Washington, D.C.: University Press of America, 1978.

Ramo, Simon. *America's Technological Slip.* New York: Wiley, 1980.

Reingold, Nathan, ed. *The Sciences in the American Context: New Perspectives.* Washington, D.C.: Smithsonian Institution Press, 1979.

Rosenberg, Charles E. *No Other Gods: On Science and American Social Thought.* Baltimore: Johns Hopkins Univ. Press, 1976.

Rosenthal, Albert H. *Public Science Policy and Administration.* Albuquerque: Univ. of New Mexico Press, 1973.

Salomon, Jean Jacques. *Science and Politics.* Cambridge: MIT Press, 1973.

Schaffter, Dorothy. *The National Science Foundation.* New York: Praeger, 1969.

Schooler, Dean, Jr. *Science, Scientists, and Public Policy.* New York: Free Press, 1971.

Schumpeter, Joseph A. *Capitalism, Socialism, and Democracy,* 3d ed. New York: Harper & Row, 1950.

Schwing, Richard C., and Walker A. Albers, eds. *Societal Risk Assessment: How Safe Is Safe Enough?* New York: Plenum, 1980.

Shapley, Deborah, and Roy Rustum. *Lost at the Frontier: U.S. Science and Technology Adrift.* Philadelphia: ISI Press, 1985.

Smith, Alice K. *A Peril and a Hope: The Scientists' Movement in America, 1945–1947.* Chicago: Univ. of Chicago Press, 1965.

Smith, C.S. *A Search for Structure: Selected Essays on Science, Art, and History.* Cambridge: MIT Press, 1981.

Spiegel-Rösing, Ina, and Derek J. de Solla Price, eds. *Science, Technology and Society.* Beverly Hills: Sage, 1977.

Stich, Stephen, and David Jackson, eds. *The Recombinant DNA Debate.* Ann Arbor: Univ. of Michigan Press, 1977.

Strickland, Stephen P. *Politics, Science and Dread Disease: A Short History of United States Medical Research Policy.* Cambridge: Harvard Univ. Press, 1972.

Studer, Kenneth E., and Daryl E. Chubin. *The Cancer Mission: Social Contexts of Biomedical Research.* Beverly Hills: Sage, 1980.

Teich, Albert H., ed. *Scientists and Public Affairs.* Cambridge: MIT Press, 1974.

Thompson, Dennis F. *The Democratic Citizen: Social Science and Democratic Theory in the Twentieth Century.* Cambridge: Cambridge Univ. Press, 1970.

―――. *John Stuart Mill and Representative Government.* Princeton: Princeton Univ. Press, 1976.

Tirman, John, ed. *The Militarization of High Technology.* Cambridge, Mass.: Ballinger, 1985.

Vidich, Arthur J., and Ronald M. Glassman, eds. *Conflict and Control: Challenge to Legitimacy of Modern Governments.* Beverly Hills: Sage, 1980.

Weart, Spencer. *Scientist in Power.* Cambridge: Harvard Univ. Press, 1979.

Weissmann, Gerald, ed. *The Biological Revolution: Applications of Cell Biology to Public Welfare.* New York: Plenum Press, 1979.

Wiesner, Jerome B. *Where Science and Politics Meet*. New York: McGraw-Hill, 1965.

Winner, Langdon. *Autonomous Technology*. Cambridge: MIT Press, 1977.

Wolfe, D. *Science and Public Policy*. Lincoln: Univ. of Nebraska Press, 1959.

Wulff, Keith M., ed. *Regulation of Scientific Inquiry: Societal Concerns with Research*. Boulder, Colo.: Westview, 1979.

Ziman, John. *Public Knowledge*. Cambridge: Cambridge Univ. Press, 1968.

Zimmerman, Burke K. *Biofuture*. New York: Plenum, 1984.

ARTICLES

Abrams, Nancy E., and R. Stephen Barry. "Mediations: A Better Alternative to Science Courts." *Bulletin of the Atomic Scientists* 33 (Apr. 1977): 50–53.

Abrams, Nancy E., and Joel R. Primack. "The Public and Technological Decisions." *Bulletin of the Atomic Scientists* 36 (June 1980): 44–48.

Adler, Reid G. "Biotechnology as an Intellectual Property." *Science* 224 (27 Apr. 1984): 357.

Alford, Robert R., and Roger Friedland. "Political Participation and Public Policy." In *Annual Review of Sociology*. Palo Alto, Calif.: Annual Review Books, 1975.

Arnstein, Sherry. "A Ladder of Citizen Participation." *Journal of the American Institute of Planning* 35 (July 1969): 216–24.

Bagamery, Anne. "No Policy Is Good Planning." *Forbes*, 18 June 1984, p. 140–45.

Baltimore, David. "Limiting Science: A Biologist's Perspective." *Daedalus* 107 (Spring 1978): 37–45.

Bayles, Michael D. "Against Professional Autonomy." *National Forum* 58 (Summer 1978): 23–26.

Beckler, David Z. "The Precarious Life of Science in the White House." *Daedalus* 103 (Summer 1974): 115–34.

Begley, Sharon, and John Carey. "Toxic Trouble in Silicon Valley." *Newsweek*, 7 Mar. 1984, p. 85.

Bennett, William. "Facts, Science and Common Lives." *Harvard Magazine* 80 (May/June 1978): 14–16.

Bereano, Philip L. "The Scientific Community and the Crisis of Belief." *American Scientist* 57 (Winter 1969): 484–501.

Boffey, Philip M. "Experiment Planned to Test Feasibility of a Science Court." *Science* 193 (9 July 1976): 129.

———. "Science Court: High Officials Back Test of Controversial Concept." *Science* 194 (8 Oct. 1976): 167–69.

———. "Scientists and Bureaucrats: A Clash of Cultures on FDA Advisory Panel." *Science* 191 (26 Mar. 1976): 1244–46.

285

Bok, Derek, "Business and the Academy." *Harvard Magazine* 83 (May/June 1981): 23–25.

Bok, Sissela. "Secrecy and Openness in Science: Ethical Considerations." *Science, Technology, and Human Values* 7 (Winter 1982): 32–41.

Bouton, Katherine, "Academic Research and Big Business: A Delicate Balance." *New York Times Magazine*, 11 Sept. 1983, p. 63.

Bozeman, Barry, "'Straight Arrow Science Policy' and Its Dangers." *Public Administration Review* 39 (Mar./Apr. 1979): 116–21.

Bozeman, Barry, and L. Vaughn Blankenship. "Science Information and Governmental Decision Making: The Case of the National Science Foundation." *Public Administration Review* 39 (Jan./Feb. 1979): 53–57.

Bozeman, Barry, and Ian Mitroff, eds. "A Symposium: Managing National Science Policy." *Public Administration Review* 39 (Mar./Apr. 1979): 111–47.

Bozeman, Barry; E. Slusher; K. Roerig. "Social Structure and the Flow of Scientific Information in Public Agencies: An Ideal Design." *Research Policy* 7 (Nov. 1978): 384–405.

Branscomb, Lewis M. "Science in the White House: A New Start." *Science* 196 (20 May 1977): 851.

Brickman, Ronald, and R.P. Arie. "Science Policy Advisory Councils in France, the Netherlands and the United States, 1955–77: A Comparative Analysis." *Social Studies of Science* 9 (Feb. 1979): 167–98.

Brooks, Harvey. "The Resolution of Technically Intensive Public Policy Disputes." *Science, Technology, and Human Values* 9 (Winter 1984): 39–50.

———. "The Scientific Advisory." In *Scientists and National Policy-Making,* edited by Robert Gilpin and Christopher Wright. New York: Columbia Univ. Press, 1964.

Brown, Donald. "Quality and Relevance." *Hastings Center Report* 5 (June 1975): 7–8.

Brown, George. "Administration Policies on Government Control of Information." *Congressional Record,* 97th Cong., 2d sess., 128, no. 16 (25 Feb. 1982), H511.

Callahan, Daniel, "Recombinant DNA: Science and the Public." *Hastings Center Report* 7 (Apr. 1977): 20–23.

Carey, William D. "Peer Review Revisited." *Science* 189 (1 Aug. 1975): 331.

———. "Science and Public Understanding." *Science* 204 (25 May 1979): 797.

Carmen, Ira H. "The Constitution in the Laboratory: Recombinant DNA Research as 'Free Expression'." *Journal of Politics* 43 (1981): 737–62.

Carroll, James D. "Participatory Technology." *Science* 171 (19 Feb. 1971): 647–53.

Casper, Barry. "Technology Policy and Democracy." *Science* 194 (1 Oct. 1976): 29–35.

"Classifying Research." *Physics Today* 37 (1984): 15, 90.

Cole, Leonard A. "Science Watch." *The Sciences* 21 (Dec. 1981): 9.

Cole, Stephen; Leonard Rubin; and Jonathan R. Cole. "Peer Review and the Support of Science." *Scientific American* 237 (Oct. 1977): 34–41.

Comar, Cyril. "Bad Science and Social Penalties" (editorial). *Science* 200 (16 June 1978): 1225.

"Connecting Industry to University Research." *Physics Today* 37 (1984): 112.

"Coupling Industry to Basic Research." *Physics Today* 37 (1984): 120.

Culliton, Barbara J. "Biomedical Research Enters the Marketplace." *New England Journal of Medicine* 304 (14 May 1981): 1195.

————. "NSF: Trying to Cope with Congressional Pressure for Public Participation." *Science* 191 (23 Jan. 1976): 274, 318.

————. "Public Participation in Science: Still in Need of Definition." *Science* 192 (30 Apr. 1976): 451–53.

————. "Science's Restive Public." *Daedalus* 107 (Spring 1978): 147–56.

Cournand, André. "The Code of the Scientist and Its Relationship to Ethics." *Science* 198 (18 Nov. 1977): 699–705.

Dadario, Emilio Q. "Science Policy: Relationships Are the Key." *Daedalus* 103 (Summer 1974): 135–42.

Davidson, Joanne. "Gloom in the Valley . . . But a Silver Lining, Too." *U.S. News and World Report,* 20 Aug. 1984, p. 38.

Delgado, Richard, et al. "Can Science Be Inopportune? Constitutional Validity of Governmental Restrictions on Race-IQ Research." *UCLA Law Review* 31 (1983): 128–225.

Delgado, Richard, and David R. Millen. "God, Galileo, and Government: Toward Constitutional Protection for Scientific Inquiry." *Washington Law Review* 53 (May 1978): 354–404.

Denny, Brewster C. "Renegotiating the Society-Academy Contract." *Science* 201 (28 Aug. 1978): 677.

"DOD University Research on the Rise." *Physics Today* 35 (1982): 50–51.

"DOE Proposal to Restrict Nuclear Information Strongly Opposed." *Physics Today* 36 (1983): 43–45.

Drucker, Peter F. "The Technological Revolution: Notes on the Relationship of Technology, Science, and Culture." *Technology and Culture* 2 (Fall 1961): 342–51.

Dunwoody, Sharon. "The Science Writing Inner Club: A Communication Link Between Science and the Lay Public." *Science, Technology, and Human Values* 5 (Winter 1980): 14–21.

————. "Science Writing Study Finds: AAAS is Master of What Makes News at its Sessions." *Newsletter — National Association of Science Writers* 28 (Nov. 1979): 1–3.

Edwards, Paul N. "Are 'Intelligent Weapons' Feasible?" *Nation* 240 (2 Feb. 1985): 110–112.

Ehrlich, Paul R. "The Benefits of Saying 'Yes'." *Bulletin of the Atomic Scientist* 31 (Sept. 1975): 49–51.

England, J. Merton. "Dr. Bush Writes a Report: *Science—The Endless Frontier.*" *Science* 191 (9 Jan. 1976): 41–46.

Ezrahi, Yaron. "The Political Resources of American Science." *Science Studies* 1 (Apr. 1971): 117–33.

"Faculty Comply but Complain about OMB Rule." *Physics Today* 34 (1981): 55–57.

"FBI Upsets AVS by Arresting East German at Meeting." *Physics Today* 37 (1984): 53–54.

Fields, Cheryl M. "Incentives Called Necessary for Industry to Invest in University Genetic Research." *Chronicle of Higher Education*, 15 June 1981.

Fischhoff, Baruch; Paul Slovic; and Sara Lichtenstein. "Lay Foibles and Expert Fables in Judgment about Risk." *American Statistician* 36 (Aug. 1982): 240–55.

Flack, Richard. "On the Uses of Participatory Democracy." *Dissent* 13 (Nov./Dec. 1966): 701–8.

Fox, Jeffrey L. "Patents Encroaching on Research Freedom." *Science* 224 (8 June 1984): 1080.

Frankel, Mark S. "The Development of Policy Guidelines Governing Human Experimentation in the United States: A Case Study of Public Policy-making for Science and Technology." *Ethics in Science and Medicine* 2 (1975): 43–59.

Fredrickson, Donald S. "The Public Governance of Science." *Man and Medicine* 3 (1978): 77–88.

Fried, Charles. "Public Input in Research" (letter). *Science* 189 (25 July 1975): 248.

Friedman, Robert S. "Representation in Regulatory Decision-Making: Scientific, Industrial, and Consumer Input on the FDA." *Public Administration Review* 38 (May/June 1978): 205–14.

Goggin, Malcolm, L. "Commission Government: Collective Decision Making in the Executive Branch." Houston: Univ. of Houston Center for Public Policy, 1984.

———. "The Life Sciences and the Public: Is Science Too Important to Be Left to the Scientists?" *Politics and the Life Sciences* 3 (Aug. 1984): 28–40.

———. "Threats to Freedom from a Tyranny of the Minority." *Politics and the Life Sciences* 3 (Aug. 1984): 68–75.

Goodell, Rae S. "Public Involvement in the DNA Controversy: The Case of Cambridge, Massachusetts." *Science, Technology, and Human Values* 4 (Spr. 1979): 36–43.

Graham, Loren R. "Concerns About Science and Attempts to Regulate Inquiry." *Daedalus* 107 (Spring 1978): 1–21.

Green, Harold P. "The Boundaries of Scientific Freedom." Presentation at the Annual Meeting of the American Association for the Advancement of Science, Denver, Colo., Feb. 1977, 17–21.

———. "Law and Genetic Control: Public Policy Questions." *Annals of the New York Academy of Sciences* 265 (1976): 170–77.

Greenberg, Daniel S. "The Myth of the Scientific Elite." *The Public Interest* 1 (Fall 1965): 51–62.

Greep, Roy O. "Science Politics, and Society." *Perspectives in Biology and Medicine* 18 (Winter 1975): 211–26.

Gullis, Robert. "Human Rights and the Scientist." *Nature* (24 Feb. 1977): 671.

Gurin, J., and Nancy E. Pfund. "Bonanza in the Biolab." *Nation* (22 Nov. 1980): 542–48.

Handler, Philip. "Public Doubts About Science." *Science* 208 (6 June 1980): 1093.

Hardin, Garrett. "Living with the Faustian Bargain." *Bulletin of the Atomic Scientists* 32 (Nov. 1976): 25–29

Hart, Herbert L. "Are There Any Natural Rights? *Philosophical Review* 64 (Apr. 1955): 175–91.

Harvard Report on Federal Restrictions. *Chronicle of Higher Education*, 9 Jan. 1985, pp. 13–17.

Heberlein, Thomas A. "Some Observations on Alternative Methods for Public Involvement: The Hearing, Public Opinion Poll, the Workshop, and the Quasi-Experiment." *Natural Resources Journal* 16 (Jan. 1976): 197–212.

Hilgartner, Stephen. "The Binary Weapons Controversy." In *Controversy: The Politics of Technical Decisions*, edited by Dorothy Nelkin, pp. 143–58. Beverly Hills: Sage, 1984.

Hirshon, Paul. "Arthur J. Little Opens High Security Lab in Cambridge to Test Hazardous Chemicals." *Boston Globe*, 20 Oct. 1983.

Hoffman, Stanley. "Participation in Perspective?" *Daedalus* 99 (Winter 1970): 177– 220.

Hoge, James. "In Praise of Science and Technology." *New Republic* (22 Jan. 1977): 21–26.

Holdren, John P. "The Nuclear Controversy and the Limitations of Decision-Making by Experts." *Bulletin of the Atomic Scientists* 32 (Mar. 1976): 20–22.

Holman, Halsted R., and Diana B. Dutton. "A Case for Public Participation in Science Policy Formation and Practice." *Southern California Law Review* 51 (Sept. 1978): 1505–34.

Holton, Gerald. "On Being Caught Between Dionysians and Apollonians." *Daedalus* 103 (Summer 1974): 65–81.

———. "Scientific Optimism and Societal Concerns." *Hastings Center Report* 5 (Dec. 1975): 39–47.

Holtzman, Eric. "Competition and the Marketplace: The Need for Balance." *BioScience* 34 (June 1984): 349.

"How Will Revisions to Export Regulations Affect Research?" *Physics Today* 35 (1982): 49–51.

Hutt, Peter Barton. "Public Criticism of Health Science Policy." *Daedalus* 107 (Spring 1978): 157–69.

"Industry-University Research Programs." *Physics Today* 37 (1984): 24–29.

289

Kahn, Tom. "Direct Action and Democratic Values." *Dissent* 13 (Jan./Feb. 1966): 22–30.

Kantrowitz, Arthur. "Controlling Technology Democratically." *American Scientist* 63 (Sept./Oct. 1975): 505–9.

———. "The Science Court Experiment: Criticisms and Responses." *Bulletin of the Atomic Scientists* 33 (Apr. 1977): 44–50.

Karmin, Monroe W., with Linda K. Lanier; Ron Scherer; Jack A. Seamonds; and Michael Bosc., "High Tech: Blessing or Curse?" *U.S. News and World Report*, 16 Jan. 1984, 38–44.

Kennedy, Edward M. "News and Comment." *Science* 189 (20 June 1975): 1187.

Kerson, Roger. "Will Pac-Man Eat Your Job?" *Michigan Voice* (July 1983): 22.

Kevles, Daniel J. "The National Science Foundation and the Debate Over Postwar Research Policy, 1942–1945: A Political Interpretation of *Science—The Endless Frontier*." *Isis* 68 (Mar. 1977): 5–26.

Kolata, Gina. "Export Control Threat Disrupts Meeting." *Science* 217 (24 Sept. 1982): 1233–34.

Krause, Elliott A. "Health and the Politics of Technology." *Inquiry* 8 (1971): 51–59.

Krimsky, Sheldon. "A Citizen Court in the Recombinant DNA Debate." *Bulletin of the Atomic Scientists* 34 (Oct. 1978): 37–43.

LaDou, Joseph. "The Not-So-Clean Business of Making Chips." *Technology Review* 87 (1984): 9.

Lambright, W. Henry, and Albert H. Teich. "Scientists and Government: A Case of Professional Ambivalence." *Public Administration Review* 38 (Mar./Apr. 1978): 133–39.

La Porte, Todd R., and Daniel Metlay. "Technology Observed: Attitudes of a Wary Public." *Science* 188 (11 Apr. 1975): 121–27.

Lasagna, Louis. "Consensus among Experts: The Unholy Grail." *Perspectives in Biology and Medicine* 19 (Summer 1976): 537–48.

Laski, Harold J. "The Limitations of the Expert." Fabian Tract No. 235. *The Fabian Society* (Feb. 1931): 1–14.

Lederman, Leon M. "The Value of Fundamental Science." *Scientific American* 251 (Nov. 1984): 40–47.

Leiserson, Avery. "Scientists and the Policy Process." *American Political Science Review* 59 (June 1965): 408–16.

Lessing, Lawrence. "The Senseless War on Science." *Fortune* 83 (Mar. 1971): 88–91.

Lester, Paldy. "Knowledge, Authority, and Responsibility: The Debate over Congressional Control of NSF Grants." *Journal of College Science Teaching* 5 (1975): 105–10.

Levine, Arthur L. "The Role of the Technoscience Administrator in Managing National Science Policy." *Public Administration Review* 39 (Mar./Apr. 1979): 122–28.

Lilienthal, David E. "Skeptical Look at 'Scientific Experts'." *New York Times Magazine*, 29 Sept. 1963,: 23, 69.

Lipsky, Michael, and Morris Lounds. "Citizen Participation and Health Care: Problems of Government Induced Participation." *Journal of Health Politics, Policy and Law* 1 (Spring 1976): 85–111.

Longino, Helen E. "Beyond 'Bad Science'." *Science, Technology and Human Values* 8 (Winter 1983): 7–17.

Luria, Salvador. "The Goals of Science." *Bulletin of the Atomic Scientists* 33 (May 1977): 28–33.

McGinn, Robert E. "In Defense of Intangibles: The Responsibility-Feasibility Dilemma in Modern Technological Innovation." *Science, Technology, and Human Values* 5 (Fall 1979): 4-10.

McGowan, Alan. "Has America Lost Faith in the Experts?" *Christian Science Monitor*, western ed., 5 Dec. 1979, p. 20.

McGucken, William. "On Freedom and Planning in Science: The Society for Freedom in Science, 1940-46." *Minerva* 16 (Spring 1978): 42–72.

Maclin, Ruth. "Moral Concerns and Appeals to Rights and Duties." *Hastings Center Report* 6 (Oct. 1976): 31–38.

MacRae, Duncan, Jr. "Science and the Formation of Policy in a Democracy." *Minerva* 11 (Apr. 1973): 228–42.

———. "Technical Communities and Political Choice." *Minerva* 14 (Summer 1976): 169–90.

Martin, L. John. "Science and the Successful Society." *Public Opinion* 4 (June/ July 1981): 16–19, 55–56.

May, Judith V. "Professionals and Clients: A Constitutional Struggle." *Sage Professional Papers in Administrative and Policy Studies* 3, Series No. 03-036, Beverly Hills and London: Sage, 1976.

Mazur, Allan. "Disputes between Experts." *Minerva* 11 (Apr. 1973): 243–62.

———. "Commentary: Opinion Poll Measurement of American Confidence in Science." *Science, Technology, and Human Values* 6 (Summer 1981): 16–19.

———. "Science Courts." *Minerva* 15 (Spring 1977): 1–14.

Mead, Margaret. "Toward a Human Science," *Science* 191 (5 Mar. 1976): 903–9.

Merton, Robert K. "The Ambivalence of Scientists." *Bulletin of the Johns Hopkins Hospital* 112 (Feb. 1963): 77–97.

———. "Behavior Patterns of Scientists." *American Scholar* 38 (Spring 1969): 197–225.

———. "The Matthew Effect in Science: The Reward and Communications System of Science Are Considered." *Science* 159 (5 Jan. 1968): 56–83.

Meselson, Matthew, and J.P. Robinson. "Chemical Warfare and Chemical Disarmament." *Scientific American* 242 (Apr. 1980): 38–47.

Milch, Jerome. "The Politics of Technical Advice." *Administrative Science Quarterly*, 22 (Sept. 1977): 526–35.

291

Mitroff, Ian I. "On Managing Science Holistically, or, Is the Management of Science Becoming More Important than the Philosophy of Science?" *Public Administration Review* (Mar./Apr. 1979): 129–33.

Mullins, Nicholas C. "Science Elite?" In *Structuralist Sociology*, edited by B. Wellman and S. Berkowitz. New York: Cambridge Univ. Press, 1981.

"NAS Panel: Most University Research Should Not be Restrained." *Physics Today* 35 (1982): 69–70.

"Needed: More Public Understanding of Science." *Physics Today* 36 (1983): 104.

Nelkin, Dorothy, "Changing Images of Science." *Harvard University Newsletter on Public Conceptions of Science* 14 (1976): 21–31.

———. "Ecologists and the Public Interest." *Hastings Center Report* 6 (Feb. 1976): 38–44.

———. "The Political Impact of Technical Expertise." *Social Studies of Science* 5 (Feb. 1975): 35–54.

———. "Scientific Knowledge, Public Policy, and Democracy: A Review Essay." *Knowledge* 11 (Sept. 1979): 106–22.

———. "Some Social and Political Dimensions of Nuclear Power: Examples from Three Mile Island." *American Political Science Review* 75 (Mar. 1981): 132–42.

———. "Technology and Public Policy." In *Science, Technology, and Society: A Cross-Disciplinary Perspective*, edited by Ina Spiegel-Rösing and Derek J. de Solla Price. Beverly Hills: Sage, 1977.

———. "Threats and Promises: Negotiating the Control of Research." *Daedalus* 107 (Spring 1978): 191–211.

Nelkin, Dorothy, and Susan Fallows. "The Evolution of the Nuclear Debate: The Role of Public Participation." *Annual Review of Energy* (1978): 275–312.

Nelkin, Dorothy, and Michael Pollak. "Ideology as Strategy: The Discourse of the Anti-Nuclear Movement in France and Germany." *Science, Technology, and Human Values* 5 (Winter 1980): 3–13.

———. "Public Participation in Technological Decisions: Reality or Grand Illusion?" *Technology Review* 80 (1978): 55–64.

Nelson, Bryce. "Scientists Increasingly Protest HEW Investigation of Advisers." *Science* 164 (27 June 1969): 1499–1504.

Noble, David F. "The Selling of a University." *Nation* (6 Feb. 1982): 1.

Norman, Colin. "Briefing: Reagan Orders Review of Controls on Research." *Science* 219 (1983): 473.

———. "How to Win Buildings and Influence Congress." *Science* 222 (16 Dec. 1983): 1211–13.

———. "Pork Barrel Scorecard." *Science* 226 (2 Nov. 1984): 519.

———. "Reagan's Science Policy." *Science* 218 (12 Nov. 1982): 659.

Nowotny, Helga. "The Role of the Experts in Developing Public Policy: The Austrian Debate on Nuclear Power." *Science, Technology, and Human Values* 5 (Summer 1980): 10–18.

"NSF To Put More Stress on Applied Science." *Physics Today* 34 (1981): 51–52.

Nunn, Clyde. "Is There a Crisis of Confidence in Science?" *Science* 198 (9 Dec. 1977): 995.

"On Letting the Gene out of the Bottle." *New York Times*, 11 Mar. 1977, A28.

"Pentagon Lowers Heat on Science Secrecy—Maybe." *Physics Today* 37 (1984): 57–59.

Perl, Martin L. "The Scientific Advisory System: Some Observations." *Science* 173 (24 Sept. 1971): 1211–15.

Petersen, James C., and Gerald E. Markle. "Politics and Science in the Laetrile Controversy." *Social Studies of Science* 9 (Feb. 1979): 139–66.

Piel, Gerald. "Inquiring into Inquiry." *Hastings Center Report* 6 (Aug. 1976): 18.

Pion, Georgine M. and Mark W. Lipsey. "Public Attitudes Toward Science and Technology: What Have the Surveys Told Us?" *Public Opinion Quarterly* 45 (Fall 1981): 303–16.

Pitkin, Hanna F., and Sara M. Shumer. "On Participation." *democracy* 2 (1982): 43–54.

Polanyi, Michael. "The Republic of Science: Its Political and Economic Theory." *Minerva* 1 (Aug. 1962): 54–73.

Prewitt, Kenneth. "Scientific Illiteracy and Democratic Theory." *Daedalus* 112 (Spring 1983): 49–64.

Price, Don K. "Money and Influence: The Links of Science and Public Policy." *Daedalus* 103 (Summer 1974): 97–113.

Ravetz, Jerome. "Scientific Knowledge and Expert Advice in Debates about Large Technological Innovations." *Minerva* 16 (Summer 1978): 273–82.

Relman, Arnold S. "Dealing with Conflicts of Interests." *New England Journal of Medicine* 310 (3 May 1984): 1182.

Relyea, Harold C. "The Evolution of Government Security Classification Policy: A Brief Overview." In U.S., Congress. Senate. Committee on Government Operations. *Hearings on Government Secrecy.* 93d Cong., 2d sess. (Washington, D.C.: Government Printing Office, 1974), 842–44.

Rettig, Richard. "The Federal Government and Medical Technology: Crossing Policy and Management Thresholds." *Policy Sciences* 11 (Feb. 1980): 343–56.

Revelle, Roger. "The Scientist and Politician." *Science* 187 (21 Mar. 1975): 1100–05.

Robertson, John A. "The Scientist's Right to Research: A Constitutional Analysis." *Southern California Law Review* 51 (Sept. 1978): 1203–79.

Roblin, Richard. "The Boston XYY Case." *Hastings Center Report* 5 (Aug. 1975): 5–8.

Rushefsky, Mark E. "The Misuse of Science in Governmental Decisionmaking." *Science, Technology, and Human Values* 9 (Summer 1984): 47–59.

Sanger, David E. "Business Rents a Lab Coat and Academia Hopes for the Best." *New York Times*, 21 Mar. 1982.

————. "Computer Work Bends College Secrecy Rules." *New York Times*, 16 Oct. 1984.

————. "Corporate Links Worry Scholars." *New York Times*, 17 Oct. 1982.

Sapolsky, Harvey M. "Science Advise for State and Local Government." *Science* 160 (19 Apr. 1968): 280–84.

Sayre, Wallace. "Scientists and American Science Policy." In *Scientists and National Policy-Making*, edited by Robert Gilpin and Christopher Wright. New York: Columbia Univ. Press, 1964.

Schaiberg, Allan. "Obstacles to Environmental Research by Scientists and Technologists: A Social Structural Analysis." *Social Problems* 24 (June 1977): 501–20.

"Science and Science Policy: A Seminar with William D. Carey." *Science, Technology, and Human Values* 10 (Winter 1985): 7–16.

"Scientific Interchange and National Security." *Physics Today* 35 (1982): 120.

Shapley, Deborah. "Intelligence Agency Chief Seeks Dialogue with Academics." *Science* 202 (27 Oct. 1978): 407–10.

————. "NSF: A 'Populist' Pattern in Metallurgy, Materials Research?" *Science* 189 (22 Aug. 1975): 622–24.

Shils, Edward. "Faith, Utility, and the Legitimacy of Science." *Daedalus* 103 (Summer 1974): 1–15.

Siegel, Karolynn, and Pamela Doty. "'Advocacy Research' vs. 'Management Review': A Comparative Analysis." *Policy Analysis* 5 (Winter 1979): 37–66.

Siekevitz, Philip. "The Scientist-Entrepreneur." *Nature* 101 (1979): 100.

Sills, David L. "A Comment on Dorothy Nelkin's 'Some Social and Political Dimensions on Nuclear Power: Examples from Three Mile Island.'" *American Political Science Review* 75 (Mar. 1981): 143–45.

Staats, Elmer B. "Federal Research Grants: Maintaining Public Accountability Without Inhibiting Creative Research." *Science* 205 (6 July 1979): 18–20.

Stech, Frank, Jr. "Scientific Rivalries: A Sign of Vitality?" *Science* 196 (20 May 1977): 830–31.

Steinfels, Peter. "Biomedical Research and the Public: A Report from the Arlie House Conference." *Hastings Center Report* 6 (June 1976): 21–35.

Stetten, DeWitt, Jr., "Freedom of Inquiry." *Genetics* 81 (Nov. 1975): 415–25.

"Stifling Scientific Communications to Protect U.S. Technology." *Physics Today* 36 (1983): 41–43.

Sun, Marjorie. "NIH Ponders Pitfalls of Industrial Support." *Science* 213 (3 July 1981): 113–14.

Sutton, John. "Organizational Controls and Professional Autonomy in Science: A Case Study of the Lawrence Livermore Laboratory." Unpublished manuscript.

Swanson, Jack. "A New Way of Life—Or Is It?" *National Observer* (23 Mar. 1970): 22.

Task Force of the Presidential Advisory Group on Anticipated Advances in

Science and Technology. "The Science Court Experiment: An Interim Report." *Science* 193 (20 Aug. 1976): 653–56.

Taylor, Alexander, L., III. "Sad Tales of Silicon Valley: High Tech Companies Encounter the Hardest Truths of the Marketplace." *Time* (3 Sept. 1984): 58–9.

Thomas, Lewis. "Hubris in Science?" *Science* 200 (30 June 1978): 1459–62.

Trachtman, Leon E. "The Public Understanding of Science Effort: A Critique." *Science, Technology, and Human Values* 6 (Summer 1981): 10–15.

Unger, Stephen H. "The Growing Threat of Government Secrecy." *Technology Review* 85 (Feb./Mar. 1982): 31–39, 84–85.

"Unwise Export Controls Can Hurt." *Physics Today* 34 (1981): 144.

Wade, Nicholas. "Background Paper." In *The Science Business: Report of the Twentieth Century Fund Task Force on the Commercialization of Scientific Research*. New York: Priority Press, 1984.

———. "Contrary to Fears, Public is High on Science." *Science* 199 (31 Mar. 1978): 1420–21.

———. "Recombinant DNA: NIH Sets Strict Rules to Launch New Technology." *Science* 190 (19 Dec. 1975): 1175–79.

Watson, James D. "DNA Folly Continues." *New Republic* (13 Jan. 1979): 12–15.

Weinberg, Alvin, M. "Science and Trans-Science. *Minerva* 10 (Apr. 1972): 209–22.

Weinberg, Steven. "Reflections of a Working Scientist." *Daedalus* 103 (Summer 1974): 33–45.

Wenk, Edward, Jr. "Scientists, Engineers, and Citizens." *Science* 206 (16 Nov. 1979): 771.

Wilensky, Harold L. "The Professionalization of Everyone?" *American Journal of Sociology* 70 (Sept. 1964): 137–57.

"Will Export Regulations Affect Academic Freedom?" *Physics Today* 34 (1981): 55–57.

Woolf, Patricia. "Fraud in Science: How Much, How Serious?" *Hastings Center Report* 11 (Oct. 1981): 9–14.

Wright, Susan. "Setting Science Policy." *Environment* 20 (May 1978): 6–41.

GOVERNMENT DOCUMENTS

American Council on Education. *America's Competitive Challenge: The Need for a National Response*. Washington, D.C.: Business-Higher Education Forum, Apr. 1983.

Executive Order 12356, "National Security Classification." The White House, Feb. 1982.

Export Administration Regulations 379.1 (a) (1979).

National Academy of Sciences. *Assessing Biomedical Technologies: An In-*

quiry into the Nature of the Process. Washington, D.C.: National Academy of Sciences, 1975 and 1977.

———. *Research with Recombinant DNA: An Academic Forum, March 7–9, 1977.* Washington, D.C.: National Academy of Sciences, 1977.

———. *Scientific Communication and National Security.* Washington, D.C.: National Academy Press, 1982.

National Science Board. *Science Indicators, 1982.* Washington, D.C.: National Science Foundation, 1983.

National Science Foundation. *University-Industry Research Relationships: Myths, Realities, and Potentials.* Washington, D.C.: Government Printing Office, 1982.

Science and Technology: Annual Report to Congress. Washington, D.C.: Government Printing Office, 1980.

U.S. Congress. House of Representatives. Committee on Government Operations. *Report on the President's Executive Order on Security Classification.* 97th Cong., 2d sess., 16 Aug. 1982. Washington, D.C.: Government Printing Office, 1982.

U.S. Congress. House of Representatives. Committee on Science and Technology. *Federal Policy, Plans and Organization for Science and Technology.* 93d Cong., 2d sess., 1974.

———. *Long Range Planning.* Washington, D.C.: Government Printing Office, May 1976.

U.S. Congress. House of Representatives. Committee on Science and Technology. Subcommittee on Investigations and Oversight. *Hearings on University/Industry Cooperation in Biotechnology.* 97th Cong., 1st sess., 16 and 17 June 1982. Washington, D.C.: Government Printing Office, 1982.

U.S. Congress. House of Representatives. Committee on Science and Technology. Subcommittee on Science, Research, and Technology. *Hearings on the Commercialization of Academic Research.* 97th Cong., 1st sess., 8 and 9 June, 1981. Washington, D.C.: Government Printing Office, 1981.

U.S. Department of State. Proposed revisions of ITAR, *Federal Register* 45, no. 246 (19 Dec. 1980): 83970–95.

U.S. Office of Technology Assessment. *Commercial Biotechnology: An International Analysis.* Washington, D.C.: Government Printing Office, 1984.

———. *Impacts of Applied Genetics.* Washington, D.C.: Government Printing Office, 1981.

U.S. President's Commission for a National Agenda for the Eighties. *Report of the Panel on Science and Technology: Promises and Dangers.* Washington, D.C.; Government Printing Office, 1981.

Name Index

Subject Index

academic freedom, 129; limits to, 42, 182, 186; as a right, 34, 48, 138, 187, 191; *see also* freedom of inquiry
academic success, criterion of, 122–23
accountability, 22, 33, 91, 147, 220, 259, 270; arguments for, 48–49, 141, 149, 188; in defense-related research, 89; of local government, 194; *see also* social responsibility
acid rain, 146, 273
administrative state, rise of the, 15
advisers, "two hat," 126
agencies, executive, 227, 264, 269; mission-oriented, 84, 86, 93, 142, 151; regulatory, 143, 154–55, 188; technoscience, 54n
agenda: for biohazards committees, 110; for corporate science, 106; regulatory, 208
alienation, 233; hypothesis, 37–39, 52n, 263
Allied Chemical, and U.C. Davis, 186
American Association for the Advancement of Science (AAAS), 29n, 129, 249
American Council on Education, 26n
American Philosophical Association (APA), 78
American Political Science Association (APSA), 228
American Society of Microbiologists, 239
Amherst, Mass., and recombinant DNA research, 53n
anti-intellectual prejudices, 131

apathetics, in the political process, 38
apathy, mass, 39–40, 234, 263–64
Arlington Advocate, 196
Arlington, Mass., 195–96
arms race, cost of, 100
Arthur D. Little (ADL), 20, 139, 194–217
artificial heart, 98, 102, 265; cost and distribution of, 18, 44, 100, 108
Artificial Heart Assessment Panel (AHAP), 110–12 passim
Artificial Heart Program, 102
artificial intelligence, 65
artificial organs, 274
asbestos, exposure to, 108
Asilomar, 165–67, 170
atomic energy, control of, 79, 86, 115
Atomic Energy Commission (AEC), 83, 169; and nuclear fallout, 148, 160, 247
atomic scientists, as lobbyists, 79
attentive public, 40, 53n, 161
attitudes of the public, toward science and technology, 16, 19–20, 163n
autonomy 41, 69–70, 75, 90–95 passim, 105, 144, 216, 220–21, 223, 227, 241, 262, 266; arguments for, 33, 47–48, 57–59, 76, 225, 228, 267; myth of, 113; threats to, 126

bacteriological warfare. *See* biological warfare
basic research, 72, 93; support for, 82, 85, 92, 125–27; cost of, 72; politics of, 93
Berkeley, Calif., 53n, 106

303

Governing Science and Technology in a Democracy was composed into type on a Compugraphic digital phototypesetter in ten point Times Roman with two points leading between the lines. Times Roman was also used as display. The book was designed by Sheila Hart, composed by Lithocraft, Inc., printed offset by Thomson-Shore, Inc., and bound by John H. Dekker & Sons. The paper on which the book is printed carries acid-free characteristics and is designed for an effective life of at least three hundred years.

THE UNIVERSITY OF TENNESSEE PRESS : KNOXVILLE